PRONTO!

Italian for Business

Alwena Lamping • Paul Durrant

PITMAN
PUBLISHING

Pitman Publishing
128 Long Acre, London WC2E 9AN

A Division of Longman Group UK Limited

First published in 1993
Reprinted 1994

© Lamping and Durrant 1993

British Library Cataloguing in Publication Data
A CIP catalogue record for this book can be obtained from the British Library

ISBN 0 273 60138 5

Typeset by PanTek Arts, Maidstone
Printed and bound by Clays Ltd, St Ives plc

The
publisher's
policy is to use
**paper manufactured
from sustainable forests**

Contents

Part One

Part Two

Introduction

The start of the 1990s saw a remarkable resurgence of interest in Italian. Following the high-profile coverage of the World Cup in Italy and the advent of the Single Market in 1993, British tourists and business people are taking to learning Italian as never before.

Unfortunately, while there is no lack of general phrasebooks and courses for tourists, there has been little or no material for the beginner who wishes to acquire a basic knowledge of business Italian. Our aim in producing *Pronto!* has been to meet this need and provide a genuine, comprehensive *ab-initio* course for BTEC and other vocational students in continuing, further and higher education, and also for business people studying alone or with a teacher and wishing to take advantage of the new opportunities to trade with one of Europe's leading industrial nations.

Italians, more than perhaps any other people in Western Europe, greatly appreciate a willingness on the part of foreign business people to relate socially and to talk 'shop', even if only on a basic level, in the language of their hosts. We hope that on completing this course you will be able to do both with confidence.

Pronto! follows the experiences of a British firm, MK Information Systems, as it negotiates a contract for the supply of computers to Lentini SpA, an Italian company based in Rome.

Part One (Units 1–4) is set in London. The limited range of situations in these early stages allows students to concentrate on basic language skills as they talk about themselves, their families and work.

Part Two (Units 5–10) moves to Rome, with learners now ready with the basic skills they have gained to deal confidently with the variety of situations encountered by the traveller abroad: at the airport, in the hotel, in the restaurant, at the bank, at the railway station and finally at the client's offices and factory.

Assignments and Role Plays are designed to allow the student to bring skills together and apply them at greater length in a more authentic work situation.

The Grammar Review brings together grammar points which may have been dealt with across several units. Students will be referred to it throughout the ten units.

Additional sections have been included for general interest.

How to use the course

All ten units follow the same pattern.

Conversazioni

Always listen to the dialogues first without referring to the text. The first time you listen you should only expect to get the general feel of the situation and the sound and shape of the words and phrases. Then, working with the text and with the *Spiegazioni* and *Vocabolarietto* on the facing page, listen to them again several times. Finally, listen again as often as possible without the text. The more times you listen, the more familiar you will become with the sounds and patterns of Italian.

v

Spiegazioni

This section highlights the key phrases of the dialogues, explains or translates the more difficult idioms, and indicates any points to be dealt with more fully in the *Grammatica* or *In Italia...* sections. Words which appear for the first time in the dialogues are listed in the *Vocabolarietto*.

When you are familiar with all the dialogues in the unit you might go straight to *Pratica*, Exercise 1, and answer the questions in Italian. But do not continue with the other exercises until you have read the *Grammatica* and *In Italia...* sections.

Grammatica

This is where you will find an explanation of those language structures which are emphasised in the unit and practised in the dialogues and exercises.

In Italia...

This section gives practical information about everyday life in Italy, in particular those aspects relevant to business.

Pratica

This begins with comprehension questions on the dialogues to be answered in Italian. Even if you have already answered them once as suggested, it is a good idea to go through them again at this stage. The listening comprehension is followed by a variety of reading, speaking and writing exercises. You will need to refer back to the *Grammatica* before tackling some of them. The *key* to the exercises is available separately.

Riassunto

This section summarises the skills you have learnt in the unit.

Acknowledgements

Both the authors thank their families for their support. Special thanks go to Daniel Lamping for his contribution to the graphics, and to Dott. Nadia Marzocco for her invaluable help.

The Publishers would like to thank the following for permission to reproduce material in this volume: Alitalia for their logo on pp. 81 and 83; Ente Provinciale per il Turismo di Roma for the section of the street plan and tube map on p.189; *La Repubblica* for the table of exchange rates on p.6 and the masthead on p.138; *Il Messaggero* for the masthead on p.138; Wasteels Travel (London) Ltd (tel. 071-834 7066) for the extract from their brochure *Italia 92* on p.186.

Every effort has been made to trace and acknowledge ownership of copyright. The Publishers will be glad to make suitable arrangements with any copyright holders whom it has not been possible to contact.

Pronuncia – Pronouncing Italian

The best way to learn how to pronounce Italian is to listen carefully to the cassette and to your teacher and to imitate their pronunciation.

The sounds of Italian are relatively easy to master as, unlike English, they are constant and do not vary according to the word in which they appear.

The Italian alphabet has 21 letters and the following guide links every letter (and some combinations of letters) to the sound in English which corresponds most closely to them.

Vowels

a	Milano / casa	**a** in barn / father
e	bello / mezzo	**e** in met / set / bell
	sera / piacere	**ay** in may / say
i	italiano / lire	**ee** in meet / **i** in police
o	otto / posso	**o** in not
	sono / solo	**o** in more
u	una / tutto	**u** in pull / **oo** in moon

Consonants

b	banca / bar	**b** in bank
c + e/i	cento / arrivederci / ciao	**ch** in chest / chin
c + other letters	caffè / Chianti / classico	**c** in classic / **k** in king
d	diretto / grande	**d** in needy
f	fortuna / fisica	**f** in fortune / **ph** in physics
g + e/i	generale / agente	**g** in general / agent
g + n	signore / lasagne	**ni** in onion (no **g** sound)
g + li	gli / famiglia	**lli** in million (no **g** sound)
g + other letters	pigro/ghetto	**g** in got/gate
h	ho/ha/che	*never pronounced*
l	lettera / chilo	**l** in letter/kilo
m	moderno / Roma	**m** in modern / Rome

n	nucleare / bene	n in nuclear / benefit
p	principale / scopo	p in principal
q	qualità / acqua	qu in quality
r	rapido / treno / per	r in Scottish bairn (rolled)
s (between two vowels)	rosa / riso	s in rose
s (elsewhere)	santo / scuola	s in saint
sc + e / i	scienza / pesce	sh in show
sc + other letters	schema / scuola / scrivere	sch in scheme / sk in skip
t	trasporto / sposato	t in transport
v	via / nove	v in victory
z	polizia / zio	ts in bits
	zero / zona	ds in cads

Double consonants

Double consonants have the same sound as one consonant but they are pronounced more emphatically and the sound is prolonged.

alla (as in the English normal limit)   mappa (top person)   nonna (unnecessary)

Stress

Most Italian words have the stress on the last vowel but one.

tuo / parlare / direttore / generale / italiano / inglese

Some words have the stress on the final vowel in which case the word has a written accent.

città / caffè / così / però / più / perché

A few words have the stress on the third vowel from the end. They do not have written accents and the only way of familiarising yourself with them is to listen carefully. Some of them are similar to English words but stressed differently.

telefono / industria / macchina

Unit 1

PIACERE!

You will learn to:

- greet people and welcome them
- address them correctly
- introduce yourself
- introduce a colleague
- say what position you hold in a company
- say your nationality
- say which languages you speak

part one

Typical management structure of a large company

Direttore Generale

Direttore Commerciale

Ufficio Vendite
(Sales)
Direttore alle Vendite
Direttore delle Esportazioni (Exports)
Venditore (Salesman)
Rappresentante (Representative)
Agente

Ufficio Marketing
Direttore del Marketing
Direttore della Pubblicità

Ufficio Acquisti
(Purchasing)
Direttore agli Acquisti
Compratore (Buyer)

Direttore Tecnico

Reparto Produzione
(Production)
Direttore della Produzione
Direttore della Manutenzione
(Maintenance)

Reparto Ingegneria
(Engineering)

Ufficio
Ricerca & Progettazione
(Research & Development)
Progettista (Design Engineer)
Ricercatore (Researcher)
Geometra (Draughtsman)

Ufficio
Controllo Qualità
Scienziato (Scientist)

Direttore Amministrativo

Ufficio Ragioneria
(Accounts)
Capo Contabile
Ragioniere/a (Accountant)

Ufficio Informatica
(IT)
Direttore dei sistemi
Analista
Programmatore

Ufficio Personale
(Personnel)
Direttore del Personale

Amministrazione
Segretaria (secretary)
Centralinista (switchboard operator)
Dattilografa (typist)

capo	head/chief
direttore	manager
reparto	department
ufficio	department/office

MK Information Systems (UK) Ltd

Ian McMillan	Direttore Generale (General manager)
Richard Craven	Direttore Commerciale (Commercial manager)
Peter Lawrence	Direttore alle Vendite (Sales manager)
Joanna Rossi	Responsabile delle Esportazioni (i/c Exports)
Laura Barlow	Direttore del Marketing (Marketing manager)
David Williams	Capo Ragioniere (Chief accountant)
Sarah Donnington	Direttore del Personale (Personnel manager)

LENTINI SpA

Antonio Bianchi	Direttore Generale
Giancarlo Lucarini	Direttore agli Acquisti (Purchasing Manager)
Marco Cardella	Direttore dei Sistemi (Systems Manager)
Salvatore Russo	Direttore Tecnico (Technical Manager)
Francesca Bastiani	Direttore della Pubblicità (Advertising Manager)
Enzo Chiari	Capo Contabile (Chief Accountant)
Laura d'Angelo	Ragioniera (Accountant)
Carla Zimonti	Segretaria (Secretary)

Within the image:
MK Information Systems (UK) Ltd
Dr Ian McMillan
General Manager
Ledbury House, 42 Greenfields
London WC2 6LA
Tel 071 836 0023
Fax 071 836 0487

LENTINI SpA
Dott. Ing. G. LUCARINI
DIRETTORE AGLI ACQUISTI
Sede legale Via Monteleone 89 00100 ROMA
Tel. 06/87694220 Fax 06/87623841

LENTINI SpA
Dott. Antonio BIANCHI
DIRETTORE GENERALE
Sede legale Via Monteleone 89 00100 ROMA
Tel. 06/87694220 Fax 06/87623841

🔊 Conversazioni

Two visitors from Lentini SpA arrive at the reception desk at MK Head Office in London. One of them, Antonio Bianchi, talks to the receptionist.

Buongiorno, signore

Antonio Bianchi:	Buongiorno, signorina. Sono Antonio Bianchi, direttore generale* della ditta Lentini.
Receptionist:	Ah, signor Bianchi. Buongiorno. Un attimo, per favore. Si accomodi.
Antonio Bianchi:	Grazie.
Receptionist:	Prego.

Ecco il signor Lawrence

Receptionist:	Signor Bianchi, ecco il signor Lawrence.
Peter Lawrence:	Benvenuto, signor Bianchi. Sono Peter Lawrence, direttore alle vendite*.
Antonio Bianchi:	Piacere. Questo è Giancarlo Lucarini, direttore agli acquisti*.
Peter Lawrence:	Molto lieto.
Giancarlo Lucarini:	Piacere.

(Later the same day)

Buona sera

Peter Lawrence:	Signor Bianchi, signor Lucarini, buona sera. Questo è Ian McMillan, direttore generale* della MK, e questa è Laura Barlow, direttore del marketing*.
Antonio Bianchi:	Piacere.
Giancarlo Lucarini:	Molto lieto.
Laura Barlow:	Molto lieta.
Ian McMillan:	Lei è il direttore generale della Lentini, vero?
Antonio Bianchi:	Sì, sì.
Ian McMillan:	E Lei è il direttore dei sistemi*?
Giancarlo Lucarini:	No, non sono il direttore dei sistemi. Sono il direttore agli acquisti*.

* Refer to the chart on p. 2 for the English equivalents of these titles.

Spiegazioni

- **Buongiorno** – Hello / Good morning / Good afternoon / Goodbye (lit. 'Good day'). Use **buongiorno** from early morning until late afternoon. It is usual to add a person's name or title, e.g. **signore, signora, signorina**. (*In Italia... page 11*)

- **Sono Antonio Bianchi** – I am Antonio Bianchi.
  Sono – I am. (See **Essere** , *Grammatica page 8*)

- **della ditta Lentini** – of Lentini (lit. 'of the Lentini company'). This is often shortened to 'della Lentini'. **della** = **di** (of) + **la** (the) (*Grammatica page 10*)

- **Signor Bianchi** – **Signore** drops the final -e when the surname is added. (*In Italia... page 11*)

- **Prego** – 'Not at all / Please don't mention it', is used much more regularly in Italian than in English.

- **il signor Lawrence** – Mr Lawrence. **Il** means 'the' (*Grammatica page 9*). Except when directly addressing a person, you use 'the' before their title.

- **Benvenuto** – Welcome. If Signor Bianchi were addressing a woman, he would say **Benvenuta**. (*Grammatica page 10*)

- When a man is introduced, the correct response is either **Piacere** or **Molto lieto**. As you will notice in the next dialogue, a woman says **Piacere** or **Molto lieta** not **lieto**.

- To introduce a man you say **Questo è** and his name.
  To introduce a woman you say **Questa è** and her name.

- **è** – is. It is part of **essere**. (*Grammatica, page 8*)
  è can also mean (**you**) **are**. It is clear from the context which one is meant.
  e (without an accent) – and.

- **Buona sera** – Good evening. Use **buona sera** from about 4 p.m. till late evening.

- **Laura Barlow, direttore del marketing** – Laura Barlow, Marketing Manager. There is a feminine form of '**direttore**', but, as in English, women in business are referred to as managers not manageresses.

- **Lei è** – you are. (*Grammatica page 8*)

- **Vero?** – aren't you? (Lit. 'true')

- **non sono** – I am not. (*Grammatica page 9*)

Vocabolarietto

un attimo	one moment	**per favore**	please
la ditta	firm / company	**sì**	yes
questo / questa	this	**no**	no
si accomodi	sit down / make yourself comfortable	**e**	and
ecco	here is	**del, della, dell' delle, degli, dei** } of the (*Grammatica page 10*)	
grazie	thank you		

🔊 Conversazioni

Nazionalità

Giancarlo Lucarini: Il signor McMillan è scozzese?

Peter Lawrence: Sì, è scozzese, è di Edimburgo. Il direttore del personale* è irlandese, io sono inglese, e David Williams, il capo contabile,* è gallese!

Giancarlo Lucarini: Davvero! L'intero Regno Unito!

Il signor Bianchi non parla inglese

Joanna Rossi: Did you have a good journey?

Antonio Bianchi: Scusi, non parlo inglese.

Joanna Rossi: Scusi, Dottore. Come sta?

Antonio Bianchi: Bene, grazie. Anche Lei parla italiano.

Joanna Rossi: Solo un po'. Studio l'italiano di sera.

Antonio Bianchi: Parla bene.

Joanna Rossi: Grazie.

Complimenti!

Antonio Bianchi: Come si chiama?

Joanna Rossi: Mi chiamo Joanna Rossi.

Antonio Bianchi: Che lavoro fa?

Joanna Rossi: Sono la responsabile delle esportazioni.

Antonio Bianchi: Signora, Lei parla molto bene l'italiano. Complimenti!

In the table of Exchange Rates (below) taken from the Italian newspaper La Repubblica *you will find many examples of adjectives of nationality.*

CAMBI INDICATIVI	In lire italiane	Rispetto al dollaro	CAMBI INDICATIVI	In lire italiane	Rispetto al dollaro
Dollaro usa	1479,340	—	Dracma greca	6,997	210,5000
Ecu	1826,690	1,2538	Escudo portoghese	10,328	142,8000
Marco tedesco	937,660	1,9145	Dollar canadese	1167,590	1,2670
Franco francese	276,380	5,3480	Yen giapponese	11,921	124,1000
Lira sterlina	2240,460	1,5153	Franco svizzero	1020,800	1,4480
Fiorino olandese	833,100	1,7742	Scellino austriaco	133,290	11,0775
Franco belga	45,530	32,4650	Corona norvegese	219,880	6,7250
Peseta spagnola	13,129	112,3000	Corona svedese	206,870	7,1900
Corona danese	242,510	6,0890	Marco finlandese	271,440	5,4250
Lira irlandese	2462,070	1,6630	Dollaro australiano	1004,470	0,6785

* Refer to the chart on p. 2 for the English equivalents of these titles.

Spiegazioni

- **Il signor McMillan è scozzese?** – Is Mr McMillan Scottish?

- **l'intero Regno Unito** – <u>the</u> whole United Kingdom (*Grammatica page 10*)

- **Non parlo inglese** – I don't speak English.
  Parlo, part of the verb **parlare,** means **I speak.**
  Because the verb ends in **-o** we know it refers to what **I** do. (*Grammatica page 8*)

- Notice that the definite article (the) is used before a language except immediately after **parlare.**
  studio l'italiano / parlo molto bene l'italiano, but **parlo italiano**
  Capital letters are not used for languages.

- **di sera** – in the evening.

- **Come sta?** – How are you?

- **Anche Lei parla italiano.** – You speak Italian as well.
  Because the verb ends in **-a** we know it means **you** speak. (*Grammatica page 8*)

- **Come si chiama?** – What is your name?
  Mi chiamo .... - My name is ......

- **Che lavoro fa?** – What work do you do?

- **Sono la responsabile delle esportazioni** – I'm responsible for exports / I'm in charge of exports.

- **molto bene** – very well

Vocabolarietto

il lavoro	work / job
il Regno Unito	UK
gallese	Welsh
inglese	English
intero	whole / entire
irlandese	Irish
scozzese	Scottish
parlare	to speak
studiare	to study
anche	also / too
bene	well
un po'	a little / a bit
Complimenti!	Congratulations!
Davvero!	Really!
Scusi	Sorry / Excuse me

Grammatica

A The Present tense

There are three groups of verbs in Italian, the infinitive endings of which are: **-are -ere, -ire**. The infinitive is the form you find in a dictionary, and corresponds to the English **to** _____

> e.g. parl<u>are</u> – to speak,
> vend<u>ere</u> – to sell
> part<u>ire</u> – to depart

The infinitive ending is _replaced_ by other endings to change the tense.

Regular verbs ending in -are

This is the largest group of verbs, and almost all verbs ending in **-are** follow exactly the same pattern.

> to say **I** _____ replace **-<u>are</u>** by **-<u>o</u>**
> to say **you / he / she** _____ replace **-<u>are</u>** by **-<u>a</u>**

	parl<u>are</u> to speak	studi<u>are</u> to study	arriv<u>are</u> to arrive
io (I)	parl<u>o</u>	studi<u>o</u>	arriv<u>o</u>
Lei (you) lui (he) lei (she)	parl<u>a</u>	stud<u>ia</u>	arriv<u>a</u>

Italian does not distinguish between 'I speak' and 'I am speaking', 'you leave' and 'you are leaving', etc.

Essere – to be

Essere is quite separate from the verbs mentioned above. It is one of a relatively small number of _irregular_ verbs. It is an important verb and should be learnt thoroughly.

(io)	sono*	I am	(noi) siamo	we are
(tu)	sei	you are	(voi) siete	you are
(Lei)	è*	you are	(loro) sono	they are
(lui/lei)	è*	he / she is		

The asterisked forms are those you have met in this Unit.

B io, tu, Lei, lui, lei – I, you, he, she (subject pronouns)

The subject pronouns are usually omitted in Italian because the ending of the verb is enough to tell us who is carrying out the action. They are only used to avoid confusion, to emphasize or to show contrast.

> **Lei** parla italiano – **you** speak Italian
> **lui** parla italiano – **he** speaks Italian
> Il direttore del personale è irlandese ma **io** sono inglese – The personnel manager is Irish but I am English

There are two ways of saying **you** in Italian when addressing one person.

> **tu** familiar – to family and close friends
> **Lei** formal – to acquaintances and strangers

The one you should use in business relationships is **Lei**. Nowadays it is usual amongst young people to use **tu**, but it is wise to keep to **Lei** until you are invited to use **tu** or until you hear others addressing you as **tu**.

Note that **Lei** is written with a capital letter. The **Lei** form of all verbs is the same as the **lui** / **lei** form.

C Negatives

To make a verb negative you put **non** in front of it.

> **Non** parlo inglese – I don't speak English
> **Non** è irlandese – He is not Irish

D Questions

Listen to the cassette and note how the voice rises at the end of a question. Unlike English, the words do not change.

> È scozzese – He is Scottish   È scozzese? – Is he Scottish?
>
> Parla italiano – You speak Italian   Parla italiano? – Do you speak Italian?

Vero (lit. 'true') is often added to a question. It is the equivalent of all English phrases like 'aren't they?', 'isn't it?', 'don't you?', etc.

E Gender

Nouns and articles

All nouns in Italian, not just people's names, are **masculine** or **feminine**.
The definite article (the) and the indefinite article (a / an) have masculine and feminine forms.

As a general rule:

Masculine nouns end in -o or -e				
il lavoro	il signore	l'ingegnere	lo stabilimento	THE
un lavoro	un signore	un ingegnere	uno stabilimento	A / AN
Feminine nouns end in -a or -e				
la ditta	la nazione	l'azienda		THE
una ditta	una nazione	un'azienda		A / AN

- **il** (m.) and **la** (f.) become **l'** before a vowel.
- **lo** and **uno** are *only* used with masculine singular nouns beginning with z or s + consonant(s), e.g. **lo stabilimento** (plant / factory), **lo zucchero** (sugar).
- **una** (f.) becomes **un'** before a vowel.

Adjectives

Adjectives also have masculine and feminine endings.
A dictionary gives you the masculine singular form which ends in <u>-o</u> or <u>-e</u>.

- <u>-o</u> changes to <u>-a</u> for the feminine
  liet<u>o</u> (m.)   liet<u>a</u> (f.)
  quest<u>o</u> (m.)   quest<u>a</u> (f.)
- Adjectives ending in <u>-e</u>, (e.g. **generale, inglese**) have the same ending for both masculine and feminine.

F Di and other prepositions with 'the'

In Italian, **di** (of / from), <u>a</u> (at / to), <u>da</u> (from), **su** (on) and <u>in</u> (in) combine with the words for '**the**'.

You have already seen examples of this with **a** and **di** in the Management Structure chart on page 2.

   di + il = del   di + la = della   di + l' = dell'   a + le = alle

The others combine in a similar way (e.g. **da + la = dalla**). They will be dealt with in later units. Do not worry about them at this stage. You will find that you gradually get used to them.

In Italia ...

Greetings

Shaking hands is an essential part of greeting someone and saying goodbye, not merely something one does when being introduced for the first time.

In the dialogues you have already heard **buongiorno** and **buona sera**. You will also come across the following.

Buona notte – good night
Arrivederci – the usual way of saying goodbye
ArrivederLa – a more formal way of saying goodbye
Ciao – a very informal way of saying hi or goodbye

Forms of address

The Italians tend to be more formal than the British and titles are used regularly, with and without the surname.

A man is addressed as **signore,** a married or older woman as **signora,** and a young unmarried woman as **signorina**. There is no Italian equivalent of Ms.

You will appear casual and rather impolite if you greet someone without using these titles. However, it is perfectly acceptable in business to refer to male colleagues by their surname only. Avoid using first names unless it is obviously acceptable.

When **signore** is used together with the surname (the equivalent of Mr) the final -e is dropped – **Buongiorno, sign<u>ore</u>** but **Buongiorno, sign<u>or</u> Lucarini**. Signora and signorina do not change.
The written abbreviations for **signore, signora** and **signorina** are **sig., sig.ra** and **sig.na**.

These are not the only titles used regularly in Italian.

Professional titles such as **ragioniere** (m.) / **ragioniera** (f.) (accountant), **ingegnere** (m. & f.) (engineer) are used as everyday titles. They drop the final -e before a surname and abbreviate in the written language to **rag.** and **ing.**

You will also hear **signor** followed by the professional title, e.g. **signor ingegnere**.

If you do not know the title of an Italian executive, you should address him / her as **dottore / dottoressa. Dottore** drops the final -e before a surname. **Dottoressa** stays unchanged - **Dottor Columbro, Dottoressa Bonelli.**

Not quite as common are the titles **Cavaliere (Cav.)** and **Commendatore (Comm.)**. They are titles awarded by the State for achievement in a particular field of work, but they are also used, as a token of respect, to people who have not officially been granted them.

Names of companies

As in English, there are several words for a company, firm or business. **Ditta, azienda, società** and **compagnia** are all widely used, and you will also hear **casa** and **impresa**.

Pratica

1 *Listen to all the conversations again and answer the following questions in Italian.*

    (i)   Il signor Lucarini è il direttore generale della Lentini?

    (ii)   Come si chiama il direttore alle vendite della ditta MK?

    (iii)   Laura Barlow è il direttore del personale?

    (iv)   Ian McMillan è scozzese?

    (v)   Il capo ragioniere è inglese?

    (vi)   Antonio Bianchi parla inglese?

    (vii) Joanna Rossi parla italiano?

    (viii) Joanna Rossi è una segretaria?

2 *Listen to the five interviews on the cassette and supply the information missing from the form. Note that in Italian, especially in a formal context, people often give their surname (cognome) before their Christian name.*

Cognome   *BONELLI*
Nome
Lavoro
Nazionalità *ITALIANA*
Residente a

Cognome
Nome   *ALESSANDRO*
Lavoro
Nazionalità
Residente a

Cognome
Nome   *PAOLO*
Lavoro
Nazionalità
Residente a *ZURIGO*

Cognome   *TREVESE*
Nome
Lavoro
Nazionalità
Residente a *PARIGI*

Cognome
Nome
Lavoro *DIRETTORE TECNICO*
Nazionalità
Residente a

NORVEGIA
SVEZIA
SCOZIA
DANIMARCA
RUSSIA
IRLANDA
INGHILTERRA
GALLES
OLANDA
POLONIA
GERMANIA
BELGIO
CECOSLOVACCHIA
AUSTRIA
UNGHERIA
FRANCIA
SVIZZERA
SLOVENIA
SERBIA
CROAZIA
BOSNIA
PORTOGALLO
SPAGNA
ITALIA
ALBANIA
GRECIA

3 *The following are on the cassette first as statements, then as questions. Listen to them and repeat them carefully. (Grammatica D)*

Laura è inglese.	Laura è inglese?
Lei è direttore alle vendite.	Lei è direttore alle vendite?
Giorgio parla francese.	Giorgio parla francese?
La ditta Lentini è italiana.	La ditta Lentini è italiana?
Il signor Bianchi è il direttore generale.	Il signor Bianchi è il direttore generale?

4 *Fill the gaps in the conversation using the words in the box.*

Sig. Morello: Buongiorno signore. _____ Carlo Morello della Società Badino.

Sig. Franchi: _____ S'accomodi, signor Morello.

Sig. Morello: Grazie._____ è Mary Wright e _____ è Franco Rossetti.

Sig.ra Wright: Molto _____

Sig. Verdi: Molto _____

Sig. Franchi: Piacere. Lei ___ inglese, signora?

Sig.ra Wright: No, _____ scozzese.

questo	questa
lieto	lieta
è	sono
sono	piacere

5 *Rearrange the following jumbled-up sentences.*

(i) bene Lei parla molto l'italiano
(ii) favore attimo per un
(iii) del è direttore irlandese il personale
(iv) italiano scusi parlo non
(v) acquisti Lucarini è agli questo Giancarlo direttore

6 (A) *Put il, la, lo or l' as required in front of the following nouns... (Grammatica E)*

ditta   lavoro   nazione   azienda   ufficio

ingegnere   signora   casa   zucchero   attimo

(B) *...and un, una, uno or un' in front of these.*

attimo   dottore   ragioniera   impresa   signorina

direttore   segretaria   capo   ditta   stabilimento

7 *In Italian, how would you ....*

- Greet Enzo Chiari in the evening.
- Say you are pleased to meet him.
- Ask him to wait a moment.
- Invite him to sit down.
- Ask him if he speaks English.
- Tell him that you are English / Welsh / Scottish / Irish.

8 *If you were asked the following questions, how would you answer? (Grammatica A and C)*

For your answer you will need:
Sì / No + the appropriate form of **parlare + non / un po' / bene / molto bene**

Esempio Parla portoghese? Sì, parlo un po'. / No, non parlo portoghese.

- Parla tedesco?
- Parla italiano?
- Parla francese?
- Parla giapponese?
- Parla spagnolo?
- Parla inglese?

9 *Introduce each of the following people in Italian. Refer to page 3 for their titles.*

Esempio Questo è Antonio Bianchi, direttore generale della Lentini.

Antonio Bianchi	Laura Barlow
Giancarlo Lucarini	Joanna Rossi
Peter Lawrence	Ian McMillan

 10 *Take part in the following conversations.*
(**A**)

Giovanni Villoresi:	Buongiorno, dottore. Lei è Marco Bonsanti, vero?
You:	(*Say you are not Marco Bonsanti and say who you are.*)
Giovanni Villoresi:	Scusi, signore. Lei non è italiano. È americano?
You:	(*Say you're English.*)
Giovanni Villoresi:	Piacere, signore. Io sono Giovanni Villoresi.
You:	(*Say you're pleased to meet him.*)

(**B**)

Franco Ruggini:	Buongiorno, signore. Parla italiano?
You:	(*Tell him you speak a little and that you are studying Italian.*)
Franco Ruggini:	Come si chiama?
You:	(*Tell him your name and say what work you do.*)
Franco Ruggini:	Molto lieto. Io sono Franco Ruggini.
You:	(*Ask him if he is the personnel manager.*)
Franco Ruggini:	No, sono ragioniere.
You:	(*Now introduce Paul King to him and explain that he does not speak Italian. Ask signor Ruggini if he speaks English.*)
Franco Ruggini:	Piacere, signor King. No, io non parlo inglese. Ma Lei parla bene l'italiano.
You:	(*Thank him and say goodbye.*)

11 *Practise introducing yourself, giving your name and nationality, saying which company you are from and what position you hold in the company.*

Now practise introducing some of the people you work with. Use the Management Structure chart on page 2 for professions / occupations / positions.

12 *The advertisements on the following page are taken from an Italian newspaper. When you have looked over them, answer the questions below.*

You know many of the words already. A few of the new words are given to help you and all the words are in the Vocabulary at the end of the book, but you should make every effort to recognise the many words that are similar in English and Italian. It helps if you read the words out loud. (Several English words like 'leader' and 'marketing' are rarely translated into Italian.)

Do not expect to understand every word at this stage.

(A) OFFERTE DI COLLABORAZIONE **(Appointments wanted)**

(i)   What is the profession of the person looking for work in Bologna? Is it a man or a woman?

(ii)   What experience does the marketing manager offer?

(iii) Which foreign languages does the commercial manager offer?

(iv)   In which sector does the electronics engineer have experience?

(v)   What sort of post is the journalist with industrial experience seeking?

(B) RICERCHE DI COLLABORATORI **(Appointments offered / Situations vacant)**

(vi)   Apart from word-processing skills, what does the secretary need to have for the multinational company?

(vii) What nationality is the firm advertising the position of Chief Accountant?

(viii) What is the position advertised by the electric motors firm based in north Rome?

(ix)   What sort of firm is advertising for agents and representatives in Northern and Central Italy?

(C) CORSI / SCUOLE **(Courses / Schools)**

(x)   What are the five languages advertised by the international language school in Via Aretino?

(xi)   What is the number to ring for information about courses in Spanish and Portuguese?

(xii) Which types of French courses are advertised?

OFFERTE DI COLLABORAZIONE

DIRETTORE COMMERCIALE
conoscenza inglese e tedesco
cerca lavoro zona Roma nord.
Casella Postale 4053 – 00182
ROMA

INGEGNERE ELETTRONICO,
esperienza settore automobilistico
cerca lavoro.
Tel. (06) 2399873

PROGRAMMATORE analista
esperienza IBM cerca lavoro
importanza internazionale.
Tel. (0337) 747610

GIORNALISTA, esperienza industriale,
cerca lavoro – pubbliche relazioni.
Tel. (059) 378104

LAUREATA Economia e Commercio
(25enne) esperta di marketing
nazionale e internazionale,
conoscenza inglese.
Tel. (06) 8705419

RAGIONIERA 28enne cerca lavoro a
Bologna. Esperienza contabilità
computerizzata.
Tel. (06) 8431209

DIRETTORE MARKETING
esperienza nazionale /
internazionale
settore telecomunicazioni
cerca lavoro interessante.
Casella Postale 155 –
00054 Fiumicino

RICERCHE DI COLLABORATORI

Importante azienda
italo-tedesca ricerca
CAPO RAGIONIERE
Curriculum a
Cas. Post. n. 917
00182 ROMA

IMPORTANTE azienda farmaceutica
cerca agenti e rappresentanti, nord /
centro Italia.
Curriculum – Fax (06) 9621248

AZIENDA motori elettrici, zona Roma
nord, cerca ingegnere meccanico.
Tel. (035) 260357

SEGRETARIA per ditta multinazionale, uso wp, conoscenza
inglese e francese.
Curriculum vitae –
Fax (06) 7943200

Prestigiosa società
leader settore
informatico
cerca
DIRETTORE VENDITE
con esperienza
internazionale.
Scrivere a
Casella Postale 5910
00100 ROMA

CORSI / SCUOLE

Parla con il mondo!

- *inglese*
- *tedesco*
- *francese*
- *spagnolo*
- *giapponese*

**Scuola internazionale
di lingue
Via P. Aretino 41
Tel. (0577) 74 90 12**

CORSI di spagnolo e portoghese
a tutti i livelli.
Tel. (06) 4431909

INGLESE professoressa madrelingua.
Tel. (06) 5468103

**Parla inglese?
No?
Perché no?**

*Corsi di lingua inglese
The English School,
Via Nomentana 2
Tel. (06) 390 1856*

FRANCESE per il turismo e per il
commercio.
Tel. (06) 8365920

Vocabolarietto

la conoscenza	knowledge
la contabilità	accountancy
il settore	sector
la zona	district
laureato / laureata	graduate
–enne	– years old
cercare / ricercare	to seek
perché	why

16

Riassunto

You can now ...

- **greet people and say goodbye**

  Buongiorno / buona sera / buona notte
  Arrivederci / arrivederLa / ciao

- **address them correctly**

  Signore / signora / signorina / signor Bianchi
  Dottoressa Bastiani / ingegnere

- **welcome somebody**

  Benvenuto / benvenuta
  Si accomodi, signore

- **introduce yourself and others**

  Sono _____
  Questo / questa è _____
  Piacere
  Molto lieto / lieta

- **say what your profession is / what position you hold at work**

  Sono direttore / ragioniere / segretaria / direttore del marketing

- **say what nationality you are**

  Sono inglese / gallese / scozzese / irlandese

- **say which languages you speak**

  Parlo un po' d'italiano
  Non parlo spagnolo
  Parlo francese bene

►► *Now, with a partner, try Role Play 1 on pages 195–6*

The abbreviations mentioned in Unit 1 are listed here, along with others you will find useful. You will find that you soon become familiar with the most common, and it is not intended that you should learn them at this stage.

alleg.	allegato (enclosure)
API	Associazione Piccole e Medie Industrie
avv.	avvocato (lawyer)
c.a.	corrente anno (this year)
CGIL	Confederazione Generale Italiana del Lavoro (Communist Trade Union)
CISL	Confederazione Italiana Sindacato Lavoratori (Christian Democrat Trade Union)
c.m / m.c.	corrente mese (this month)
c/o	conto (account)
CONFINDUSTRIA	Confederazione dell'Industria Italiana
dir.	direttore (director)
dott.	dottore (doctor)
ecc.	eccetera (etcetera)
Egr. Sig.	Egregio Signore (Dear Sir)
F.lli	Fratelli (Brothers)
FS	Ferrovie dello Stato (Italian Railways)
Gent. Sig.ra	Gentile Signora (Dear Madam)
ing.	ingegnere (engineer)
IVA	Imposta sul Valore Aggiunto (VAT)
L. it.	lire italiane (Italian lire)
L. st.	lire sterline (pound sterling)
mitt.	mittente (sender)
mq	metro quadro (square metre)
ns.	nostro, nostra (our, ours)
Ns. Rif.	Nostro Riferimento (Our Ref)
p.es / p.e.	per esempio (for example)
prof.	professore (professor)
PT	Poste e Telegrafi (Post Office)
rag.	ragioniere / a (accountant)
RAI	Radiotelevisione Italiana
s.a.	scorso anno (last year)
SA	società anonima (limited company)
Sig.	signore (Mr)
Sig.na	signorina (Miss)
Sig.ra	signora (Mrs / Ms)
SIP	Società Italiana per l'Esercizio Telefonico
Snc	società in nome collettivo (general partnership)
SpA	società per azioni (public limited company)
spett.	spettabile (esteemed)
spett. ditta	spettabile ditta (Dear Sirs, Messrs)
Srl	società a responsabilità limitata (private limited compnay)
UIL	Unione Italiana del Lavoro (Socialist Trade Union)
u.s.	ultimo scorso (last month)
Vs.	Vostro, Vostra (your, yours)
Vs/	Vostra lettera (Your letter)

Unit 2

DOVE LAVORA?

You will learn to:
- say where you are from and where you live
- say where you work
- ask other people about their work and their family
- offer / accept a drink
- use the numbers from 1 to 30

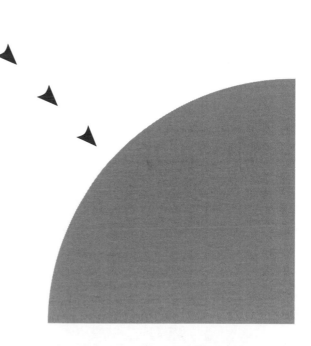

📼 Conversazioni

Tè o caffè?

Joanna Rossi:	Prende un tè, dottore? O un caffè?
Antonio Bianchi:	Volentieri – un caffè. No, no ... prendo un tè.
Joanna Rossi:	Infatti, il caffè inglese non è molto buono! Con o senza latte? O al limone?
Antonio Bianchi:	Preferisco il tè al limone. Senza zucchero.

Dove lavora?

Joanna Rossi:	Dove lavora? Alla sede centrale della Lentini?
Antonio Bianchi:	Sì, lavoro a Roma da venti* anni. E Lei, da quanto tempo lavora qui?
Joanna Rossi:	Da quattro* anni.

È interessante?

Antonio Bianchi:	Lavora all'ufficio vendite, vero?
Joanna Rossi:	Sì. Organizzo la pubblicità per il mercato estero e parlo con i clienti esteri.
Antonio Bianchi:	È un lavoro interessante?
Joanna Rossi:	Sì, è interessante ma sono molto occupata.

Dove abita?

Joanna Rossi:	Dove abita? A Roma?
Antonio Bianchi:	No, abito a Ostia, vicino a Roma. E Lei, abita a Londra?
Joanna Rossi:	No, non abito a Londra. Da cinque* mesi abito a Richmond.
Antonio Bianchi:	Dov'è Richmond? È lontano?
Joanna Rossi:	No, non è molto lontano. È a dieci* chilometri.

* For numerals 1–30 refer to *Grammatica page 26*.

Spiegazioni

- **Prende un tè?** – Would you like some tea? **Prende** is a form of the verb **prendere** (to take). (*Grammatica page 24*)

- **Volentieri** – I'd love some (Lit. 'willingly')

- **Molto buono** – very good. The ending of **molto** meaning **very** does not change.

- **Preferisco il tè al limone** – I prefer tea with lemon. **Preferisco** is a form of the verb **preferire** (to prefer). (*Grammatica page 24*)

- **Dove lavora?** Where do you work?

- **Lavoro a Roma da venti anni** – I have been working in Rome for twenty years.
  To say you have been doing something for a period of time or since a particular time you use the present tense followed by **da**.
  Lavoro qui **da dieci anni** – I have been working here *for ten years*.
  Lavoro qui **da settembre** – I have been working here *since September*.

- **a Roma** – in Rome. It can also mean 'to Rome'.
  In Italian you never say **in** + a town or city; **a Londra** means 'in London' or 'to London'.

- **anni** – years. In Italian you do not add an -s to form the plural, you change the final vowel instead. Look out for **mesi** (months), **clienti esteri** (overseas customers) and **chilometri** (kilometers) in the conversations on the facing page. (*Grammatica page 25*)

- **E Lei, da quanto tempo lavora qui?** – And how long have *you* been working here?

- **Che lavoro fa?** – What is your job? **Fa** comes from **fare** (to do / make). (*Grammatica page 25*)

- **Dov'è?** = (**dove + è**) – Where is?

- **È a dieci chilometri** – It's 10 km away

Vocabolarietto

l'anno	year	**abitare**	to live
il caffè	coffee	**lavorare**	to work
il cliente	customer	**organizzare**	to organize
il latte	milk	**preferire (-isc)**	to prefer
il limone	lemon	**prendere**	to take
il mercato	market		
il mese	month	**quanto**	how much
la pubblicità	publicity / advertising	**vicino a**	near
la sede (centrale)	head office	**alla = a + la**	at the
il tè	tea	**all' = a + l'**	
il tempo	time	**per**	for
lo zucchero	sugar	**con**	with
		senza	without
buono	good	**o**	or
estero	foreign / overseas	**ma**	but
interessante	interesting	**dove**	where
lontano	far	**infatti**	in fact / quite so
occupato	busy	**molto**	very

▦ Conversazioni

Antonio Bianchi presenta Giancarlo Lucarini a Joanna Rossi

Antonio Bianchi:	... Lucarini! Signora Rossi, Le presento Giancarlo Lucarini.
Joanna Rossi:	Molto lieta.
Giancarlo Lucarini:	Piacere.

Lucarini non è romano, è fiorentino

Joanna Rossi:	Lei lavora con il dottor Bianchi?
Giancarlo Lucarini:	Sì, lavoro presso la Lentini da quasi tre* anni.
Joanna Rossi:	Abita a Ostia anche Lei?
Giancarlo Lucarini:	No. Io ho un piccolo appartamento a Roma, vicino all'ufficio, e una casa a Firenze.
Joanna Rossi:	A Firenze?
Giancarlo Lucarini:	Sì, lavoro a Roma ma sono fiorentino. Mi capisce? Sono di Firenze. Mia moglie abita a Firenze. Anche lei è fiorentina.

La famiglia

Joanna Rossi:	Ha figli?
Giancarlo Lucarini:	Abbiamo una figlia.
Joanna Rossi:	E Lei, dottor Bianchi, ha figli?
Antonio Bianchi:	Ne ho tre* – un* maschio e due* femmine.
Joanna Rossi:	Quanti anni hanno?
Antonio Bianchi:	Mio figlio Carlo ha quindici* anni, mia figlia Anna tredici*, e la piccola Olivia solo cinque*. Ecco una fotografia.
Joanna Rossi:	Che bella famiglia!
Antonio Bianchi:	Lei è sposata?
Joanna Rossi:	Sì, mio marito è giornalista. È italiano – di Napoli.
Antonio Bianchi:	Che coincidenza! Anche mia moglie è napoletana!

* For numerals 1–30 refer to *Grammatica page 26.*

Spiegazioni

- **Le presento** – Let me introduce ___ to you (lit. 'to you I introduce ___').

- **Ho un piccolo appartamento** – I have a small flat. **Ho** is a form of **avere** (to have). Other forms of **avere** in this conversation are **ha** (you have, he / she has), **abbiamo** (we have), and **hanno** (they have). (*Grammatica page 24*)

- **Mi capisce?** – Do you understand me? **Capisce** is from **capire** (to understand) (*Grammatica page 24*). Note that <u>me</u> usually goes in front of the verb in Italian.

- **Ha figli? Ne ho tre – un maschio e due femmine** – Do you have any children? I have three (of them), a boy and two girls. **Ne**, which here means 'of them', can also mean 'of it' / 'some' / 'any'.
  Figli is the plural of **figlio** and the literal translation is 'sons'. But it is used to mean 'children', and the masculine plural form is used in Italian if there are sons and daughters, even if two of the children are girls.
  The word for a younger child is **bambino** and, again, the masculine plural form, **bambini**, is used for boys and girls together, as well as just boys.

- **Quanti anni hanno?** – How old are they?
  In Italian, to say how old someone is, you use **avere** + number of years + **anni**.
  Ho 25 anni – I am 25 years old. Mio figlio ha 15 anni – My son is 15.

- **Che bella famiglia!** – What a lovely family!

- **Mio marito è giornalista** – My husband is a journalist. In Italian you do not use the indefinite article (a / an) when giving your profession.

- Nouns ending in **-ista**.
  There are many nouns ending in **-ista** which you will recognise without the need for a dictionary.
  e.g. artista, dentista, terrorista, socialista, specialista, realista,
       femminista, farmacista, turista, pessimista, ottimista, ciclista,
  They do not follow the rule that words ending in **-a** are feminine. You can have **il giornalista** (m.) and **la giornalista** (f.)
  Not *all* English words ending in -ist are like these.
  e.g. scientist – **scienziato**, (industrial) chemist – **chimico**, physicist – **fisico**.

- **Che coincidenza!** – What a coincidence!

Vocabolarietto

l'appartamento	flat	**mio**	my
la casa	house	**napoletano**	from Naples / Neapolitan
la famiglia	family	**piccolo**	little
la figlia	daughter	**sposato**	married
il figlio	son		
la fotografia	photograph	**capire (-isc)**	to understand
il marito	husband	**presentare**	to introduce
la moglie	wife		
		presso	at / for (a company / place)
bello	fine / beautiful	**quasi**	nearly / almost
fiorentino	from Florence	**solo**	only

Grammatica

A The Present tense

The endings for -ere and -ire verbs differ slightly from the -are pattern you learnt in Unit 1.

Regular verbs ending in -ere

vendere – to sell	
(io)	vend<u>o</u>
(Lei)	vend<u>e</u>
(lui / lei)	vend<u>e</u>

Regular verbs ending in -ire

There are two types of -ire verbs.

1. Verbs like **partire** the endings of which in the singular are exactly the same as the **-ere** verb endings.
2. Verbs like **capire** which insert **-isc** before the ending.*

	1. **Partire** – to leave	2. **Capire** – to understand
(io)	part<u>o</u>	cap<u>isco</u>
(Lei)	part<u>e</u>	cap<u>isce</u>
(lui / lei)	part<u>e</u>	cap<u>isce</u>

*-ire verbs taking **-isc** before the ending will be indicated in the Vocabolarietto.

Avere – to have

In Unit 1 you learnt **essere**. **Avere** is another irregular verb and it is especially important that you know it well.

(io)	**ho**	I have	(noi)	**abbiamo**	we have
(tu)	**hai**	you have	(voi)	**avete**	you have
(Lei)	**ha**	you have	(loro)	**hanno**	they have
(lui / lei)	**ha**	he / she has			

Note that in English we ask **Have you —? Do you have —?** or **Have you got —?**
In Italian all that is necessary is **Ha__?** e.g. **Ha figli?**

Fare – to make / to do

Fare (also irregular) will be dealt with in more detail in later units, but it is included here because it is used to ask someone what their work is – **Che lavoro fa?**
If you are asked this question, your answer could be either of the following:

(i) **Sono** + profession   Sono avvocato (lawyer)

(ii) **Faccio** + the + profession   Faccio l'avvocato

(io)	**faccio**	I do	(noi)	**facciamo**	we do
(tu)	**fai**	you do	(voi)	**fate**	you do
(Lei)	**fa**	you do	(loro)	**fanno**	they do
(lui / lei)	**fa**	he / she does			

B Plurals

In Italian all nouns, adjectives and the definite article (the) have a plural.

Nouns and articles

MASCULINE

SINGULAR	il mercato	il signore	l'ingegnere	lo stabilimento
PLURAL	i mercati	i signori	gli ingegneri	gli stabilimenti

FEMININE

SINGULAR	la ditta	la nazione	l'azienda
PLURAL	le ditte	le nazioni	le aziende

Adjectives

Adjective endings change in the same way as noun endings.

MASCULINE			FEMININE		
SINGULAR	italiano	inglese	SINGULAR	italiana	inglese
PLURAL	italiani	inglesi	PLURAL	italiane	inglesi

Any adjective used to describe a noun must agree with that noun.

MASC. SING. il piccol<u>o</u> appartamento   MASC. PLUR. i piccol<u>i</u> appartament<u>i</u>
FEM. SING.   la piccol<u>a</u> cas<u>a</u>   FEM. PLUR.   le piccol<u>e</u> cas<u>e</u>

Position of Adjectives

As a general rule, adjectives go after the noun they describe.

C Numbers 1–30

These numbers are on the cassette after the *Conversazioni*.

0	zero				
1	uno	11	undici	21	ventuno
2	due	12	dodici	22	ventidue
3	tre	13	tredici	23	ventitré
4	quattro	14	quattordici	24	ventiquattro
5	cinque	15	quindici	25	venticinque
6	sei	16	sedici	26	ventisei
7	sette	17	diciassette	27	ventisette
8	otto	18	diciotto	28	ventotto
9	nove	19	diciannove	29	ventinove
10	dieci	20	venti	30	trenta

In Italia ...

Despite the importance of addressing professional people by their appropriate title and avoiding undue familiarity, a strictly business approach might be seen as curt or even impolite in Italy where conversation is important. Italians show an interest in people and talk about their family with the interest the British reserve for the weather, so do not be reluctant to ask questions.

Campanilismo

Di dov'è? – Where are you from? If asked this question you might answer 'sono inglese / scozzese', or you might say 'abito a Bristol'.

If you ask an Italian where he is from, he is more likely to say 'sono di Firenze', than 'abito a Firenze', revealing a sense of belonging to that particular city rather than just living there. Equally as common would be 'sono fiorentino' (or milanese, romano, napoletano, veneziano, etc.). In fact, this is often seen as more significant than being 'Italian'. This attachment to one's native city, known as **campanilismo** (from **campanile** – 'bell tower'), is easy to understand if we remember that Italy has only existed as a unified country since the 1860s. Until that time it was a collection of independent city-states, each with its particular identity, character and dialect.

These regional identities are still strong today. In particular, there is a marked social and economic contrast between Northern and Southern Italy. This shows few real signs of being eradicated despite massive government aid to combat underdevelopment, unemployment, poverty and organised crime in the South. The contrast extends to attitudes to work and to life in general, and an awareness of regional differences is fundamental to successful business in Italy.

Northern Italy

Northern Italy includes Lombardy (Lombardia), Piedmont (Piemonte), Liguria, Veneto, Emilia Romagna and Tuscany (Toscana) – all rich in industry, agriculture and commerce. Milan (Milano) is considered the financial, commercial, fashion and banking capital of Italy. It is one of Europe's leading centres for trade fairs and has the largest stock exchange in Italy.

Turin (Torino) is Italy's industrial capital, and Genoa (Genova), a major industrial city, its largest port. It has two container terminals with a third under construction and there is a long tradition of British imports through Genoa.

Central Italy

Rome (Roma), in Central Italy, is the capital city and the seat of government. Rome is where around 70 per cent of national commercial organisations and most State agencies and public utilities have their administrative headquarters.

Southern Italy

Southern Italy, including Sardinia (Sardegna) and Sicily (Sicilia), is known as the **Mezzogiorno**. There is considerable funding here to stimulate industrial investment in a traditionally underdeveloped agricultural area.

Naples (Napoli), with the greatest density of population in Italy, is the largest industrial centre in the South and an important port with container facilities.

Sicily's main industries are oil and petrochemical refining, primary chemical production and citrus fruits. Palermo and Catania are the chief industrial centres.

Sardinia's economy is centred on mining, the petrochemical and metallurgical industries, and a developing tourist trade.

Practica

1 *Listen to all the conversations again and answer the following questions in Italian.*

(i) Dove lavora Antonio Bianchi?
(ii) Da quanto tempo lavora qui?
(iii) Abita a Roma?
(iv) E Lucarini, abita a Roma?
(v) Che lavoro fa Joanna Rossi?

(vi) È sposato Giancarlo Lucarini?
(vii) Di dov'è sua moglie?
(viii) Quanti figli hanno?
(ix) Quanti anni ha Carlo Bianchi?
(x) Che lavoro fa il marito di Joanna Rossi?

2 *Vero o falso? Listen to some people talking about themselves and then decide whether the following statements are true (vero) or false (falso).*

	VERO	FALSO
Renato Franchi lives near Rome.	☐	☐
Salvatore Antonello is an accountant from Naples.	☐	☐
Caterina Frosoni has worked in Milan for five years.	☐	☐
Paolo Giordano has been married for six months.	☐	☐
Laura Varetti speaks French and German.	☐	☐
Guido Viscardi is a dentist.	☐	☐

3 **(A)** *This weather report from Meteoradio gives the maximum temperatures for the following Italian cities in February. Write them down in figures. (Grammatica C)*

TORINO	_____	L'AQUILA	_____
MILANO	_____	CAMPOBASSO	_____
VENEZIA	_____	NAPOLI	_____
TRIESTE	_____	BARI	_____
BOLZANO	_____	POTENZA	_____
GENOVA	_____	REGGIO CALABRIA	_____
BOLOGNA	_____	PALERMO	_____
FIRENZE	_____	CAGLIARI	_____
PERUGIA	_____		

(B) *Now try some arithmetic. Add up the pairs of numbers.*

(C) *Listen to the passage on the cassette and fill in the missing statistics.*

Da ———— anni lavoro presso la società Angeletti. La sede centrale è a Torino, Corso Umberto ————, telefono ————————.

Io lavoro allo stabilimento San Giovanni, a ——— chilometri da Mantova. Abbiamo ———————— dipendenti a San Giovanni.

4 *Decide what Alessandra, Marco and Francesca have to drink.*

Alessandra ———————— Marco ———————— Francesca ————————

5 *Complete the following sentences with the appropriate form of the verbs in brackets. (Grammatica A, Units 1 and 2)*

    (i)   La signora Moro ————————l'opuscolo. (leggere)

    (ii)   Lei ————————il francese? (studiare)

    (iii)   Io ————————————un'esposizione. (organizzare)

    (iv)   Io ————————————i prodotti in Italia. (vendere)

    (v)   Agnelli ————————————oggi. (partire)

    (vi)   Santoro ————————————il tè al limone. (preferire)

    (vii) Io ————————————un caffè. (prendere)

    (viii) Lei, quanti figli ————————? (avere)

    (ix)   Io non ————————————. (capire)

    (x)   Io non ————————————il numero di telefono. (avere)

Vocabolarietto

l'esposizione (f.)	exhibition
l'opuscolo	brochure
il prodotto	product
oggi	today

6 *If necessary, change the adjectives in brackets to make them agree with their nouns. (Grammatica B)*

La dottoressa Bellini non è (italiano), è (svizzero). Lavora all'ufficio (estero) della Marchem, una società (chimico) in Lombardia, una regione (ricco) e (industriale) nel nord dell'Italia.

La dottoressa è (sposato) da dieci anni e ha due bambini (piccolo). Ha un appartamento a Milano ma preferisce la (piccolo) casa di Lucca, una (bello) città toscana.

7 *You are talking to someone who is not sure of his facts. Correct him in each of the following, altering the singular / plural endings as necessary. (Grammatica B)*

Esempio   Un maschio e due femmine?   No, due maschi e una femmina.

- (i)   Una casa e due appartamenti?
- (ii)   Una sorella e due fratelli?
- (iii)   Un inglese e due italiani?
- (iv)   Un romano e due milanesi?
- (v)   Una segretaria e due direttori?

8 *The answer to each of these questions will be one more than the number mentioned in the question.*

Esempio   Lavora a Torino da dieci anni?   No, da undici anni.

- (i)   Lavora qui da otto anni?
- (ii)   Ha cinque filiali in Germania?
- (iii)   Lei organizza quattro esposizioni in Europa quest'anno?
- (iv)   Studia l'italiano da sei mesi?
- (v)   È sposato da tre anni?
- (vi)   Abita a ventiquattro km da Torino?
- (vii)   La città è a diciassette km da qui?
- (viii)   È direttore generale da quattordici anni?

9 *Rearrange these jumbled-up sentences.*

- (i)   anni lavoro da Roma a dieci
- (ii)   lontano molto non no è
- (iii)   ma fiorentino lavoro Roma a sono
- (iv)   quanti figlio Suo anni ha?
- (v)   a casa piccolo vicino una appartamento Roma Firenze ho e un a

10 *In Italian, how would you ask someone:*

- – Where they work.
- – How long they have been working here.
- – If the work is interesting.
- – Where they live.

- – If they are married.
- – If they have children.
- – If they would like some coffee.
- – If they understand.

Take part in the following conversations.

    (A) *You strike up a conversation with a lady at the airport.*

You:	(*Introduce yourself and find out her name.*)
Signora:	Mi chiamo Luisa Brown.
You:	(*Ask if she is English.*)
Signora:	No. Mio marito è inglese. Io sono italiana.
You:	(*Ask if she lives in Rome.*)
Signora:	No, non abito a Roma. Abito vicino a Firenze. E Lei, di dov'è?
You:	(*Tell her where you are from and where you live now.*)
Signora:	Ma parla molto bene l'italiano.
You:	(*Say you have been studying Italian for two months.*)
Signora:	Solo due mesi? Complimenti!
You:	(*Thank her and ask if she has any children.*)
Signora:	Sì. Ho quattro figli – un maschio e tre femmine. Ecco una fotografia.
You:	(*Say what a beautiful family she has.*)

    (B) *You meet Giancarlo Lucarini ...*

You:	(*Ask him if he is the commercial manager.*)
Giancarlo Lucarini:	No. Sono direttore agli acquisti.
You:	(*Apologise, then find out how long he has been working for Lentini.*)
Giancarlo Lucarini:	Da sei anni.
You:	(*Ask if it is a big company.*)
Giancarlo Lucarini:	Abbastanza grande.
You:	(*Ask if the head office is in Rome.*)
Giancarlo Lucarini:	Vicino a Roma, a Pomezia.
You:	(*Ask if he prefers tea or coffee.*)
Giancarlo Lucarini:	Preferisco il caffè. Grazie.
You:	(*With or without milk? Sugar?*)
Giancarlo Lucarini:	Con zucchero, senza latte.

12 *Here are the Bianchi, d'Angelo and Russo family trees:*

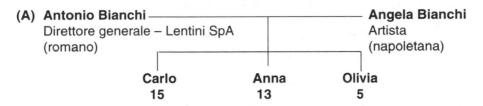

(A) Antonio Bianchi — **Angela Bianchi**
Direttore generale – Lentini SpA   Artista
(romano)   (napoletana)

Carlo   Anna   Olivia
15   13   5

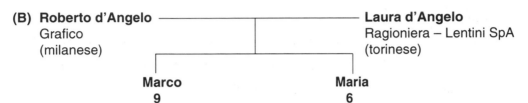

(B) Roberto d'Angelo — **Laura d'Angelo**
Grafico   Ragioniera – Lentini SpA
(milanese)   (torinese)

Marco   Maria
9   6

(C) Salvatore Russo — **Giovanna Russo**
Direttore tecnico – Lentini SpA   Professoressa
(bolognese)   (fiorentina)

Francesca   Barbara   Fabrizio   Enzo
17   14   10   8

(A) *Antonio Bianchi è direttore generale della ditta Lentini. È sposato. Sua moglie si chiama Angela, è di Napoli. Angela fa l'artista.*
Ha tre figli, un maschio e due femmine. Suo figlio Carlo ha 15 anni, sua figlia Anna 13 anni, e Olivia 5 anni.

(B) *Fill in the gaps*

Laura d'Angelo, di Torino, è _____presso la Lentini. È _____. Suo

_____si chiama Roberto, è di _____. Roberto fa il _____.

Laura ha _____figli, un _____e una _____. Suo figlio _____ha

_____anni e sua _____Maria _____anni.

(C) *Now see if you can do the same for Salvatore Russo and his family.*

13 *Finally, use what you have learnt in Units 1 and 2 to write about 30 words in Italian about yourself. You may want to use **fratello** (brother), **sorella** (sister), **padre** (father), **madre** (mother).*

Riassunto

You can now ...

- **talk about yourself and your family**

  Lavoro a ...
  Lavoro per ... da ... anni.
  Abito a ..., vicino a / lontano da / a 25 km.
  (Non) sono sposato
  Ho due figli / non ho figli / bambini.

- **ask other people about themselves**

  Di dov'è?
  Dove abita?
  Dove lavora?
  Da quanto tempo?
  È sposato?
  Ha figli?
  Quanti anni ha?

- **offer someone refreshment**

  Prende un caffè / un tè?
  Con o senza latte / zucchero?

- **accept / refuse refreshment**

  Volentieri! Prendo ...
  Grazie, no.
  Preferisco ...

- **use the numbers 1 to 30**

► ► *Before moving on to Unit 3, turn to Assignment 1, page 183 to practise the skills you have learnt in Units 1 and 2.*

Unit 3

PRONTO!

You will learn to:
- use the telephone (1)
- make simple arrangements
- tell the time
- describe a schedule
- use the numbers 30 +

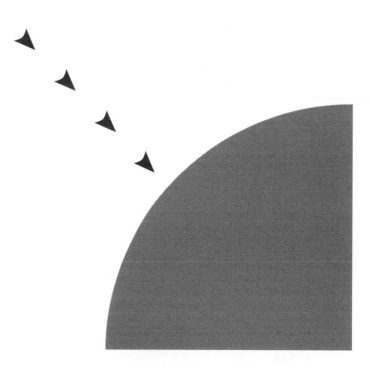

📼 Conversazioni

Lunedì, Bianchi telefona al suo ufficio a Roma, ma l'ingegner Russo non c'è

Centralinista:	Pronto! Ditta Lentini. Mi dica.
Antonio Bianchi:	Buongiorno, Carla. Sono Antonio Bianchi. C'è l'ingegner Russo?
Centralinista:	Mi dispiace, signore. L'ingegnere non c'è stamattina. Vuole lasciare un messaggio?
Antonio Bianchi:	Quando torna, gli dica di telefonarmi. Il numero di telefono è 071 836 0023, interno 45.
Centralinista:	071 836 0023, interno 45. Va bene. Arrivederci, signor Bianchi.
Antonio Bianchi:	Arrivederci, Carla.

Martedì, Russo chiama Bianchi a Londra

Operator:	MK Information Systems. Good morning.
Salvatore Russo:	Buongiorno, signorina. Parla italiano?
Operator:	Sì, signore. Chi parla?
Salvatore Russo:	Sono Salvatore Russo della ditta Lentini. Vorrei parlare con il signor Bianchi.
Operator:	Un attimo, signor Russo. Le passo il signor Bianchi.
Antonio Bianchi:	Buongiorno, Russo. Senta, vorrei il documento tecnico 120A.
Salvatore Russo:	Nessun problema, Dottore, lo mando subito via fax. Ha il numero del fax della MK?
Antonio Bianchi:	Sì, eccolo – 071 836 0487.
Salvatore Russo:	071 836 0487. Bene.
Antonio Bianchi:	Arrivederci, Russo. Grazie.

Spiegazioni

- **Lunedì**– Monday, **martedì** – Tuesday. (All the days of the week are in *Grammatica page 43*)

- **Pronto** is the equivalent of 'hello' on the telephone. (lit. 'ready')

- **Mi dica** – Can I help you? (lit. 'Tell me')
  You will hear **Mi dica** very often in shops, restaurants, banks, hotels, etc.

- **Sono Antonio Bianchi** – It's Antonio Bianchi / Antonio Bianchi speaking.
  Sono + your name is the way to identify yourself on the telephone.
  Do not attempt to translate the English 'this is ...' or 'it's ... speaking' into Italian.

- **C'è l'ingegner Russo?** – Is Russo there? **Russo non c'è** – Russo isn't here.
  The more usual meaning of **C'è** is 'there is'. Similarly, **non c'è** 'there is not'.

- **Vuole lasciare un messaggio?** – Do you want to leave a message?
  Vuole + Infinitive – do you want to ... / would you ... / would you like to ...

- **Gli dica di telefonarmi** – Tell him to call me.
  Gli dica di + Infinitive – Tell him to ....

- **Va bene** – All right / That's fine / OK

- **Chi parla?** – Who's calling?

- **Vorrei parlare con ...** – I would like to speak to ...
  Vorrei + Infinitive – I would like to ...
  Vorrei il documento ... – I'd like the document ...

- **Le passo ...** – I'll put you through to ...

- **tecnico** – technical
  Most of the adjectives which end in *-ic* and *-ical* in English, end in *-ico* in Italian.
  e.g. automatico, meccanico, elettrico, chimico, pneumatico, politico, microscopico,
      geografico, alcolico, artistico, economico, classico, grafico.

- **Nessun problema** – No problem. **Problema** is masculine even though it ends in **-a**. The
  plural is **problemi**. A few other words ending in **-ma** behave the same way,
  e.g. programma, sistema, dilemma, telegramma.

- **Lo mando subito via fax** . I'll fax it immediately. (lit. 'I'll send it by fax'). You will also
  hear **per fax**.
  Lo – it. Refers to **il documento** (*Grammatica page 41*)

- **Eccolo** – Here it is. Lo used again to mean **it**.

Vocabolarietto

il documento	document	**telefonare**	to telephone
l'interno	extension	**tornare**	to return
il messaggio	message		
il numero	number	**chi?**	who?
il telefono	telephone	**quando**	when
l'ufficio	office	**stamattina**	this morning
		subito	immediately / right away
chiamare	to call		
lasciare	to leave	**mi dispiace**	I'm sorry
mandare	to send	**senta**	listen

Conversazioni

Joanna Rossi chiede a Antonio Bianchi quando torna in Italia

Joanna Rossi: Buongiorno, Antonio. Come sta oggi?

Antonio Bianchi: Buongiorno, Joanna. Molto bene, grazie, e Lei?

Joanna Rossi: Non c'è male. Quando tornate in Italia?

Antonio Bianchi: Giovedì pomeriggio. Partiamo per l'aeroporto alle due.

Joanna Rossi: Ci vediamo domani?

Antonio Bianchi: Purtroppo, credo di no. Ho un appuntamento con il signor McMillan alle nove, poi c'è la riunione all'ufficio tecnico alle dieci e mezzo. Il pomeriggio andiamo tutti alla mostra a Earl's Court.
Ma Lei, quando viene in Italia? Forse in giugno con Peter?

Joanna Rossi: Magari!... Allora, Antonio, buon viaggio e arrivederci.

Antonio Bianchi: Arrivederci, Joanna. Alla prossima volta!

Anche Enzo Chiari, il capo ragioniere, vuole sapere quando torna in Italia

Antonio Bianchi: Buongiorno, Chiari, come sta?

Enzo Chiari: Benissimo, grazie. Mi dica, Dottore, a che ora tornate a Roma venerdì?

Antonio Bianchi: Torniamo giovedì sera. Arriviamo a Fiumicino alle diciotto e trenta, ora italiana.

Enzo Chiari: Allora ci vediamo venerdì in ufficio? Vorrei controllare le cifre mensili. Va bene?

Antonio Bianchi: Sì, certo. Arrivederci, Chiari, a venerdì.

Enzo Chiari: Buongiorno, Dottore.

Spiegazioni

- **Come sta?** – How are you? Note the various ways of answering **Come sta?** in the conversations on this page. Antonio Bianchi says **molto bene** ('very well'), Joanna Rossi says **non c'è male** ('not too bad'), and Enzo Chiari says **benissimo** ('terrific').
  Sta is from the irregular verb **stare** which means 'to be' when referring to health. It is written out in full in the Grammar Review on page 207.

- **Quando tornate in Italia?** – When are you going back to Italy? Note the plural ending **-ate** because Joanna Rossi is referring to Bianchi and Lucarini. (*Grammatica page 40*)

- **In Italia** can mean 'to Italy' or 'in Italy'. To say *in* or *to* a country or a region you use **in** – e.g. **in Sicilia** means 'in Sicily' or 'to Sicily'.

- **giovedì pomeriggio** – on Thursday afternoon. You do not translate the word **on** before a day or a date. The days of the week are on the tape after the conversations, and written out on page 43.

- **Partiamo ... alle due** – we are leaving ... at two o'clock. **-iamo** is the **we** ending for verbs. (*Grammatica page 40*). Telling the time is on page 42.

- **ci vediamo domani?** – Shall we see each other tomorrow?

- **Credo di no** – I don't think so. The opposite is **Credo di sì** – I think so.

- **andiamo tutti a ...** – we are all going to ...

- **Quando viene in Italia?** – When are you coming to Italy? **Viene** is from **venire** – to come (*Grammatica page 40*)

- **Allora** – well then. You will come across many 'filling-in' words in Italian. They are difficult to translate as there is no exact equivalent in English, apart from 'Well then / right / now then'. Listen out for them in the dialogues and try to use them when you speak.

- **Buon viaggio** – I hope you have a pleasant journey / Bon voyage! (lit. good journey)

- **Alla prossima volta** – Until the next time (we meet).

- **A venerdì** – See you on Friday. **A** followed by a day, a date or a time means 'see you on ...'.

- **ora italiana** – Italian time.
  Local time in winter (**ora solare**) is GMT + 1 hour.
  From the last Sunday in March until the last Sunday in September, Italian Summer Time (**ora legale**) is GMT + 2 hours.

Vocabolarietto

l'aeroporto	airport	**prossimo**	next	**domani**	tomorrow
l'appuntamento	appointment	**tutto**	all	**in giugno**	in June
la cifra	figure				
la mattina	morning	**andare**	to go	**certo**	of course
la mostra	exhibition	**chiedere**	to ask	**forse**	perhaps
il pomeriggio	afternoon	**controllare**	to check	**magari!**	if only!
la riunione	meeting	**credere**	to believe	**purtroppo**	unfortunately
la sera	evening				
la volta	time / occasion	**sapere**	to know		
		vedere	to see		
mensile	monthly	**venire**	to come		

39

Grammatica

A Verbs

Present tense of regular verbs – tu, noi, voi, loro

In this unit we meet the four remaining Present tense endings

tu	you (familiar)
noi	we
voi	you (when addressing more than one person)
loro	they

	-are verbs e.g. **parlare** to speak	-ere verbs e.g. **vendere** to sell	-ire verbs e.g. **partire** to leave	capire to understand
tu	parl<u>i</u>	vend<u>i</u>	part<u>i</u>	capisc<u>i</u>
noi	parl<u>iamo</u>	vend<u>iamo</u>	part<u>iamo</u>	cap<u>iamo</u>
voi	parl<u>ate</u>	vend<u>ete</u>	part<u>ite</u>	cap<u>ite</u>
loro	parl<u>ano</u>	vend<u>ono</u>	part<u>ono</u>	capisc<u>ono</u>

- You have now met all the Present tense endings for regular verbs.

- For verbs like **capire**, remember that the **noi** and **voi** forms do *not* take **-isc** before the ending.

- In the **loro** form of all regular verbs the stress falls on the syllable before the **-ano /
-ono** ending – e.g. pàrlano, vèndono, pàrtono, capìscono.

- Make an effort to learn these Present tense endings quickly and you will soon be using them correctly without needing to stop and think. You will find them set out for you in the Grammar Review section, where they appear in the traditional order:

io, tu, Lei / lui / lei, noi, voi, loro

This is the order in which all verbs will be presented from now on.

Two more irregular verbs

Andare – to go	
vado	andiamo
vai	andate
va	vanno
va	

Venire – to come	
vengo	veniamo
vieni	venite
viene	vengono
viene	

40

B Direct object pronouns – him, her, it, them

Masc. **lo** him, it   **li**   them
Fem.   **la** her, it   **le**   them

They all go *in front of the verb* in Italian:

Vuole <u>il documento?</u>	<u>Lo</u> mando subito via fax.
Chi organizza <u>la pubblicità.</u>	<u>La</u> organizzo io.
Capisce <u>i messaggi?</u>	<u>Li</u> capisco bene.
Controllate <u>le cifre?</u>	<u>Le</u> controlliamo oggi.

C Numbers 30 + (on cassette after the Conversazioni)

40	quaranta	200	duecento
50	cinquanta	1.000	mille
60	sessanta	1.100	millecento
70	settanta	1.500	millecinquecento
80	ottanta	2.000	duemila
90	novanta	10.000	diecimila
100	cento	100.000	centomila
101	centouno	1.000.000	un milione
102	centodue	2.000.000	due milioni
110	centodieci	1.000.000.000	un miliardo
150	centocinquanta		

- Numbers are written out as single words - e.g. **quarantadue**, *not* **quaranta due**

- The last vowel of **venti, trenta, quaranta**, etc. is dropped before **uno** and **otto**
  e.g **cinquantuno, settantotto**

- 'One hundred' is **cento**, never **un cento**.
  Cento does not change. 100 – **cento**, 200 – **duecento**, 300 – **trecento**, etc.
  but 1.100 – **millecento**, 1.200 – **milleduecento**, etc., never **undici cento** as in the English 'eleven hundred'.
  The year 1993 is **millenovecentonovantatrè**.

- 'One thousand' is **mille**, never **un mille**.
  Mille changes to **mila** in the plural, 2.000 – **duemila**, 5.000 – **cinquemila**.
  The full stop is used to separate thousands.

- The comma (**virgola**) is used for the decimal point – e.g. 7,5 = **sette virgola cinque**.

D Che ora è? / Che ore sono? – What time is it?

In Italy it is normal to use the 24-hour clock in all business and official communications. It makes telling the time very easy and straightforward.

02 00
sono le due

08 00
sono le otto

09 00
sono le nove

17 00
sono le diciassette

Minutes past the hour are simply added after **e**.

07 10
sono le sette e dieci

08 30
sono le otto e trenta

10 24
sono le dieci e ventiquattro

14 35
sono le quattordici e trentacinque

In everyday conversation, the 12-hour clock is used, and there is another way of saying a quarter past, half past and minutes *to* the hour.

sono le otto e mezzo (or mezza)

sono le undici e un quarto

sono le cinque meno venti

sono le due meno un quarto

sono le sei meno dieci

Note that in answer to **Che ora è?** or **Che ore sono?** the answer always begins with **Sono le ...** except:

è l'una	è mezzogiorno	è mezzanotte
it is one o'clock	it is midday	it is midnight

To say 'at' a particular time, use **alle**.

> alle otto – at 8 o' clock
> alle quattordici e trenta – at 14.30

Note the question **A che ora ...?** – At what time ...?

To say 'from' / 'to' a particular time use **dalle** / **alle**.

> dalle dieci alle quattordici – from 10.00 to 2.00

Note

The word **ore** can be inserted after **le**, **alle** and **dalle**. It does not alter the meaning at all.

> Sono le ore otto – It is eight o'clock
> La riunione comincia alle ore dieci e trenta – The meeting starts at 10.30
> Dalle ore venti alle ore ventidue – From 8 p.m. to 10 p.m.

Time in a general sense is **tempo**.
> Non c'è tempo – There's no time

Time of day is **ora**.
> È ora di andare – It's time to go

Time, meaning occasion, is **volta**.
> La prima volta – The first time

E I giorni della settimana

The days of the week, starting with Monday are:

> **lunedì, martedì, mercoledì, giovedì, venerdì, sabato, domenica**

Listen to them on the cassette after the numbers and note where the stress is. They are written without a capital letter in Italian and they are all masculine except **domenica**.

To the days you can add **mattina** (or **mattino**), **pomeriggio** or **sera**.

> lunedì mattina – Monday morning
> venerdì pomeriggio – Friday afternoon
> sabato sera – Saturday evening

In Italia ...

Hours of business

- *Business hours* in Italy vary from north to south. In the North they are generally 08.30 / 09.00 to 13.00 and 14.00 to 17.30 / 18.00. In Central, and particularly Southern Italy, they are often 08.30 to 13.00, and 16.30 to 20.00.

- *Government offices* are usually open 08.30 to 13.45, Monday to Saturday.

- *Banks* are open 08.30 to 13.20 and 15.00 to 16.00, Monday to Friday.

- *Shop opening hours* may vary slightly according to locality and time of year, but are generally 09.00 to 13.00 and 16.00 to 19.30, Monday to Saturday. Many shops close on Monday morning.

Telephoning

All telephone numbers in Italy have an area code starting with 0. The code for Rome is 06, Milan 02, Florence 055. This code is followed by a local number. If calling within the area, omit the area code.

Local numbers are either given as single digits, e.g. 3597601 (tre cinque nove sette sei zero uno) or in groups of two or three digits, 45 73 02 (quarantacinque settantatrè zero due), 336 81 96 (trecentotrentasei ottantuno novantasei).

To ring Italy from Britain the prefix is 010 39 followed by the number without the initial 0. Italian visitors to England can avoid potentially embarrassing charges on the host's telephone bill by using **Italia in Diretta,** a system enabling calls to be charged to the caller's home number. The number to ring is 0800 89 0039

> **Chiamate con pagamento a destinazione**
> **(Reverse charge call)**
>
> Senza moneta, pagamento a carico del destinatario
>
> **ITALIA IN DIRETTA**   **0800-89-0039**
>
> Operatore internazionale britannico   **155**
>
> **Teleselezione internazionale**
> Senza operatore, pagata nel Regno Unito
>
> 010 39 prefisso distrettuale (senza formare il primo 0) + numero locale
> Tariffa ridotta: sabato e domenica, tutto il giorno,
> (ora locale)   da lunedì a venerdì, dalle 20.00 alle 8.00
>
>

To ring Britain from Italy the prefix is 00 44 followed by the number without the initial 0. A similar system to Italia in Diretta is available by ringing 172 00 44 where you will be connected to an operator in Britain. If you are calling from a payphone you will need a 200 lire coin or a telephone token (**un gettone**) which is returned on completion of the call.

Call boxes in Italy increasingly operate with the **carta telefonica** (phone card), on sale from post offices, bars and tobacconists'.

Numero Verde denotes a freephone number.

Pratica

1 *Listen to all the conversations again and answer these questions in Italian.*

  (i)   Con chi vuole parlare il dottor Bianchi?

  (ii)   Qual è il numero di telefono della MK?

  (iii)   Qual è il numero del documento tecnico?

  (iv)   Quando tornano Bianchi e Lucarini in Italia?

  (v)   A che ora partono per l'aeroporto?

  (vi)   A che ora è l'appuntamento con Ian McMillan?

  (vii)   Dove va il dottor Bianchi alle dieci e mezzo?

  (viii) Dove vanno il pomeriggio?

  (ix)   A che ora arrivano a Fiumicino giovedì?

  (x)   Dove va il dottor Bianchi venerdì?

2 *Vero o falso?*

	VERO	FALSO
It is early morning.		
The caller's name is Vittorio Crovari.		
Lucia Lubrano is on holiday.		
The caller leaves a message for Signora Lubrano.		
Renato Bellofiore is at lunch.		

3 *Write down in English the travel arrangements for Giovanni, Alessandra and Franca.*

	Giovanni	Alessandra	Franca
Day of departure			
Time of departure			
Time of arrival			

4 *Make a note of the telephone, extension and fax numbers mentioned. Remember that phone numbers are not always given in single digits.*

SANSONI FRATELLI SpA   MODENA

Sede legale 41100 Modena Corso Umberto 8
CROVARI Vittorio – Direttore Acquisti

| Tel. | Interno | Fax |

Stabilimento San Giuseppe,
41194 Modena Via San Giuseppe
LUBRANO Lucia – Direttore Produzione

| Tel | Interno | Fax |

---

5 (**A**) *The Lentini Sales Manager is briefing his Sales team. Complete the briefing with the appropriate form of the verb in brackets. (Grammatica A)*

I clienti francesi _____(arrivare) oggi a mezzogiorno. Non _____(parlare) italiano ma _____(capire) tutti l'inglese. Dopo la riunione i clienti _____(andare) a Napoli; _____(partire) alle ore 18.

(**B**) *Later he meets an old friend.*

Ciao, Giorgio! Dove _____(andare)? _____(Venire) al bar con noi? _____ (Prendere) un caffè o _____(preferire) un tè?

(**C**) *Russo rings from Rome to find out when Lucarini and Bianchi are returning to Italy. Fill in the gaps in the conversation with the **noi** or **voi** form of the verbs. (Grammatica A)*

Russo:	E quando _____ (tornare) a Roma? Domani?
Lucarini:	Sì, _____ (partire) domani pomeriggio.
Russo:	A che ora _____ (partire)?
Lucarini:	Alle ore 15. _____(Arrivare) in Italia alle 16.23.
Russo:	_____ (Essere) contenti della visita?
Lucarini:	Molto contenti. Oggi _____ (avere) un appuntamento con l'Amministratore Delegato e poi _____ (andare) alla mostra.

6 *Practise saying the following telephone numbers, some in single digits, and others in pairs or groups of three. (Grammatica C)*

CARABINIERI 85291
POLIZIA DI STATO 4686
POLIZIA STRADALE 557 79 05
VIGILI URBANI 67691

SOCCORSO STRADALE ACI 116
GUARDIA MEDICA 482 67 41
AMBULANZA CROCE ROSSA 51 00
CENTRO ANTIVELENI 49 06 63

In caso di emergenza

Soccorso pubblico di emergenza
113

7 *Ring Lentini and ask to speak to the following people. (Grammatica C)*

Esempio Vorrei parlare con il signor Bianchi. Mi passi l'interno 30 per piacere.

(i)   the General Manager

(ii) the Chief Accountant

(iii) the Purchasing Manager

(iv) the Technical Manager

(v)   the Publicity Manager

Antonio Bianchi	(Direttore generale)	Interno 30
Giancarlo Lucarini	(Direttore agli acquisti)	Interno 124
Laura d'Angelo	(Ragioniera)	Interno 93
Marco Cardella	(Direttore dei sistemi)	Interno 150
Salvatore Russo	(Direttore tecnico)	Interno 68
Enzo Chiari	(Capo Ragioniere)	Interno 44
Francesca Bastiani	(Direttore della pubblicità)	Interno 86

8 *Answer the following questions as in the example. The answer will always be two days later than the day mentioned in the question. (Grammatica E)*

Esempio Torna in Italia giovedì? No, sabato.

(i)   Lei va a Torino sabato?

(ii)   Ci vediamo domenica?

(iii) Andiamo alla mostra mercoledì?

(iv)   Giovanni arriva sabato?

(v)   Quando va in Germania – martedì?

(vi)   Quando torna in Inghilterra – lunedì?

(vii) Enrico e Giorgio partono venerdì?

(viii) L'appuntamento con il ragioniere è per mercoledì?

9 *In Italian, how would you:*

- Identify yourself on the telephone.
- Say you would like to speak to signora Visconti.
- Say you would like to leave a message for Carlo Rossi.
- Give your telephone number.
- Greet someone on the phone and offer to help.
- Ask who is calling.
- Say that you are sorry but Mr Lawrence isn't here.
- Ask if they would like to leave a message.

10 *Take part in the conversations.*

(**A**) *You ring a firm in Italy to talk to signor Colombo*

Centralinista: Pronto. Buongiorno. Mi dica.

You: (*Greet her politely and ask to speak to signor Colombo.*)

Centralinista: Un attimo, signore. Chi parla?

You: (*Say who you are.*)

Centralinista: Mi dispiace, il signor Colombo non c'è oggi.
Vuole lasciare un messaggio?

You: (*Say you don't, thank her and say goodbye.*)

(**B**) *You wish to speak to signora Celentano*

Centralinista: Pronto. Mi dica.

You: (*Greet her politely and ask if signora Celentano is there.*)

Centralinista: La signora è occupata in questo momento.

You: (*Say you would like to leave a message.*)

Centralinista: Certo, signore. Mi dica.

You: (*Say you would like the new brochure (**l'ultimo opuscolo**).*)

Centralinista: Certo, signore.

You: (*Thank her and say goodbye.*)

(**C**) *You receive a call from an Italian customer*

You: (*Say hello and ask if you can help.*)

Enrico Zaina: Buongiorno, signore. Posso parlare con la signora Henderson?

You: (*Say you are sorry – she is not there. She's going to London today.*)

Enrico Zaina: A che ora parte?

You: (*Say she's leaving at 11.30.*)

Enrico Zaina: Quando torna?

You: (*Tell him she's coming back on Thursday.*)

Enrico Zaina: Grazie, signore. Buongiorno.

You: (*Say he's welcome and then say goodbye.*)

11 (A) *Read the following schedule out loud. Check with the cassette afterwards.*
(Grammatica D)

> lunedì – incontro con il capo contabile alle 09.00. Poi, dalle 11.45 alle 12.30 c'è la
> visita dello stabilimento.
>
> martedì – alle 10.30 appuntamento con la signora Ferrara della Società Gardini.
>
> mercoledì – libero
>
> giovedì – il pomeriggio alle ore 15.00 c'è una riunione all'ufficio commerciale. La sera
> andiamo al ristorante alle 19.30.

Vocabolarietto

l'incontro	meeting
il ristorante	restaurant
lo stabilimento	plant / factory
la visita	visit
libero	free
poi	then

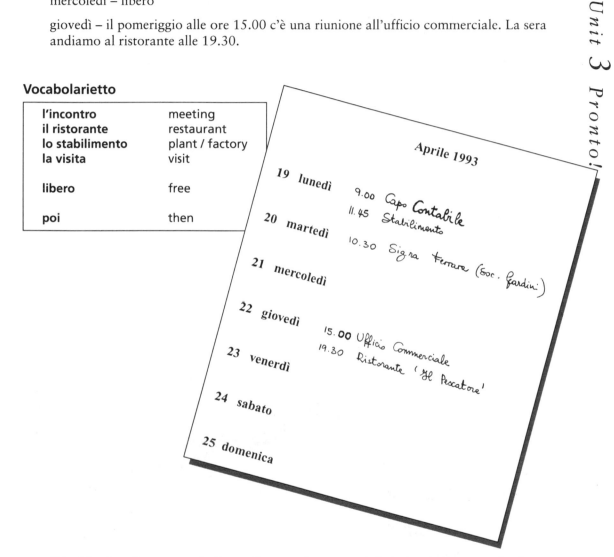

Aprile 1993

19 lunedì — 9.00 Capo Contabile / 11.45 Stabilimento

20 martedì — 10.30 Sig.ra Ferrara (Soc. Gardini)

21 mercoledì

22 giovedì — 15.00 Ufficio Commerciale / 19.30 Ristorante 'Il Pescatore'

23 venerdì

24 sabato

25 domenica

(B) *Massimo Tranto, an Italian colleague about to visit Britain, rings you and asks
you what arrangements you have made for him for Tuesday and Wednesday.*

Using the programme shown on the next page, tell him what is planned for his visit.

Note the use of '**riunione**', the general word for a meeting, and '**incontro**', a more
personal meeting with only one or two other persons.

Tuesday
09.00   Meeting with Ian McMillan, General Manager
09.45   Appointment with Peter Lawrence, Sales Manager
11.30   Visit to the factory in Watford
14.15   Visit to the exhibition in London

Wednesday
09.15   Meeting with John Webster, Engineering Manager
09.45 – 12.30 Meeting in the Technical Department
14.00   Visit to the works
17.45   Appointment with Susan Wright from Mechtronics
20.00   Restaurant

12 *See how much information you can glean from these various signs and notices. A few key words are given to help you.*

(**A**) *Both sides of an Italian telephone card are reproduced here. Can you work out:*

– the cheapest time to make a call during the week?
– the cheapest time on Sundays?
– the peak time for weekday calls?
– the saving by phoning on Sunday morning instead of the same time on Saturday?

(B) *The answers to these questions are in the signs below.*

- When will the office reopen?
- Is the Architecture Museum open in the afternoons?
- On which day is it closed?
- What time does the bank open in the afternoon?
- When is the SANA '93 exhibition open?

ESPOSIZIONE SANA '93

APERTO

martedì, mercoledì, venerdì
dalle ore 10 alle ore 19

MUSEO D'ARCHITETTURA

Orario: 9.30 – 13.30
martedì & giovedì anche 14.30 – 17.00
chiuso lunedì. Ingresso Lire 5.000
Piazza di Siena, tel. 5311065

Questo ufficio è

CHIUSO

fino alle ore 9
di mercoledì

**BANCA NAZIONALE
delle COMUNICAZIONI**

Orario di sportello

Feriali	ore 08.30 – 13.30
	ore 14.55 – 15.55
Festivi	chiuso

Vocabolarietto

(giorni) feriali	weekdays	aperto	open
(giorni) festivi	Sundays / public holidays	chiuso	closed
l'ingresso	entrance		
l'orario	timetable	fino a	until
lo sportello	counter		

Riassunto

You can now ....

- **make a telephone call**

  Sono ....
  C'è ....?
  Vorrei parlare con ....
  Mi passi ....
  Vorrei lasciare un messaggio.
  Gli dica di ....

- **receive a telephone call**

  Pronto! Mi dica.
  Chi parla?
  Le passo ....
  Vuole lasciare un messaggio?

- **give and understand telephone numbers**

  Il numero è cinque, due, zero, sei ....
  Il numero è zero ottantuno ....

- **tell the time**

  Che ore sono? Sono le otto / le diciassette.

- **discuss travel plans**

  Quando parte?
  Parto venerdì, alle ore diciotto.
  Arriviamo a Fiumicino a mezzogiorno.
  A che ora arrivano i clienti?

- **make simple arrangements**

  Ci vediamo domani? / Ci vediamo martedì?
  A che ora?
  Alle dieci va bene?

- **make social conversation**

  Come sta?
  Benissimo / non c'è male / molto bene, grazie.
  E Lei?

▶▶ *Now, with a partner, try Role Play 2 on pages 195–196*

Unit 4

RESTI IN LINEA

You will learn to:
- use the telephone (2)
- relay a simple message
- make appointments / plans
- talk about the past (1)
- apologise

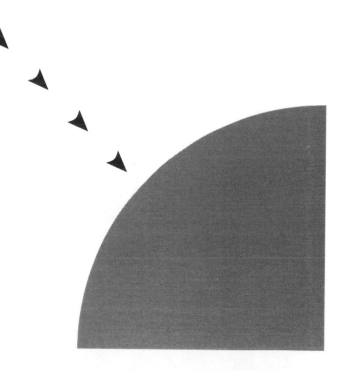

⊡ Conversazioni

Joanna Rossi telefona alla ditta Lentini per discutere la visita del signor Lawrence in giugno. L'ufficio è chiuso e la signora Rossi lascia un messaggio sulla segreteria telefonica

Lentini: Ditta Lentini. Buongiorno. Ci dispiace ma oggi l'ufficio è chiuso per ferie. Se desiderate lasciare un messaggio siete pregati di parlare dopo il segnale acustico.

Joanna Rossi: Qui parla Joanna Rossi della ditta MK Information Systems in Inghilterra. Il numero di telefono è 071 836 0023, interno 17. Vorrei parlare con l'ingegner Lucarini per discutere la visita del signor Lawrence alla Lentini. Per favore, mi richiami appena possibile.

Il giorno dopo, la segretaria dell'ingegnere richiama Joanna Rossi

Joanna Rossi: Pronto. Ufficio vendite estere. Joanna Rossi.

Segretaria: Buongiorno. Sono Carla Zimonti, segretaria dell'ingegner Lucarini. Lei ha telefonato ieri.

Joanna Rossi: Infatti. È a proposito della visita del signor Lawrence in giugno. Attualmente lui è in Germania, a Francoforte, dove abbiamo una nuova filiale. Ha telefonato ieri – vuole cambiare la data del suo arrivo alla Lentini dal 13 giugno al 14 perché c'è una fiera commerciale a Francoforte il 13 giugno – una fiera molto importante.

Segretaria: Allora, vediamo... L'ingegnere è fuori sede oggi. Quando torna posso controllare sull'agenda per quella settimana. Però, non prevedo nessuna difficoltà.

Joanna Rossi: Grazie mille.

Segretaria: Prego. Arrivederci, signora.

Joanna Rossi: Arrivederci.

Spiegazioni

- **Joanna Rossi telefona alla Lentini** – In Italian you telephone *to* someone.

- **Ci dispiace** – We are sorry. Both **Scusi** and **mi / ci dispiace** mean 'sorry'. **Mi / ci dispiace** is used to express regret or sorrow, and **Scusi** is used to excuse oneself after a minor mishap or mistake, and also to attract attention ('excuse me' in English). I'm really / very sorry is **Mi dispiace proprio**.

- **Siete pregati di parlare dopo il segnale acustico** – You are requested to speak after the tone.

- **Qui parla Joanna Rossi della MK** – This is Joanna Rossi of MK speaking. An alternative to **Sono Joanna Rossi**. Not to be confused with **Chi parla?** – Who's calling?

- **Per favore, mi richiami** – Please call me back.

- **appena possibile** – as soon as possible.

- **Lei ha telefonato ieri** – You telephoned yesterday. (*Grammatica page 58*)

- **È a proposito della visita del signor Lawrence** – It's about Mr Lawrence's visit. **A proposito** on its own means 'by the way' / 'incidentally'.

- **in giugno** – in June. The months are on the cassette after the *Conversazioni* and in *Grammatica page 59*.

- **Attualmente** – currently / at the present time (*not* actually).

- **perché c'è una fiera commerciale** – because there is a trade fair. **Perché** here means 'because', but in the Questions in *Pratica 1* you will see that it is also the Italian for 'Why?'

- **È fuori sede** – He is out of the office.

- **Posso controllare sull'agenda** – I can check in the diary. **Posso** + infinitive – I can / I may.

- **Non prevedo nessuna difficoltà** – I don't anticipate any difficulty.

Vocabolarietto

l'agenda	diary	cambiare	to change
l'arrivo	arrival	desiderare	to wish
la data	date	discutere (discusso)	to discuss
la difficoltà	difficulty	prevedere (previsto)	to anticipate / foresee
le ferie (pl.)	holidays	richiamare	to call back
la fiera	(trade) fair		
la filiale	branch		
la segreteria telefonica	answering machine		
la settimana	week	dopo	after
		ieri	yesterday
Francoforte	Frankfurt	perché	why / because
		però	however
nuovo	new	sull' = su + l' }	on the
possibile	possible	sulla = su + la }	
quello	that		

📼 Conversazioni

In maggio, Joanna Rossi telefona all'ingegner Lucarini per confermare i dettagli della visita del signor Lawrence. Ma non è facile!

Centralinista:	Pronto. Hotel Olimpia.
Joanna Rossi:	Ah, scusi, ho sbagliato numero. Buongiorno.

Centralinista:	Pronto. Ditta Lentini. Buongiorno.
Joanna Rossi:	Buongiorno, signorina. Qui parla Joanna Rossi della MK in Inghilterra. Mi passi l'ingegner Lucarini, per favore.
Centralinista:	Resti in linea. Le passo il suo ufficio.

Segretaria:	Pronto. Mi dica.
Joanna Rossi:	Pronto. Sono Joanna Rossi della MK. Vorrei parlare con l'ingegner Lucarini.
Segretaria:	Ah, signora Rossi! Un attimo, prego... . Mi dispiace, l'ingegnere è in riunione. Posso aiutare io?
Joanna Rossi:	Tutto è in ordine per la visita del 14 giugno?
Segretaria:	Sì, sì. Ha ricevuto la mia lettera, spero.
Joanna Rossi:	No, non ho ricevuto niente.
Segretaria:	Come mai? Ho scritto la settimana scorsa... no, due settimane fa. Che seccatura! Ma non si preoccupi, signora. Ho organizzato tutto. Ho prenotato una camera singola all'albergo Aretusa dal 14 al 18 giugno. Ho telefonato ieri all'albergo per confermare la prenotazione. Posso inviare tutte le informazioni via fax adesso. Va bene?
Joanna Rossi:	Va benissimo. Grazie mille e arrivederci.
Segretaria:	Prego. Arrivederci, signora Rossi.

Spiegazioni

- **per confermare i dettagli della visita del signor Lawrence** – to confirm the details of Mr Lawrence's visit.
  The English 's to denote possession does not exist in Italian. (*Grammatica page 58*)

- **ho sbagliato numero** – I've got the wrong number.

- **Mi passi ...** – Put me through to ...

- **Resti in linea** – Hold the line.

- **Un attimo, prego** – One moment, please. Here, **prego** is used to mean 'please'.

- **L'ingegnere è in riunione** – The engineer is in a meeting.

- **Posso aiutare io?** – Can *I* help? Notice the use of **io** to emphasise I.

- **ho ricevuto** – I have received   **ha ricevuto?** have you received?
  ho scritto – I have written / I wrote
  ho organizzato – I have organised
  ho prenotato – I have booked
  ho telefonato – I have telephoned
  (*Grammatica page 58*)

- **non ho ricevuto niente** – I haven't received anything.

- **Come mai?** – How come? / Why ever not?

- **Che seccatura!** – What a nuisance!

- **Non si preoccupi** – Don't worry.

- **dal 14 al 18 giugno** – from 14th till 18th of June. (Months are *on page 59*)

- **le informazioni** – information. The plural is used in Italian. The singular **un' informazione** means one specific piece of information.

- **Va benissimo!** – That's wonderful / marvellous!

Vocabolarietto

l'albergo	hotel	**prenotare**	to book / reserve
la camera	room	**ricevere**	to receive
il dettaglio	detail	**sbagliare**	to make a mistake
la lettera	letter	**scrivere (scritto)**	to write
la prenotazione	booking	**sperare**	to hope
facile	easy	**adesso**	now
scorso	last	**fa**	ago
singolo	single	**in ordine**	in order
		niente	nothing
aiutare	to help		
confermare	to confirm	**al = a + il**	to the
inviare	to send	**dal = da + il**	from the

Grammatica

A The Perfect tense

To talk about something that happened in the past, we use:

The Present tense of **avere** + the Past Participle of the verb expressing the action

The past participle is formed by changing:

-are to **-ato**	lavorare > lavor<u>ato</u>	parlare > parl<u>ato</u>
-ere to **-uto**	vendere > vend<u>uto</u>	ricevere > ricev<u>uto</u>
-ire to **-ito**	finire > fin<u>ito</u>	fornire > forn<u>ito</u>

<u>ho</u> telefonato	I telephoned / have telephoned
<u>hai</u> prenotato	you booked / have booked
<u>ha</u> ricevuto	you received / have received he / she received / has received
<u>abbiamo</u> venduto	we sold / have sold
<u>avete</u> finito	you finished / have finished
<u>hanno</u> capito	they understood / have understood

Many **-ere** past participles are irregular: for example, the past participle of **scrivere** (to write) is **scritto.**

From now on, irregular past participles will be included with the verb in the Vocabolarietto section, e.g. **leggere** (**letto**) – to read

Note

(i)   Italian does not distinguish between 'telephoned', 'sold' and 'have / has telephoned' and 'have / has sold'.

(ii)   When the perfect tense is formed in this way with **avere,** the **-o** ending of the past participle is the same for masculine and feminine, singular and plural.

(iii)   Not <u>all</u> verbs form the perfect tense in this way. In Unit 5 you will see that verbs dealing with motion (to go, come, arrive, etc.) form their perfect tense another way.

B Possession

Italian does not have the equivalent of the English '<u>s</u> to denote possession. For example, 'Giovanni'<u>s</u> office' is translated as 'the office of Giovanni' – l'ufficio *di* Giovanni.

Anna'<u>s</u> car = the car of Anna – la macchina <u>di</u> Anna
Today'<u>s</u> newspaper = the newspaper of today – il giornale <u>di</u> oggi

When the definite article (the) comes after **di**, the two words combine. You have already seen examples of this in Units 1, 2 and 3 – e.g. direttore <u>del</u> marketing.

the manager's office	il	l'ufficio <u>del</u> direttore
the firm's address	la	l'indirizzo <u>della</u> ditta
	l'	l'indirizzo <u>dell'</u> azienda
the State Railways	lo	le Ferrovie <u>dello</u> Stato
the customers' needs	i	i bisogni <u>dei</u> clienti
the agents' responsibilities	gli	le responsabilità <u>degli</u> agenti
sales analysis	le	analisi <u>delle</u> vendite

C I mesi dell'anno

Like the days of the week, the months are written without a capital letter.

gennaio	luglio
febbraio	agosto
marzo	settembre
aprile	ottobre
maggio	novembre
giugno	dicembre

When saying or writing the date you use **il** + number + month

25th January – **il venticinque gennaio** (written 'il 25 gennaio')
16th April – **il sedici aprile** (written 'il 16 aprile')
From the 16th until the 20th of March – **dal 16 al 20 marzo**

The only exception is the first of the month – **il primo** + month

1st June – **il primo giugno** (written 'il 1 giugno')

CALENDARIO

GENNAIO
Lunedì	.	4	11	18	25	.
Martedì	.	5	12	19	26	.
Mercoledì	.	6	13	20	27	.
Giovedì	.	7	14	21	28	.
Venerdì	1	8	15	22	29	.
Sabato	2	9	16	23	30	.
Domenica	3	10	17	24	31	.

MAGGIO
Lunedì	.	3	10	17	24	31
Martedì	.	4	11	18	25	.
Mercoledì	.	5	12	19	26	.
Giovedì	.	6	13	20	27	.
Venerdì	.	7	14	21	28	.
Sabato	1	8	15	22	29	.
Domenica	2	9	16	23	30	.

SETTEMBRE
Lunedì	.	6	13	20	27	.
Martedì	.	7	14	21	28	.
Mercoledì	1	8	15	22	29	.
Giovedì	2	9	16	23	30	.
Venerdì	3	10	17	24	.
Sabato	4	11	18	25	.
Domenica	5	12	19	26	.

FEBBRAIO
Lunedì	1	8	15	22	.
Martedì	2	9	16	23	.
Mercoledì	3	10	17	24	.
Giovedì	4	11	18	25	.
Venerdì	5	12	19	26	.
Sabato	6	13	20	27	.
Domenica	7	14	21	28	.

GIUGNO
Lunedì	.	7	14	21	28
Martedì	1	8	15	22	29
Mercoledì	2	9	16	23	30
Giovedì	3	10	17	24	.
Venerdì	4	11	18	25	.
Sabato	5	12	19	26	.
Domenica	6	13	20	27	.

OTTOBRE
Lunedì	.	4	11	18	25
Martedì	.	5	12	19	26
Mercoledì	.	6	13	20	27
Giovedì	.	7	14	21	28
Venerdì	1	8	15	22	29
Sabato	2	9	16	23	30
Domenica	3	10	17	24	31

MARZO
Lunedì	1	8	15	22	29	.
Martedì	2	9	16	23	30	.
Mercoledì	3	10	17	24	31	.
Giovedì	4	11	18	25	.
Venerdì	5	12	19	26	.
Sabato	6	13	20	27	.
Domenica	7	14	21	28	.

LUGLIO
Lunedì	.	5	12	19	25
Martedì	.	6	13	20	27
Mercoledì	.	7	14	21	28
Giovedì	1	8	15	22	29
Venerdì	2	9	16	23	30
Sabato	3	10	17	24	31
Domenica	4	11	18	25	.

NOVEMBRE
Lunedì	1	8	15	22	29
Martedì	2	9	16	23	30
Mercoledì	3	10	17	24	.
Giovedì	4	11	18	25	.
Venerdì	5	12	19	26	.
Sabato	6	13	20	27	.
Domenica	7	14	21	28	.

APRILE
Lunedì	.	5	12	19	26
Martedì	.	6	13	20	27
Mercoledì	.	7	14	21	28
Giovedì	1	8	15	22	29
Venerdì	2	9	16	23	30
Sabato	3	10	17	24	.
Domenica	4	11	18	25	.

AGOSTO
Lunedì	.	2	9	16	23	30
Martedì	.	3	10	17	24	31
Mercoledì	.	4	11	18	25	.
Giovedì	.	5	12	19	26	.
Venerdì	.	6	13	20	27	.
Sabato	.	7	14	21	28	.
Domenica	1	8	15	22	29	.

DICEMBRE
Lunedì	.	6	13	20	27
Martedì	.	7	14	21	28
Mercoledì	1	8	15	22	29
Giovedì	2	9	16	23	30
Venerdì	3	10	17	24	31
Sabato	4	11	18	25	.
Domenica	5	12	19	26	.

GENNAIO
Lunedì	.	3	10	17	24	31
Martedì	.	4	11	18	25	.
Mercoledì	.	5	12	19	26	.
Giovedì	.	6	13	20	27	.
Venerdì	.	7	14	21	28	.
Sabato	1	8	15	22	29	.
Domenica	2	9	16	23	30	.

MAGGIO
Lunedì	.	2	9	16	23	30
Martedì	.	3	10	17	24	31
Mercoledì	.	4	11	18	25	.
Giovedì	.	5	12	19	26	.
Venerdì	.	6	13	20	27	.
Sabato	.	7	14	21	28	.
Domenica	1	8	15	22	29	.

SETTEMBRE
Lunedì	.	5	12	19	26
Martedì	.	6	13	20	27
Mercoledì	.	7	14	21	28
Giovedì	1	8	15	22	29
Venerdì	2	9	16	23	30
Sabato	3	10	17	24	.
Domenica	4	11	18	25	.

FEBBRAIO
Lunedì	.	7	14	21	28
Martedì	1	8	15	22	.
Mercoledì	2	9	16	23	.
Giovedì	3	10	17	24	.
Venerdì	4	11	18	25	.
Sabato	5	12	19	26	.
Domenica	6	13	20	27	.

GIUGNO
Lunedì	.	6	13	20	27
Martedì	.	7	14	21	28
Mercoledì	1	8	15	22	29
Giovedì	2	9	16	23	30
Venerdì	3	10	17	24	.
Sabato	4	11	18	25	.
Domenica	5	12	19	26	.

OTTOBRE
Lunedì	.	3	10	17	24	31
Martedì	.	4	11	18	25	.
Mercoledì	.	5	12	19	26	.
Giovedì	.	6	13	20	27	.
Venerdì	.	7	14	21	28	.
Sabato	1	8	15	22	29	.
Domenica	2	9	16	23	30	.

MARZO
Lunedì	.	7	14	21	28
Martedì	1	8	15	22	29
Mercoledì	2	9	16	23	30
Giovedì	3	10	17	24	31
Venerdì	4	11	18	25	.
Sabato	5	12	19	26	.
Domenica	6	13	20	27	.

LUGLIO
Lunedì	.	4	11	18	25
Martedì	.	5	12	19	26
Mercoledì	.	6	13	20	27
Giovedì	.	7	14	21	28
Venerdì	1	8	15	22	29
Sabato	2	9	16	23	30
Domenica	3	10	17	24	31

NOVEMBRE
Lunedì	.	7	14	21	28
Martedì	1	8	15	22	29
Mercoledì	2	9	16	23	30
Giovedì	3	10	17	24	.
Venerdì	4	11	18	25	.
Sabato	5	12	19	26	.
Domenica	6	13	20	27	.

APRILE
Lunedì	.	4	11	18	25
Martedì	.	5	12	19	26
Mercoledì	.	6	13	20	27
Giovedì	.	7	14	21	28
Venerdì	1	8	15	22	29
Sabato	2	9	16	23	30
Domenica	3	10	17	24	.

AGOSTO
Lunedì	1	8	15	22	29
Martedì	2	9	16	23	30
Mercoledì	3	10	17	24	31
Giovedì	4	11	18	25	.
Venerdì	5	12	19	26	.
Sabato	6	13	20	27	.
Domenica	7	14	21	28	.

DICEMBRE
Lunedì	.	5	12	19	26
Martedì	.	6	13	20	27
Mercoledì	.	7	14	21	28
Giovedì	1	8	15	22	29
Venerdì	2	9	16	23	30
Sabato	3	10	17	24	31
Domenica	4	11	18	25	.

In Italia ...

Trade fairs – Fiere / Esposizioni / Mostre

Some of Europe's best known and most prestigious trade fairs are held in Italy. Every year several hundred fairs, covering the full range of industrial and consumer goods, are held there. Milan is now one of the world's leading trade fair centres, with about 85 specialised exhibitions a year, more than half of them international.

Information about Italy's trade fairs and the special facilities available to British exporters can be obtained from the Fairs & Promotions Branch, Dean Bradley House, 52 Horseferry Road, London SW1P 2AG.

A particularly useful publication is the *Italian Year* handbook of trade fairs and conferences, compiled annually for the year ahead by Alitalia and ENIT and obtainable from Alitalia in London or from BBE Publishing, via Montebello 21, 10124 Torino, Italy.

Public holidays – Le ferie

Public holidays in Italy are 1 and 6 January, Easter Monday, 25 April, 1 May, 15 August, 1 November, 8, 25 and 26 December.

There are also local official holidays in each town on the Feast Day of the local Patron Saint – 24 June in Turin and Genoa, 29 June in Rome, 19 September in Naples, 7 December in Milan.

When a public holiday happens to be on a Tuesday or a Thursday, many people take an extra day's holiday on the Monday or Friday. This is known as **fare il ponte** ('bridging the gap') and can be very disruptive.

The main holiday season, when you will find business drastically disrupted, is from late July to early September.

Postal services and communications

Post offices (**uffici postali**) are open from 08.30 to 13.45, Monday to Friday and from 08.30 to 12.00 on Saturday. In the larger cities the main post office stays open until 19.30 / 20.00. Stamps (**i francobolli**) are sold in tobacconists' shops as well as at post offices.

A poste restante service is available at main post offices. Letters should be addressed c/o **Fermo Posta** followed by the name of the town and the **CAP** (post code). You will need your passport when collecting your letters from the Fermo Posta counter. You can also arrange for money to be sent to you at this counter by international telegraphic money orders.

Information on all postal services is available from 08.00 to 20.00 every day by telephoning 160.

A word of caution: the Italian postal service is not renowned for its speed, and it is as well to be aware of the alternatives.

There is a national (P.I.) and an international (EMS CAI – POST) rapid courier service for urgent documents and /or goods. There are offices in most large cities. Rome, Milan and Naples also have a city rapid courier service (P.U.).

A fax service is available in main post offices and also at most large hotels.

In Milan, the **Servizio Telegrafico** in the central post office, Via Cordusio 4, accepts telexes, faxes and telegrams for transmission to Britain. This service is available 24 hours a day. Also in Milan, the British Chamber of Commerce for Italy offers visiting British business people the opportunity to use its fax service in the Head Office (Via Agnello 8) for a modest charge.

Pratica

1 *Listen to all the conversations again and answer these questions in Italian.*

(i) Perché Joanna Rossi telefona alla ditta Lentini?

(ii) Come si chiama la segretaria dell'ingegner Lucarini?

(iii) Dov'è la nuova filiale della MK?

(iv) Perché il signor Lawrence vuole cambiare la data del suo arrivo in Italia?

(v) Perché la signorina Zimonti non controlla subito sull'agenda?

(vi) Prevede difficoltà, la signorina Zimonti?

(vii) Quando Joanna Rossi telefona per la seconda volta, dov'è Lucarini?

(viii) Joanna Rossi ha ricevuto la lettera della segretaria?

(ix) Quando ha scritto questa lettera la signorina Zimonti?

(x) Dove ha prenotato una camera per Peter Lawrence?

2 *Listen to the telephone message and decide whether* a, b *or* c *is the correct ending for these statements.*

(i) The caller is
- (a) ☐ Cesare Calabresi
- (b) ☐ Cesare Calabresi's secretary
- (c) ☐ Benedetti Fratelli

(ii) Cesare Calabresi is currently in
- (a) ☐ France
- (b) ☐ Frankfurt
- (c) ☐ Florence

(iii) He is there
- (a) ☐ at a trade fair
- (b) ☐ on business
- (c) ☐ on holiday

(iv) He returns to Genoa on
- (a) ☐ May 5
- (b) ☐ May 15
- (c) ☐ May 25

(v) His visit to England is planned for
- (a) ☐ June 3
- (b) ☐ July 3
- (c) ☐ July 13

(vi) The object of the call is to

(a) ☐ discuss the arrival date

(b) ☐ confirm the arrival date

(c) ☐ change the arrival date

3 *An Italian contact rang while you were out and left a message on your answerphone giving the dates of some trade fairs in Italy. Listen to the cassette and write down the dates of the following fairs. (Grammatica C)*

Milano	Grafitalia	_____
Roma	Mostra delle Nuove Tecnologie	_____
Bologna	Informatica	_____
Milano	ABACUS 93	_____
Roma	Esposizione Internazionale di Roma	_____
Milano	Settimana Internazionale di Fiera	_____
Modena	Commercio in Piazza	_____
Piacenza	Mostra Mercato delle Telecomunicazioni	_____
Torino	Salone Internazionale dell'Innovazione	_____
Verona	Elettroexpo	_____

4 *Fill in the gaps using the past participle of the verb in brackets. (Grammatica A)*

Esempio Ho _____ una camera all'albergo. (prenotare)
Ho *prenotato* una camera all'albergo.

(i) Franco ha _____ un messaggio? (lasciare)

(ii) Lei ha _____ al proprietario? (telefonare)

(iii) Ho _____ . (finire)

(iv) Ho _____ un appuntamento con il titolare. (fissare)

(v) Abbiamo _____ la macchina. (vendere)

(vi) Hai _____ i campioni? (controllare)

(vii) Non ho _____ bene. (capire)

(viii) Francesca ha _____ la fattura? (leggere)

(ix) Il cliente tedesco ha _____ alle due. (richiamare)

(x) I clienti francesi hanno _____ la merce. (ricevere)

Vocabolarietto

il campione	sample
la fattura	invoice
la merce	goods / merchandise
il proprietario	owner
il titolare	owner
fissare un appuntamento	make an appointment

5 *You have been asked to pass on some messages. Paul Ashton, who was due to meet an Italian agent, has been called out of the office unexpectedly. He has left you the list below and asked you to tell the agent what he has done that week.*

(i)   How would you tell the agent what Paul has done?

(ii) How would Paul himself tell him what he has done?

Phoned the commercial manager

Left a message on the answerphone

Spoke to the owner

Checked the German documents

Faxed the information to Brussels

Organised the exhibition

Booked a room for the French customer

Changed date of the visit

Wrote letter to sig. Maroni

Paid the 2 invoices.

pagare – to pay
Bruxelles – Brussels

6 *Fill the gaps with one of the following. They can be used more than once. (Grammatica B)*

di   del   della   dell'   dello   dei   degli   delle

(i)   È l'indirizzo _____ azienda madre? No, _____ filiale tedesca.

(ii)   Ha controllato sull'agenda _____ direttori?

(iii) La famiglia _____ Lucarini abita a Firenze.

(iv)   Ho un appuntamento all'ufficio _____ acquisti oggi.

(v)   Le passo la segretaria _____ ufficio tecnico.

(vi)   Vorrei confermare la data _____ fiere a Bologna e a Genova.

(vii) È a proposito _____ visita _____ signor Bianchi.

(viii) Questa è Lucia, la moglie _____ Gianni.

7 *From the following, choose the most suitable response for each of the statements / questions.*

Magari! **Volentieri.** **Mi dispiace.**

Che seccatura! **Va benissimo.** **Piacere.**

Prego. **Buon viaggio.**

(i)   Partiamo per la Germania domani.

(ii)   Prende un caffè?

(iii)   Ho prenotato una camera per Lei all'Albergo Romae. Va bene?

(iv)   Le presento la dottoressa Astolfi.

(v)   Ho ricevuto le informazioni. Grazie.

(vi)   Non ho ricevuto i campioni.

(vii)   La banca è chiusa oggi e domani.

(viii) Lei va in Italia quest'anno?

8 *Imagine the conversation when Lucarini's secretary tells him about Joanna Rossi's telephone calls. This dialogue is best worked out with a partner.*

Segretaria:	Tell Lucarini that Mrs Rossi rang from MK.
Lucarini:	Ask what time she rang.
Segretaria:	Say she rang at two o'clock yesterday and left a message.
Lucarini:	Ask if she (i.e. the secretary) rang back.
Segretaria:	Tell him that you rang Mrs Rossi at ten o'clock today.
Lucarini:	Ask if she has confirmed Lawrence's visit.
Segretaria:	Tell him Mrs Rossi changed the date of the visit.
Lucarini:	Ask when Peter Lawrence is arriving.
Segretaria:	Tell him he's arriving on 14th June.
Lucarini:	Ask if she has checked the diary.
Segretaria:	Say that you have and that it's fine.
Lucarini:	Thank her.

(A) *With Franca Bellofiore who is about to visit your company in England.*

Franca Bellofiore:	Pronto. Buongiorno. Qui parla Franca Bellofiore.
You:	(*Greet her, ask how she is, and ask if she has received the letter.*)
Franca Bellofiore:	Molto bene grazie. Ma no, non ho ricevuto niente.
You:	(*Say you're sorry, and then tell her that you have organised the meeting and the visit to the factory.*)
Franca Bellofiore:	Il 16 maggio, vero?
You:	(*Say no, the 17th – Thursday the 17th May.*)
Franca Bellofiore:	Il diciassette ... a che ora?
You:	(*Tell her that the meeting is at nine o'clock, and the visit to the factory is at 11.30.*)
Franca Bellofiore:	Bene. Ho un appuntamento a Londra alle quattro. Allora, ci vediamo il diciassette maggio, alle nove. Arrivederci, signore.
You:	(*Say goodbye and wish her a good journey.*)

(B) *You are Charles Smith, an agent for Osbornes plc, talking to Mauro Rossani's secretary.*

Smith:	(*Introduce yourself and ask to speak to Mauro Rossani.*)
Segretaria:	Mi dispiace, signore , il dottor Rossani non c'è. Posso aiutarLa io?
Smith:	(*Ask if you can make an appointment with Mr Rossani on Thursday.*)
Segretaria:	Non posso controllare la sua agenda in questo momento, signore.
Smith:	(*Ask if he's in a meeting.*)
Segretaria:	No, è fuori sede oggi.
Smith:	(*Ask if you can ring back tomorrow.*)
Segretaria:	Sì, certo, signor Smith.
Smith:	(*Ask at what time.*)
Segretaria:	Il dottore sarà in ufficio dalle otto e trenta fino alle undici domani mattina.
Smith:	(*Thank her and say goodbye until tomorrow.*)

10 *A fax received by John Smith just before a visit to Giannetti in Italy (see opposite). Read it through carefully, using the vocabulary at the end of the book for any new words you do not understand. When you have read it, answer the questions on page 68 in English.*

Giannetti F.lli SpA

Sede Amministrativa 20154 MILANO Viale Michelangelo 23
Tel 02/8923471 Fax 02/8967302

TRASMESSO VIA FAX il:	10 febbraio 1993
DA:	Giovanna SENATORE (Ufficio Vendite)
PAGINE:	2
ALLA CORTESE ATTENZIONE DI:	John Smith, Direttore Acquisti
LOCALITA':	I.M.P. Ltd, Chester, Inghilterra
OGGETTO:	Visita alla Società Giannetti

Confermiamo il Suo arrivo mercoledì 17 febbraio. Abbiamo prenotato una camera singola con bagno presso l'Albergo San Marco, Piazza della Repubblica, dal 17 al 19 febbraio.

Alleghiamo il programma.

Programma

mercoledì 17 febbraio
ore 16.34   Arrivo Milano Linate

giovedì 18 febbraio
ore 09.30   Sede amministrativa Giannetti F.lli SpA
                 Incontro con l'avv. LUCCHETTI Sergio (Direttore Generale)
ore 11.00   Incontro con la dott. RUBINI Daniela (Direttore vendite estere)
ore 13.00   Pranzo
ore 14.30   Reparto tecnico

venerdì 19 febbraio
ore 09.30   Visita fabbrica Ferruzzo, Monteleone
                 Incontro con l'ing. CARLOTTI Mauro (Direttore produzione)
ore 15.45   Partenza Milano Linate

(i)   What information is John Smith given about his hotel booking?

(ii) Who will he meet in Head Office?

(iii) What time is his meeting with the Export Sales manager?

(iv) Where is he going at 2.30 on Thursday afternoon?

(v)   Which day is his visit to the factory and who will he meet there?

11 *Look at the advertisements on the opposite page.*

Notice how many English words ending in -tion and -ction end in -zione in Italian, and how similar they are.

(In Italian the stress falls on the -o of -zione.)

(**A**) *Find the Italian for*

Communication _____

Conversation _____

Distribution _____

Enumeration _____

Installation _____

Regulation _____

Repetition _____

Resolution _____

Selection _____

Transmission _____

Not all words with these endings correspond exactly. Note the following.

Manutenzione – Maintenance

Riparazione – Repairs

Progettazione – Planning

(**B**) *What are the three main advantages given for buying the VFX 350 Fax? (Excluding the technical characteristics.)*

(**C**) *What is the significance of the words 'Numero Verde' in two of the advertisements?*

telefonia
Eurotel
il piacere della comunicazione

VENDITA • DISTRIBUZIONE
PROGETTAZIONE • ISTALLAZIONE
MANUTENZIONE • RIPARAZIONE

00150 ROMA   Via Chiabrera 43

Tel (06) 9765551   Fax (06) 9784104

TELEFAX - VFX 350
✳✳✳✳✳

TECNOLOGIA ESCLUSIVA

12 MESI DI GARANZIA

PREZZO INTERESSANTE

CARATTERISTICHE TECNICHE

- ■ trasmissione differita
- ■ trasmissione confidenziale
- ■ selezione della risoluzione
- ■ riduzione automatica dei documenti
- ■ polling multistazione
- ■ regolazione dei grigi
- ■ numerazione delle pagine

Informazioni
commerciali

Pronto?

....CFR 3000
la comunicazione a
3 dimensioni

il telefono

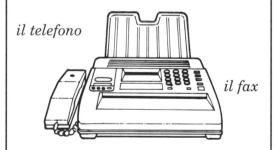

il fax

la segreteria telefonica

Belcom Srl

il sistema telefonico
per il piccolo ufficio

- • accesso diretto alle linee esterne
- • conversazioni interne segrete
- • ripetizione dell'ultimo numero selezionato
- • selezione abbreviata

Sede amm. va 00100 ROMA Via Giovanni XXIII 121

Tel (06) 7815834   Fax (06) 7935671

Ufficio vendita 00153 ROMA Via Cologno 58/60

Tel (06) 3369811   Fax (06) 3601892

Riassunto

You can now ...

- **talk about what you have done**

  Ho scritto a ...
  Ho telefonato a ...
  Ha controllato sull'agenda?
  Non abbiamo ricevuto i campioni.
  Avete ricevuto le informazioni?

- **use and understand telephone expressions**

  Resti in linea.
  Siete pregati di parlare dopo il segnale acustico.
  Ho sbagliato numero.
  Mi passi la signora ...
  Le passo il Suo ufficio.
  Mi richiami appena possibile.

- **make appointments / plans**

  Vorrei fissare un appuntamento con ...
  Vorrei cambiare la data dell'appuntamento dal 13 al 14 giugno.

- **relay messages**

  L'ingegnere è fuori sede oggi.
  Lucarini è in riunione.
  È a proposito di ...
  Non si preoccupi – non prevedo nessuna difficoltà.

- **apologise**

  Scusi.
  Mi dispiace / ci dispiace.
  Mi dispiace proprio.

►► *Before moving on to Unit 5, turn to Assignment 2, page 183 to practise the skills you have learnt in the last two units. Task 2 (telephoning) is on the cassette after Unit 4.*

Bravissimo! **You have now completed Part I of the course.**

- You have acquired enough of the basic skills of Italian to talk about yourself, your family and your work.

- You have learnt something of the country and the way Italians behave in social and business situations.

- You can speak about past events amd make simple business and travel arrangements.

Avanti! **Now follow Peter Lawrence on his visit to Rome in Part II of** *Pronto!*

- You will learn to deal with a variety of new situations such as any business person or traveller would encounter in Italy: at the airport, in the bar, in the hotel, at the bank, at the restaurant, at the railway station and finally at the factory and offices of Lentini SpA.

Buon viaggio! Buon lavoro! e Buona fortuna!

ARRIVO A ROMA

You will learn to:
- talk about the past (2)
- give simple instructions and commands
- spell out names

part two

📼 Conversazioni

All'ufficio informazioni dell'aeroporto Leonardo da Vinci

Peter Lawrence:	Scusi, signore, c'è un messaggio per me?
Impiegato:	A che nome?
Peter Lawrence:	Lawrence.
Impiegato:	Lor...? Come si scrive?
Peter Lawrence:	L - A- W - R - E - N - C - E.
Impiegato:	Aspetti un attimo, signor Lawrence ... No, mi dispiace, non c'è niente.
Peter Lawrence:	Grazie lo stesso. C'è un telefono qui?
Impiegato:	Sì, guardi, è lì, in fondo a sinistra.
Peter Lawrence:	Grazie tante.
Impiegato:	Prego. Arrivederci, signore.

Peter Lawrence trova la cabina telefonica e telefona alla ditta Lentini. Lucarini non c'è, e la centralinista lo passa alla signora Bastiani

Francesca Bastiani:	Signor Lawrence, buongiorno. Sono Francesca Bastiani. Mi dispiace, ma Lucarini è uscito cinque minuti fa. Lei, dov'è? Da dove chiama?
Peter Lawrence:	Sono arrivato! Sono all'aeroporto.
Francesca Bastiani:	Ah, ecco Lucarini! È tornato. (*A Lucarini*) Giancarlo! Peter Lawrence è arrivato... Dov'è?... A Fiumicino.
Giancarlo Lucarini:	Allora, senta, Peter – aspetti nel bar vicino all'uscita. Prenda un caffè. Arrivo. Non si preoccupi, arrivo fra mezz'ora.
Peter Lawrence:	D'accordo. Ho capito. Ci vediamo al bar vicino all'uscita.
Giancarlo Lucarini:	Sì. A più tardi. Ciao.

Al bar

Peter Lawrence:	Un caffè lungo e un panino al formaggio.
Cassiera:	Caffè lungo, panino al formaggio – tremilaseicento lire. Grazie. ... Signore! Prenda lo scontrino.

Spiegazioni

- **A che nome?** – In what name?
  Nome here refers to the whole name, i.e. Christian and surname.

- **Come si scrive?** – How is that written? / How do you spell that? (*Grammatica page 80*)

- **Aspetti** – Wait
  Guardi – Look
  These have a different ending from the usual Lei form because they are commands
  (*Grammatica page 79*)

- **Non c'è niente** – There's nothing. In Italian, to translate 'nothing' or 'not anything' you
  use <u>non</u> before the verb and <u>niente</u> after the verb. More about this in later units.

- **Grazie lo stesso** – Thanks anyway (lit. 'thanks the same').

- **Grazie tante** – Thank you so much.
  You can also say **grazie mille** or **molte grazie** for 'thank you very much'.

- **È lì** – it's over there. **Lì** and **là** both mean 'there'. **Qui** and **qua** mean 'here'.

- **Da dove chiama?** – Where are you calling from?
  Note the difference: **chiamo** – I call, **mi chiamo** – my name is (lit. 'I call myself').

- **è uscito** – he has gone out
  sono arrivato – I have arrived   } (*Grammatica page 78*)
  è tornato – he has returned

- **Dov'è?** Note that **dov'è** can mean 'Where are you?' and 'Where is he?'.

- **Senta!** – Listen!
  Prenda – Take / Have   } (*Grammatica page 79*)
  Non si preoccupi – Don't worry

- **Arrivo fra mezz'ora** – I'll be there in half an hour. **Fra** means 'in' or 'within' when
  talking about time. Take care not to confuse it with **fa** which means 'ago'.

- **D'accordo** – Agreed.
  D'accordo is similar in meaning and usage to **va bene**.

- **A più tardi** – Till later / See you later.

- **Un caffè lungo** – Coffee that is weaker than a **caffè** (lit. 'a long coffee'). (*In Italia page 81*)

Vocabolarietto

la cabina telefonica	call box	**aspettare**	to wait
il formaggio	cheese	**guardare**	to look
la mezz'ora	half an hour	**uscire**	to go out
il panino	bread roll		
lo scontrino	receipt	**a sinistra**	on the left
l'uscita	exit	**in fondo**	at the end
		nel = in + il	in the
lungo	long		
stesso	same		

📼 Conversazioni

Finalmente Giancarlo Lucarini arriva all'aeroporto

Giancarlo Lucarini: Peter! Benvenuto a Roma! Come sta?

Peter Lawrence: Molto bene, Giancarlo. Piacere di rivederLa. S'accomodi. Prende un caffè?

Giancarlo Lucarini: No, niente, grazie. Andiamo subito all'albergo. Mi dia la valigia. Ha solo questa piccola?

Peter Lawrence: Sì, soltanto questa qui e la mia valigetta.

Giancarlo Lucarini: Allora, andiamo. La macchina è parcheggiata di fronte.

Nella macchina, Lawrence spiega perché è in ritardo e Lucarini dice che ha un appuntamento alle tre

Giancarlo Lucarini: Ha fatto buon viaggio? Ma, insomma no, Lei è in ritardo ... ha avuto qualche problema?

Peter Lawrence: Sì, c'è uno sciopero oggi in Francia e ho dovuto aspettare tre ore a Heathrow.

Giancarlo Lucarini: Che seccatura! Ma anch'io ho un problema. Ho dimenticato di disdire un appuntamento per oggi pomeriggio. Devo essere in ufficio alle tre in punto.

Peter Lawrence: Pazienza!

Giancarlo Lucarini: È la prima volta che viene in Italia?

Peter Lawrence: No. Sono venuto qui in vacanza nel 1990 con mio fratello. Siamo andati in Toscana.

Giancarlo Lucarini: Siete andati a Firenze – la più bella città d'Italia?

Peter Lawrence: Sì, abbiamo visitato Firenze, Siena, Pisa, Lucca ...

Giancarlo Lucarini: Ma non è mai stato a Roma?

Peter Lawrence: No, a Roma non sono mai stato.

Giancarlo Lucarini: Siamo arrivati. Eccoci all'albergo Aretusa.

Spiegazioni

- **Piacere di rivederLa** – Delighted to see you again.

- **Mi dia la valigia** – Give me your case. **Dia** is the Imperative form of **dare** (to give) (*Grammatica page 79*)

- **Questa piccola** – This small one. **Questo**, without a noun, translates 'this one'. It is often reinforced by adding **qui** ('here'), as in **questa qui** – this one (i.e. case) here.

- **Andiamo** – Let's go.

- **Lucarini dice che ...** – Lucarini says that ... **Dice** is from **dire** (*Grammatica page 80*)

- **Ha fatto buon viaggio?** – Did you have a good journey? **Fatto** is the irregular past participle of **fare**.

- **insomma**. Another 'filling-in' word, used when summing up. Roughly equivalent to 'on reflection' in this instance.

- **Ha avuto qualche problema?** – Have you had some problems? **Qualche** – some / a few is always followed by a *singular* noun.

- **ho dovuto ... + Infinitive** – I had to ...

- **Devo essere in ufficio alle tre in punto** – I have to be in the office at three o'clock on the dot.

- **Pazienza!** (lit.) Patience. In English we would say 'Not to worry!' / 'That's life!' / 'It can't be helped!'

- **sono venuto** – I came
  siamo andati – we went
  siete andati? – did you go?
  siamo arrivati – we have arrived
  } (*Grammatica page 78*)

- **nel millenovecentonovanta** – in 1990. In Italian **il** is used with the date.

- **Firenze, la più bella città d'Italia** – Florence, the most beautiful city in Italy.

- **Non è mai stato a Roma?** – You have never been to Rome?
  No, a Roma non sono mai stato. – I have never been to Rome.

- **Eccoci** = Ecco + ci – Here we are.

Vocabolarietto

la macchina	car	**fare un viaggio**	to go on a journey
lo sciopero	strike	**parcheggiare**	to park
la valigetta	briefcase	**spiegare**	to explain
la valigia	suitcase		
il viaggio	journey	**finalmente**	finally / at last
		solo }	only
la Francia	France	**soltanto**	
dare	to give	**di fronte**	opposite
dimenticare (di)	to forget (to)	**in ritardo**	late
dire (detto)	to say / to tell	**in vacanza**	on holiday
disdire (disdetto)	to cancel	**mai**	never
dovere	to have to	**nella – in + la**	in the

Grammatica

A. The Perfect tense with essere

As you saw in Unit 4, most verbs form their perfect tense with **avere**. We have seen more examples in this unit:

e.g. ho capito, ho dovuto, ho dimenticato, ha fatto, ha avuto

However, a small number of verbs form their perfect tense with **essere** instead of **avere**. They are mainly verbs describing *movement*. For these you use:

The Present tense of **essere** + the Past Participle of the verb expressing the action

<u>sono</u> arrivato	I arrived / have arrived
<u>sei</u> uscito	you went out / have gone out
<u>è</u> partito	you left / have left he left / has left
<u>siamo</u> andati	we went / have gone
<u>siete</u> tornati	you came back / have come back
<u>sono</u> venuti	they came / have come

This pattern is only used with a few verbs, some of which are listed below. There is a complete list in the Grammar Review on page 207.

Irregular past participles are given in brackets.

andare	to go	**arrivare**	to arrive
essere (stato)	to be	**partire**	to leave
rimanere (rimasto)	to stay	**riuscire**	to succeed / manage
tornare / ritornare	to return	**uscire**	to go out
venire	to come		

N.B. With **essere** verbs, when the subject is feminine, the final **-o** of the past participle changes to **-a.**

Pietro è partit<u>o</u> / Laura è partit<u>a</u>
Sono arrivat<u>o</u> (m.) / Sono arrivat<u>a</u> (f.)

When the subject is plural, the final vowel is **-i** for the masculine or for a combination of masculine and feminine, and **-e** for the feminine.

I clienti sono arrivat<u>i</u> (m. or m. & f.)
Le lettere sono arrivat<u>e</u> (f.)

B The Imperative – Telling / asking someone to do something

For giving instructions in the Lei form, the endings are:

-i for regular -are verbs
-a for other verbs

Aspettare – to wait	Aspetti – Wait
Scusare – to excuse	Scusi – Excuse me
Richiamare – to call back	Mi richiami – Call me back

Prendere – to take	Prenda – Take
Sentire – to listen	Senta – Listen

Irregular verbs often have irregular imperative forms.

Andare – to go	Vada! – Go!
Venire – to come	Venga! – Come!
Dare – to give	Dia! – Give!

Using this form of the verb is perfectly polite and does not sound as abrupt in Italian as in English.

C A and in with the definite article

In the Conversazioni for this unit you have come across more examples of **a** (at / to) and **in** (in) combined with the various forms of the, e.g. **all**'aeroporto, **nel** bar.

Here is the complete list.

A		IN	
a + il	al direttore	in + il	nel bar
a + la	alla sede centrale	in + la	nella zona
a + l'	all'esposizione	in + l'	nell' ufficio
a + lo	allo studente	in + lo	nello stabilimento
a + i	ai treni	in + i	nei documenti
a + gli	agli impiegati	in + gli	negli aeroporti
a + le	alle ore quattordici	in + le	nelle città

D Irregular verbs dire and dare

Verbs like **disdire** (to cancel) and **contraddire** (to contradict) follow the same pattern.

Dire – to say / to tell

dico	diciamo
dici	dite
dice	dicono
dice	

Dare – to give

do	diamo
dai	date
dà	danno
dà	

E Come si scrive?

When you telephone Italy and are asked your name, you will probably be asked to spell it out as English names often present difficulties.

You know already how to pronounce the individual letters (*Pronunciation guide pages vii–viii*) but you should also know that in Italian each letter is represented by the name of a city.

Here is a list of the cities usually used. There are, no Italian cities beginning with H, J, K, Q, X, W or Y, and for these, the names of the letters are usually used instead.

However, you will hear W represented by Washington.

A	a	Ancona	N	enne	Napoli
B	bi	Bologna	O	o	Otranto
C	ci	Como	P	pi	Palermo
D	di	Domodossola	Q	cu	–
E	e	Empoli	R	erre	Roma
F	effe	Firenze / Forlì	S	esse	Savona
G	gi	Genova	T	ti	Torino
H	acca	–	U	u	Udine
I	i	Imola	V	vu	Venezia
J	i lunga	–	W	doppia vu	Washington
K	cappa	–	X	ics	–
L	elle	Livorno	Y	ipsilon	–
M	emme	Milano	Z	zeta	Zara

To spell out the name Thomas you would say: T come Torino, acca, O come Otranto, M come Milano, A come Ancona, S come Savona.

In Italia ...

Aeroporti d'Italia

Scheduled air services from Britain to Italy are operated principally by Alitalia (AZ) and British Airways. Normal flight time from London to Italy is around two hours. Domestic flights in Italy are operated by the Alitalia group which includes ATI, and by Alisarda and Aligiulia. They attract many special rates and most reservations for domestic flights can be made, changed or cancelled up to two hours before take-off time.

Airport procedures today are, of course, standard in most major European airports. In Italy the signs to look out for are **Controllo Passaporti** (Passport Control), **Ritiro Bagagli** (Luggage Reclaim), **Dogana** (Customs), **Uscita** (Exit), **Accettazione** (Check-in) and **Uscite** (Gates).

Taxi ranks are usually right outside the Arrivals terminal, but taxis can be very expensive particularly as some Italian airports are quite a way from the cities – Fiumicino is 35 km from Rome. If you do take a taxi, make sure that it is an official one with a meter.

Aeroporti di Roma
Gruppo **Alitalia**

Nuovo Aeroporto Leonardo da Vinci: fra i grandi scali europei, il più comodo.

Some airports have a good coach link service to the city centre. The line between Milan and Linate airport operates every quarter of an hour. There is also a coach link between Milan Central Station and Malpensa (46 km); allow plenty of time before your flight departure. In Rome there is a combined Metro / Rail link between Fiumicino airport and the Stazione Termini.

Caffè

Caffè in Italy is a small, strong black coffee served in a small cup. It is also called **espresso**. Topped with hot frothy milk it becomes a **cappuccino**.
A milder version served with a lot of hot milk is called **caffelatte**, and a coffee with just a dash of milk is **caffè macchiato**.
Caffè lungo is not just a larger cup of coffee – it is a coffee served in a larger cup with more hot water added to make it weaker.
The opposite is **caffè ristretto**, a small, very concentrated black coffee – barely a mouthful.
Caffè corretto is a coffee laced with alcohol.

The usual procedure in an Italian bar, especially in a busy establishment at an airport or a station, is to order and pay at the **cassa** (till), then to take your **scontrino** (receipt) and present it to the **barista** (barman), repeating the order. It is usual to leave small change on a saucer on the counter.

Signs like the following indicate that you should pay at the **cassa**.

MUNIRSI DELLO SCONTRINO ALLA CASSA GRAZIE

SI ACCOMODI ALLA CASSA PREGO

Pratica

1 *Listen to all the conversations again and answer these questions in Italian.*

    (i)   Dov'è il telefono all'aeroporto?

    (ii)   Dov'è il bar?

    (iii) Quando Peter Lawrence telefona, Lucarini è in ufficio?

    (iv) Con chi parla?

    (v)   Com'è la valigia di Peter – è grande o piccola?

    (vi) Perché è in ritardo Peter?

    (vii) Quanto tempo ha dovuto aspettare a Heathrow?

    (viii) Perché Lucarini deve andare in ufficio alle tre?

    (ix) Dov'è andato Peter nel 1990?

    (x)   È mai stato a Roma ?

2 *Listen to some airport announcements and supply the missing information.*

VOLO NUMERO	DESTINAZIONE	ORA
	Parigi	
BA 412		09.15
	Londra	
		18.45

3 *Listen to some names being spelt out and write them down in the spaces below.*
(Grammatica E)

    (i) ————————————   (ii) ————————————

    (iii) ————————————   (iv) ————————————

    (v) ————————————   (vi) ————————————

Before going on to Exercise 4, practise spelling out your own name and the name of the company you work for, using the telephone alphabet.

4 *Listen to this advertisement for Alitalia and fill in the missing statistics.*

Volate in vacanza, in _____ destinazioni in Europa,
con le nuove Formule Alitalia.

Se avete meno di _____ anni o più di _____ , le tariffe
sono molto vantaggiose.

Per esempio, andata e ritorno da Milano: Parigi,
Vienna e Berlino _____ lire.

Da Roma: Atene _____ , Vienna e Berlino
_____ , Parigi e Londra _____ .

> ## Alitalia
> Lavoriamo per farci scegliere
>
> *Formula Europa
> da 350.000 lire*

5 *Complete this conversation with one of the verbs from the box. Each one can only be used once. (Grammatica A)*

Francesca: A che ora _____ da Roma?

Adriano: Alle cinque e mezza. Lei _____ a Castelfranco oggi?

Francesca: No, _____ alla stazione in ritardo.

Adriano: Peccato! Ma Paolo _____ a Bologna, vero?

Francesca: Sì, Paolo _____ alle tre.

Adriano: Bene.

> è andato
> è andata
> è tornato
> è partito
> sono arrivata

6 *This is how Peter Lawrence might describe his journey to Italy. Complete his account using the perfect tense of these verbs. Don't forget that verbs marked with * form their perfect tense with ESSERE. (Grammatica A) The first sentence is done for you.*

andare*(2)   arrivare*   aspettare   dimenticare   dovere   parlare   partire*

telefonare   tornare*   venire*

Sono partito da casa alle sette. Alle sette e mezzo _____ all'aeroporto di

Heathrow dove _____ aspettare due ore.

Alle due _____ finalmente a Roma.

_____ alla Lentini e _____ con la signora Bastiani.

Poi _____ al bar vicino all'uscita. Lucarini _____ all'aeroporto e

_____ all'albergo in macchina. Lucarini _____ in ufficio perché

_____ di disdire un appuntamento.

7 *The centralinista at this busy office has to deal with telephone calls for employees who, for various reasons, are not available. (Grammatica A)*

The following have asked her to tell callers where they have gone ...

Esempio Guido Pozzi / aeroporto = Mi dispiace, il signor Pozzi è andato all'aeroporto.

(i) Fabrizio Orlandi / banca

(ii) Gina Renzi / ufficio postale

(iii) Aldo Monti / ambasciata greca

(iv) Eva Ciani e Enzo Ricci / esposizione

(v) Anna Finzi e Claudia Berti / Palazzo dei Congressi

(vi) Adriano Rinaldi / stabilimento

.... and these people have left the following, rather vague, messages.

(vii) Gina Cabrimi / went out ten minutes ago

(viii) Alessandro Di Silvestre / on holiday

(ix) Cristina Salvetti / in a meeting

(x) Vincenzo Forte e Marta Geri / out of the office today

8 *For each of the countries / towns listed below answer the question 'Lei è mai stato in / a...?', using the cues given.*

Esempio Parigi   on business / 1992
Sono andato a Parigi per affari nel millenovecentonovantadue

(i)	Francia	twice / on business / 1991
(ii)	Berlino	last week / with sales manager
(iii)	Atene	once / 2 years ago
(iv)	Danimarca	once / on business
(v)	Italia	on holiday / with wife / 1989
(vi)	Scozia	once / on holiday
(vii)	Germania	four times last year / on business and on holiday
(viii)	Bruxelles	10th March / on business

9 *Finish each of the half sentences in list (A) with a phrase from list (B).*

(A)   (B)

(i)   Ho dimenticato   (a)   aspettare due ore all'aeroporto.

(ii)   Mi dispiace, ma ho   (b)   venti minuti fa.

(iii) Laura è uscita   (c)   di telefonare alla signora Bastiani.

(iv)   Arrivo   (d)   di rivederLa.

(v)   Piacere   (e)   fra quindici minuti.

(vi)   Il dottor Bianchi ha dovuto   (f)   dimenticato l'appuntamento.

10 (A) *Use the Lei imperative form of the verb in brackets to ask or tell someone to do something. (Grammatica B)*

(i)   (Aspettare) all'uscita dell'aeroporto.

(ii)   (Guardare) questa lettera.

(iii) (Telefonare) subito alla signora Ferrara.

(iv)   (Controllare) l'agenda del dottor Moro, per favore.

(v)   Mi (richiamare) domani mattina.

(vi)   (Sentire), devo partire adesso.

(B) *How would you ask / tell someone:*

–   to leave a message
–   to return immediately
–   to sit down
–   not to worry
–   to put you through to dottor Bianchi

11 *Take part in the following conversations.*

(A) *At the airport information desk.*

Impiegato:	Buongiorno, signore. Mi dica.
You:	(*Ask if there is a message for you.*)
Impiegato:	Il Suo nome?
You:	(*Tell him your name is McPhail.*)
Impiegato:	Come si scrive?
You:	(*Spell out McPhail.*)
Impiegato:	M, C, P? H? ... Lei è americano?

You:	*(Tell him you are Scottish and ask again if there is a message for you.)*
Impiegato:	Allora, vediamo ... sì, signor McPhail, deve telefonare al signor Parini. Ha lasciato questo numero, 055 86 46 03.
You:	*(Repeat the number as you write it down, and ask if there is a telephone there.)*
Impiegato:	Sì, ecco ... in fondo a sinistra.
You:	*(Thank him and say goodbye.)*

(B) *With Franca Bellofiore who is visiting your company in England.*

You:	*(Greet her, welcome her to London and say you are pleased to see her again.)*
Franca Bellofiore:	Buongiorno.
You:	*(Ask if she had a good journey.)*
Franca Bellofiore:	Sì, molto bene grazie.
You:	*(Ask her if she would like a cup of coffee.)*
Franca Bellofiore:	Volentieri. Grazie.
You:	*(Ask if it is her first visit to England.)*
Franca Bellofiore:	No, sono venuta qui in vacanza l'anno scorso.
You:	*(Ask where in England.)*
Franca Bellofiore:	York – una bellissima città... A che ora comincia la riunione?
You:	*(Say it starts at 2.30 and suggest that you both go.)*

Riassunto

You can now ...

- **talk about where you have been**

  Sono stato a ...
  Sono andato a .... / siamo andati a ...
  Sono arrivato / partito alle ...
  Siamo arrivati due ore fa
  A che ora è arrivato?

- **spell out names**

  A come Ancona, etc.

- **give simple instructions and commands**

  Aspetti!
  Non si preoccupi!
  Guardi!
  Prenda!

- **welcome visitors**

  Piacere di rivederLa!
  Ha fatto buon viaggio?

► ► *Before going on to Unit 6, turn to Assignment 3 on page 185 and practise making some travel arrangements for a visit to Italy.*

Unit 6

IN ALBERGO

You will learn to:
- book accommodation
- enquire about facilities
- ask for / follow directions
- say you have to do something
- ask if you can / may do something
- ask someone to do something for you
- cope in a bank
- compose a simple letter

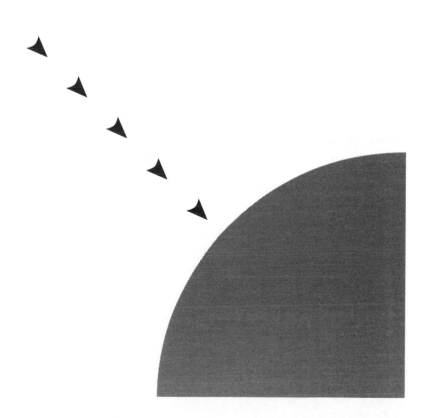

▣ Conversazioni

Peter Lawrence e Giancarlo Lucarini arrivano all' Albergo Aretusa

Giancarlo Lucarini:	Buongiorno.
Impiegato:	Buongiorno, signori. Desiderano?
Giancarlo Lucarini:	Ho prenotato una camera per questo signore.
Impiegato:	Bene. Il suo nome?
Giancarlo Lucarini:	Lawr ...
Peter Lawrence:	Mi chiamo Lawrence. L - A ...
Impiegato:	Sì, sì. Una camera singola con doccia. Per quante notti?
Peter Lawrence:	Quattro – fino a venerdì mattina, il diciotto.
Impiegato:	Perfetto. Numero 224, al secondo piano. Ecco le chiavi. L'ascensore è lì, a destra. Mi può lasciare un documento, per cortesia.
Peter Lawrence:	Ecco il mio passaporto.
Peter Lawrence:	Devo telefonare in Inghilterra. C'è un telefono nella camera?
Impiegato:	Certo, signore. Ogni camera ha il telefono diretto, bagno privato, televisione a colori e aria condizionata.
Peter Lawrence:	Avete un ristorante qui?
Impiegato:	C'è soltanto il bar per la prima colazione, signore. Ma ci sono molti ristoranti nella zona. Le posso raccomandare il Gatto Blu, a due passi.
Giancarlo Lucarini:	Lo conosco bene. Peter, mi scusi, devo scappare. Ma stasera, andiamo a cenare insieme al Gatto Blu?
Peter Lawrence:	Ottima idea! Facciamo le otto?
Giancarlo Lucarini:	D'accordo, alle otto. Arrivederci a stasera.

Spiegazioni

- **Desiderano?** – Can I help you? / What would you like?
  Often in hotels, restaurants, banks, etc. to indicate formality, you will hear the **Loro** form of the verb used instead of the **voi** form to mean 'you' in the plural.

- **Il suo nome?** The receptionist asks 'His name?' but **Il Suo nome** (written with a capital S) can also mean 'your name', which is why both Lawrence and Lucarini answered. (*Grammatica page 97*)

- **Per quante notti?** – For how many nights? (*Grammatica page 97*)

- **al secondo piano** – on the second floor.

- **Mi può lasciare un documento?** – Can you leave me a document? (i.e. some means of identification.)
  Può is from **potere** ('to be able to'). (*Grammatica page 96*)

- **per cortesia** – please. There are several ways of saying please in Italian. You will also hear **per favore** and **per piacere**.

- **Ogni camera** – Each / every room. **Ogni** is invariable (i.e. it does not change).

- **Avete ...?** Have you got ...? Instead of **ha, avete** is often used in hotels or shops when the question is not specifically intended for one person.

- **la prima colazione** – breakfast. Often called simply **la colazione**. 'To have breakfast' is **fare colazione**.

- **Ci sono molti ristoranti** – there are many restaurants. (*Grammatica page 97*)

- **Le posso raccomandare il Gatto Blu** – I can recommend the Gatto Blu (to you). **Le** means 'to you' and is usually placed before the verb.

- **a due passi** – very near (lit. 'two steps away').

- **Lo conosco bene** – I know it well.

- **Andiamo a ...** – Shall we go and ...
  Facciamo le otto – Let's make it 8 o'clock. (*Grammatica page 97*)

Vocabolarietto

l'aria condizionata	air conditioning	diretto	direct
l'ascensore (m)	lift	ottimo	excellent
il bagno	bath / bathroom	privato	private
la chiave	key		
la doccia	shower	cenare	to dine
l'idea	idea	conoscere (conosciuto)	to know
la notte	night	raccomandare	to recommend
il piano	floor	scappare	to dash off
la televisione a colori	colour TV		
la zona	area / district	perfetto!	perfect!
		insieme	together
		stasera	this evening

📼 Conversazioni ░░░░░░░░░░░░░░░░░░░░░░░░░░░░

Mentre Peter aspetta l'ascensore, ascolta una conversazione fra l'impiegato e due altri ospiti

Impiegato:	Buongiorno, signora, signore.
Signore:	Ha una camera doppia per stasera?
Impiegato:	Volete una camera a due letti o matrimoniale?
Signore:	Matrimoniale, con bagno.
Impiegato:	Un attimo, prego ... Abbiamo la camera 316, al terzo piano. Soltanto per stasera, signore?
Signore:	Sì. Quanto costa la camera?
Impiegato:	Centoventimila lire per notte.
Signore:	Va bene. Dobbiamo partire domani mattina, abbastanza presto. A che ora possiamo fare colazione? La prima colazione è compresa, vero?
Impiegato:	Potete fare colazione a partire dalle sette al bar qui al pianterreno. Ma non è compresa, è a parte.
Signore:	Possiamo avere la sveglia alle sei e mezzo per favore?
Impiegato:	Certo. Mi dà i passaporti, per cortesia, signore. Ecco la chiave.
Signore:	Grazie.
Impiegato:	Prego.

Cognome	LAWRENCE
Nome	PETER
Nato il 12 ottobre 1954 **a** OXFORD	
Nazionalità	INGLESE
Passaporto No	L601109
Abitante a	LONDRA
in	INGHILTERRA
Data d'ingresso in Italia	14 giugno 1993

Spiegazioni

- **aspetta l'ascensore** – waits for the lift.
  ascolta una conversazione – listens to a conversation.
  A few verbs in Italian include the English preposition.
  Cercare (to look <u>for</u>) and **guardare** (to look <u>at</u>) are other examples.

- **ospiti** – guests.
  The word **ospite** can mean either a guest or a host. It can be either masculine or feminine.

- **Volete** – do you want, is part of **volere** (to want / wish). (*Grammatica page 96*)

- **A due letti o matrimoniale?** – Twin beds or double bed?

- **al terzo piano** – on the third floor. For ordinal numbers see *Grammatica page 98*.

- **Dobbiamo** + Infinitive – we have to / we must. (*Grammatica page 96*)

- **a partire dalle 7** – from 7 o'clock onwards.

- **al pianterreno** – on the ground floor. You will also see **piano terreno**.

- **Possiamo avere la sveglia alle sei e mezzo?** – Can you call us at 6.30?

Vocabolarietto

il letto	bed
altro	other
compreso	included
doppio	double
ascoltare	to listen to
abbastanza	quite / fairly
fra	between
mentre	while
a parte	separate
presto	early

📼 Conversazioni

Più tardi, all'uscita

Peter Lawrence:	Scusi, signore, c'è una banca qui vicino?
Impiegato:	Ce ne sono due in Via del Corso, ma tutte le banche sono chiuse a quest'ora.
Peter Lawrence:	Lo so, ma con l'Eurocard posso ...
Impiegato:	Ah, ho capito. Allora ... vediamo ... ci sono molte banche nella zona, ma se c'è un Bancomat, non lo so. Se no, può andare al Grand Hotel dove accettano carte di credito.
Peter Lawrence:	Dov'è? È lontano da qui?
Impiegato:	No, non è troppo lontano – cinque minuti a piedi. Deve attraversare questa strada, prendere la prima a sinistra, andare sempre dritto fino al semaforo, e il Grand Hotel è sulla destra.
Peter Lawrence:	Grazie tante.
Impiegato:	Prego. Buona passeggiata!

Quindici minuti più tardi, Peter non ha ancora trovato il Grand Hotel

Peter Lawrence:	Scusi, signora. Per andare al Grand Hotel?
Signora:	Continui sempre dritto, fino al semaforo in fondo. Poi giri a destra e il Grand si trova all'angolo.
Peter Lawrence:	Grazie.
Signora:	Prego.

Finalmente, al Grand Hotel

Impiegato:	Dica?
Peter Lawrence:	Accettate l'Eurocard?
Impiegato:	Certo, signore.
Peter Lawrence:	Vorrei incassare 50 sterline. Quant'è il cambio oggi?
Impiegato:	Un attimo, prego. Lira sterlina ... 2.240 lire. Mi dia il suo passaporto. Vuole firmare qui, signore. Dunque ...112.000 lire.
Peter Lawrence:	Grazie. Buongiorno.

Spiegazioni

- **Più tardi** – later. **Più** means 'more'.

- **qui vicino** and **nella zona** both mean 'in the area / round here'.

- **Ce ne sono due** – there are two (of them). The **ci** of **ci sono** changes to **ce** before **ne**.

- **tutte le banche** – all banks. To keep the hard /c/ and /g/ sounds in words ending in **-ca, -co, -ga** and **-go**, you insert <u>h</u> in the plural. **Banca** becomes **ban<u>che</u>**, **albergo** becomes **alberg<u>hi</u>**. (*Pronuncia page vii*)

- **Lo so** – I know (lit. 'I know it'). **So** is from **sapere** (to know).

- **Vediamo** – Let's see. (*Grammatica page 97*)

- **Può + Infinitive** – you can ... (*Grammatica page 96*)

- **cinque minuti a piedi** – five minutes' walk (lit. 'five minutes on foot').

- **Deve + Infinitive** – you have to ... (*Grammatica page 96*)

- **la prima a sinistra** – the first on the left. The word **strada** ('street') is understood.

- **fino al semaforo** – up to the traffic lights. **Fino a** is used both for time ('until') and for place ('as far as').
  Note that **semaforo** is singular.

- **Buona passeggiata!** – Enjoy your walk!

- **Per andare a...?** – How do I get to ...? (lit. 'To get to ...?').

- **il Grand si trova** – the Grand is. He could also have said '**Il Grand è**', but when talking about where places are situated, you often use **si trova** in Italian.

- **Dica** – Can I help you? A variation on **Mi dica** (lit. 'Tell me').

- **Quant'è il cambio oggi?** – What is the exchange rate today?

- **Lira sterlina** (often simply **sterlina**) – pound sterling. The £ sign, L. and **Lit.** are all used for the Italian lira. If you refer back to the list of exchange rates on page 6 you will find the Italian names for the major currencies.

Vocabolarietto

l'angolo	corner	girare	to turn
la banca	bank	incassare	to cash
il Bancomat	cash dispenser		
il cambio	rate of exchange	a piedi	on foot
la passeggiata	walk	a / sulla / destra	on the right
il semaforo	traffic lights	a / sulla / sinistra	on the left
la strada	street	sempre dritto	straight on
		troppo	too
accettare	to accept	se	if
attraversare	to cross	ancora	yet / still
continuare	to continue / carry on	dunque	so / then
firmare	to sign		

Grammatica

A Potere Dovere Volere

These three irregular verbs are extremely useful and should be learnt thoroughly. The verb following each of them is in the infinitive.

	POTERE	DOVERE	VOLERE
(io)	posso	devo	voglio
(tu)	puoi	devi	vuoi
(Lei)	può	deve	vuole
(lui / lei)	può	deve	vuole
(noi)	possiamo	dobbiamo	vogliamo
(voi)	potete	dovete	volete
(loro)	possono	devono	vogliono

Potere – to be able to

Posso parlare con ...? – Can I speak to ...?
Potete fare colazione alle sette – You can have breakfast at seven o'clock.

Use **mi può ...** to ask someone to do something for you.

   Mi può richiamare più tardi? – Can you call me back later?

Posso? on its own corresponds to 'may I?'.

The Perfect Tense, **ho potuto**, corresponds to 'I was able to' and 'I have been able to'.

Dovere – to have to

Devo telefonare in Inghilterra – I must / have to phone England.
Dobbiamo partire domani – We must / have to leave tomorrow.

Devo ...? can be used for 'Should I ...?' or 'Do I ...?'.

   Devo firmare qui? – Do I have to sign here?

The Perfect Tense, **ho dovuto**, corresponds to 'I had to'.

Volere – to want

Vuole is used to mean 'Would you?' or 'Would you like to ...?'
Vuole lasciare un messaggio? – Would you like to leave a message?

The Perfect Tense, **ho voluto**, corresponds to 'I wanted to'.

B -iamo

The -iamo ending of a verb has various corresponding forms in English. You already know that **andiamo** means 'we go' or 'we are going'. It can also mean 'Let's go!' or 'Shall we go?'

Andiamo a* cenare a ...	Let's go and have dinner at ...
Facciamo le otto.	Let's make it eight o'clock.
Mangiamo?	Shall we eat?
Speriamo!	Let's hope so!

* To say 'Let's go and ...' you need **a** between **andiamo** and the Infinitive of the other verb.

C Molto Troppo Quanto

Molto has two meanings. When it means 'very', it is invariable (i.e. it does not change).

Il lavoro non è **molto** interessante / Sono **molto** occupata

Molto can also mean 'a lot of' / 'much' / 'many'. When used in this way **molto**, like other adjectives, agrees with its noun.

Molto lavoro **Molta** confusione **Molti** ristoranti **Molte** banche

Similarly, **troppo** is invariable when the meaning is 'too'.

Non è **troppo** lontano / La camera è **troppo** cara

When followed by a noun, meaning 'too much' / 'too many', **troppo** agrees with that noun.

Troppo lavoro **Troppa** confusione **Troppi** ristoranti **Troppe** banche

Quanto is invariable when the meaning is 'how much' followed by a verb:

Quanto costa?

When followed by a noun, meaning 'how much' / 'how many?', **quanto** agrees with that noun.

Quanto tempo? / **Quanta** birra? / **Quanti** giorni? / **Quante** notti?

D Possessive adjectives – my, your, his, her

● Talking about one member of the family.

my	mio / mia
your (tu)	tuo / tua
your (Lei)	Suo / Sua
his / her	suo / sua

mio marito	my husband	tua moglie	your wife
suo figlio	his / her son	Sua figlia	your daughter

- In all other cases the possessive adjective must be preceded by the definite article (the).

my	il mio / la mia / i miei / le mie
your	il tuo / la tua / i tuoi / le tue
your	il Suo / la Sua / i Suoi / le Sue
his / her	il suo / la sua / i suoi / le sue

- The possessive adjective agrees with what is owned, *not* the owner.
  'My family' is always **la mia famiglia,** regardless of whether the owner is male or female. Therefore, there is no difference in Italian between the words for 'his' and 'her'. **La sua camera** can mean 'his room' or 'her room'. It is usually clear from the context whether 'his' or 'her' is meant.

- The word for 'your' (formal) is the same as the word for 'his /her'. The only difference is that it is written with a capital letter.
  Il suo nome – her name / his name. **Il Suo nome** – your name.

- In Italian possessive adjectives are used less often than in English.
  If it is obvious whose the object in question is, then the possessive is not used.
  In Italian you say '**Ho rischiato la vita**' for 'I risked my life', you ask for '**La chiave, per favore**' in a hotel whereas in English you would probably say 'My key, please'.

E Ordinal numbers

1st	primo	6th	sesto
2nd	secondo	7th	settimo
3rd	terzo	8th	ottavo
4th	quarto	9th	nono
5th	quinto	10th	decimo

From 11 onwards you replace the final vowel of the cardinal number with **-esimo.**

11th	undicesimo	100th	centesimo
20th	ventesimo	1000th	millesimo
25th	venticinquesimo	nth	ennesimo
50th	cinquantesimo		

Ordinal numbers agree with the noun like adjectives: il secon**do** piano / la secon**da** strad**a.**

La prima volta – the first time; **l'ennesima volta** – the umpteenth time.

Remember that it is only for the <u>first</u> of the month (e.g. **il primo marzo**) that you use ordinal numbers in Italian. Thereafter, **il due marzo, il tre marzo,** etc.

In Italia ...

Hotels

Italy's 40,000 hotels are graded from 1 to 5 stars (**stelle**). The terms **albergo** and **hotel** (pronounced *otel*) are interchangeable. A **pensione** (guesthouse) offers more modest accommodation.

Four- and five-star hotels can be booked through travel agents in England, and this is advisable in the holiday season. Otherwise, the tourist office in the airport or main railway stations, usually called **Azienda di Turismo** or **Azienda di Soggiorno**, will supply lists of accommodation with prices and telephone numbers. They may even ring a hotel for you to ensure the availability of accommodation. If you arrive when these are closed, the **Ufficio Informazioni** will at least be able to supply the list of accommodation.

Hotel prices are fixed with the Provincial Tourist Board, and include service charges, **IVA** (VAT) at the current rate, and other State taxes. Hotels are obliged to display the room price in the room itself, usually on the back of the door. Prices quoted are per room, and breakfast is not included, unless this is specifically stated.

When you register at the hotel, you are required to present identification, usually your passport, for police registration.

Banks

Banking hours have been referred to already in Unit 3. In addition to public holidays (see In Italia ... Unit 4) you will find three more days – 14th August, 24th and 31st December – which are half-day bank holidays. Be prepared too for closed doors on the name day of the local saint of the town you are in. Outside banking hours (**orario di sportello**) money can be changed at the exchange office, **il cambio**, in city railway termini and in most large hotels.

A bank is **una banca** in Italian, but some of the older houses still refer to themselves by the old name of **un banco**. Whether in a **banca** or a **banco**, obtaining money is likely to be a more frustrating experience in Italy than in Britain. The cash dispenser, **il bancomat**, is less ubiquitous (though where it exists it will often accept Eurocard), and getting in and out of a bank is less straightforward than in Britain, used as we are to walking straight in through open doors to a single orderly queue to wait for the next free counter (**lo sportello**).

In Italy security at the bank doors is often elaborate and may even involve leaving all bags with the guard. Once inside the customer must find his own way to the correct counter and wait. The counter transaction will take longer as every item is computerized by the clerk while you wait. Once all forms have been completed you will be directed to another queue at the **cassa** for your cash.

Out in the street cash is still king in Italy. Credit cards are less widely accepted, while paying by cheque for small amounts is comparatively rare. Should you, as a foreigner, open a current account (**un conto corrente estero**) it will be assumed you are aware that writing a cheque with inadequate provision is an imprisonable offence. Particular care should be taken by the motorist as motorway service stations more often than not do not accept British credit cards.

Pratica

1 *Listen to all the conversations again and answer these questions in Italian.*

    (i)   Qual è il numero della camera del signor Lawrence?

    (ii)   La sua camera è con bagno o con doccia?

    (iii)   Per telefonare in Inghilterra, dove va il signor Lawrence?

    (iv)   C'è un ristorante nell'albergo?

    (v)   La prima colazione è compresa nel prezzo della camera?

    (vi)   A che ora possono fare colazione gli ospiti?

    (vii)   Dove si trova la camera 316?

    (viii) Il Grand Hotel è lontano dall'Aretusa?

    (ix)   Quante sterline desidera incassare il signor Lawrence?

    (x)   Quant'è il cambio?

 2 *The hotel receptionist is likely to be one of the first Italians you will need to understand on your arrival. Listen to the tape and write down in the spaces below the details for each room.*

The first one, Signor Rossi, is done for you.

Name	Room number	Floor	Single / double	Bath / shower	Price (lire)
ROSSI	13	1	single	bath	60.000
CONTI					
MAZZETTI					
SMITH					
GELLI					

3 *Listen to the directions on the cassette and follow each route on the map. Indicate in the spaces below the letter which marks each destination.*

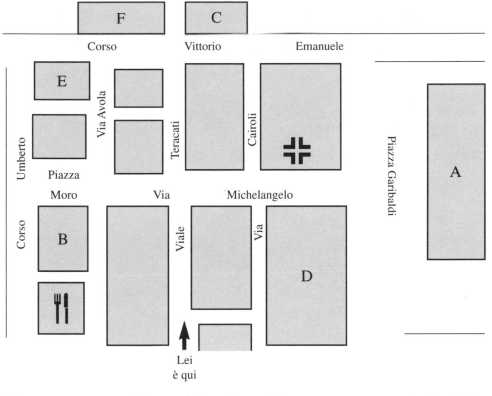

(i) _____ Il Banco di Napoli   (ii) _____ La Stazione

(iii) _____ La Posta Centrale   (iv) _____ L'Albergo Olimpia

 4 (A) *Two hotel guests phone down to reception for some information.*
Make a note of the telephone numbers – two numbers for each office.

   (i)   Assessorato del Turismo   _____   _____

   (ii) Ufficio Turistico di Roma _____   _____

(B) *A hotel guest asks the receptionist how to get to Fiumicino Airport.*
Listen to the conversation, refer to the tube map on page 189, and make a note of the important points.

   • Take the tube, line _____
   • Change at _____ station.
   • The journey time is _____
   • The cost of the ticket is _____

5 *Write these figures out (e.g. L.10.000 – diecimila lire). You will need to do this if writing out a cheque from an Italian account.*

L. 50.000
L. 75.000
L. 46.500
L. 90.200
L. 120.000

6 *Complete the sentences using a similar form of the following verbs to the one used in the example. (Grammatica B)*

andare, cominciare, guardare, mangiare, partire, parlare

Esempio Anna non è ancora arrivata. Allora, <u>aspettiamo</u> un po'.

(i) Abbiamo un appuntamento in ufficio alle tre e mezzo.
Allora, ——————— alle tre.

(ii) Scusi, io non parlo bene inglese.
Allora, ——————— italiano.

(iii) Siamo tutti qui?
Allora, ———————

(iv) Gli spaghetti sono pronti?
Allora, ——————— subito.

(v) Il signor Russo è arrivato?
Allora, ——————— i documenti.

(vi) Ha trovato un buon ristorante?
Allora, ——————— a cena stasera.

7 In your diary is a reminder to ring signora Azzano. You have jotted down notes of the points you wish to raise with her. Write what you will say in Italian. You will need an appropriate form of POTERE or DOVERE in all of them. *(Grammatica A)*

> - I have to go to Naples today,
> - can come to the office tomorrow.
> - couldn't phone yesterday,
> - had to work until 6pm.
>
> Charles Kington and I
> - can't stay until Friday.
> - have to leave on Thursday.
>
> Ask her if she can
> - change the appointment
> - check the invoice.
>
> Remind her that she must
> - speak to the agents.
> Tell her they can't
> - come to the exhibition.

8 Fill the gaps in these conversations using the appropriate possessive adjective – *mio, la Sua, le mie,* etc. *(Grammatica D)*

Impiegato:	Mi dà _____ (your) carta d'identità, signore.
Mario Conti:	Non ho una carta d'identità, ma ecco _____ (my) passaporto.
Impiegato:	Queste sono _____ (your) valige?
Mario Conti:	No. Io ho solo _____ (my) valigetta. Ah, _____ (my) amico è arrivato. Piacere di rivederLa, Giorgio. Come sta? E _____ (your) famiglia?
Giorgio:	Benissimo. _____ (my) sorella Franca adesso lavora presso _____ (my) company.
Mario:	E _____ (her) figlio?
Giorgio:	Fabrizio? È studente all'università di Firenze. Ha comprato _____ (his) prima macchina oggi!

9 *Take part in the following conversations.*

(**A**) *You are at the airport trying to book a hotel from the list you were given at the Ufficio Informazioni.*

Portiere:	Hotel Centrale. Pronto.
You:	(*Ask if he has a room.*)
Portiere:	Solo per questa notte?
You:	(*Say that you want a room for two nights.*)
Portiere:	Un attimo, prego. Con o senza bagno privato?
You:	(*Say with a bathroom and ask the price.*)
Portiere:	90.000 lire al giorno.
You:	(*You'll take it, so say it's fine and find out where it is.*)
Portiere:	Via San Marco 25. Da dove telefona?
You:	(*Tell him you are at Fiumicino airport.*)
Portiere:	Allora, siamo solo a dieci minuti dall'aeroporto. Deve prendere un tassì. Il Suo nome signore?
You:	(*Give your name, spelling it out, thank him and say goodbye.*)

(**B**) *On a different occasion, you go to the reception desk of a large city-centre hotel and speak to the receptionist.*

Impiegata:	Buongiorno, signore. Desidera?
You:	(*Ask if they have a room free.*)
Impiegata:	Per quante notti?
You:	(*Say for three nights. You want a single room with a shower. Find out the price.*)
Impiegata:	100.000 lire, signore.
You:	(*Ask if breakfast is included.*)
Impiegata:	No, signore, è a parte. Costa 6.000 lire.
You:	(*Say you'll take the room, but without breakfast.*)
Impiegata:	Va bene. Camera 122 al primo piano. Ecco la chiave. Mi può lasciare il passaporto, per piacere?
You:	(*Hand your passport over and ask if they can change £50 for you.*)
Impiegata:	Mi dispiace, signore. C'è una banca all'angolo, ma è chiusa a quest'ora.
You:	(*Express your annoyance about this, then enquire if there is a telephone as you have to phone England.*)
Impiegata:	Può telefonare in Inghilterra dalla Sua camera, signore.

You: (*Thank her and say goodbye.*)

10 *Look at these hotel advertisements and answer the questions below.*

Hotel Milano ✱✱✱

Di moderna costruzione, situato in posizione tranquilla a quindici minuti dal centro storico.
Tutte le camere con telefono, frigobar, aria condizionata, balcone. Sala TV e congressi, ascensore, bar. Ristorante con due menù a scelta, cucina casalinga. Bevande comprese nelle tariffe.
Parcheggio privato a pagamento (gratuito in bassa stagione). Offerte speciali maggio & ottobre. Prezzi IVA compresa.

Hotel ROMAE ✱✱

Nuovo hotel situato nel centro commerciale, a pochi passi dal centro storico. Le camere sono arredate modernamente, e dispongono tutte di servizi privati, telefono diretto e TV. Organizzazione ed informazioni per: gite turistiche, compagnie aeree, ristoranti, opera. Garage a richiesta.

Hotel Le Torri ✱✱✱✱✱

Qualità ☆ Lusso ☆ Eleganza
Aperto tutto l'anno.
200 camere con salotto, trasformabili in uffici:
telefono diretto ☆ servizio fax ☆ segreteria multilingue.
Sale per congressi, esposizioni, riunioni.
Zona centrale, a 20 km dagli aeroporti di Roma.
Ampio parcheggio interno.

(i)   Is Hotel Milano in the town centre?

(ii)   When do their special offers apply?

(iii) Are prices inclusive of VAT?

(iv)   Is Hotel Romae in or near:

    (a) the commercial centre?

    (b) the historic centre?

(v)   Do Hotel Milano and Hotel Romae both have telephone and TV in all rooms?

(vi)   When is Hotel Le Torri open?

(vii) Name three of the services which make it an attractive venue for a conference / presentation.

(viii) What is advantageous about its position?

Riassunto

You can now ....

- **book accommodation**

  Ha / avete una camera?
  singola / doppia / matrimoniale,
  per tre notti / per stasera,
  con / senza bagno.
  La colazione è compresa?

- **enquire about the facilities**

  C'è un telefono nella camera?
  Avete un ristorante?
  C'è una banca qui vicino?
  A che ora posso fare colazione?
  Posso avere la sveglia alle sette?

- **find your way around**

  Scusi, signora, dov'è ....
  Per andare a ...?
  A destra / a sinistra / sempre dritto
  Non è lontano – cinque minuti a piedi.

- **say you have to do something**

  Devo telefonare in Inghilterra.
  Dobbiamo partire presto.

- **ask if you can / may do something**

  Posso lasciare un messaggio?
  Posso cambiare 50 sterline?

- **ask someone to do something for you**

  Può controllare la fattura?
  Mi può dire...

- **suggest doing something**

  Andiamo a cena al ristorante.
  Facciamo le otto.

- **cope in a bank**

  Vorrei incassare / cambiare lire sterline.
  Quant'è il cambio?
  Devo firmare qui?

►► *Now, with a partner, try Role Play 3 on pages 197–8*

BUON APPETITO!

You will learn to:
- order a meal
- use appropriate social courtesies
- express preferences
- ask for advice

📟 Conversazioni

Sono le otto di sera. Peter Lawrence e Giancarlo Lucarini sono arrivati al Gatto Blu

Giancarlo Lucarini:	Buona sera.
Cameriere:	Buona sera, signori. Un tavolo per due?
Giancarlo Lucarini:	No, siamo in tre – aspettiamo qualcuno.
Cameriere:	Da questa parte, signori. Si accomodino, prego.
Giancarlo Lucarini:	Mi piace questo ristorante. La cucina è ottima – tutta casalinga. Si mangia bene ma non si spende troppo! Senta, Peter, ho invitato una collega a cena. Non Le dispiace?
Peter Lawrence:	Niente affatto! Più siamo, meglio è.
Giancarlo Lucarini:	Bravo, Peter! Ah, eccola! Francesca, buona sera.
Francesca Bastiani:	Scusate. Sono un po' in ritardo ... che traffico!
Giancarlo Lucarini:	Non fa niente! Peter, Le presento la mia gentilissima collega Francesca Bastiani, direttore della pubblicità.
Peter Lawrence:	Molto lieto, signora.
Francesca Bastiani:	Francesca... Piacere, Peter. Benvenuto a Roma.
Cameriere:	Signori, siete pronti?
Giancarlo Lucarini:	Allora, Peter, cosa gradisce?
Peter Lawrence:	Eh, non so. Che cosa mi consiglia?
Giancarlo Lucarini:	Quali sono i piatti del giorno?
Cameriere:	Come primo abbiamo minestrone*, tortelloni*, spaghetti alle vongole*, risotto ai funghi*... Il risotto è buonissimo oggi.
Peter Lawrence:	Prendo il risotto.
Giancarlo:	Per me gli spaghetti. E per te, Francesca?
Francesca:	Il minestrone.

* *See In Italia ..., page 117.*

Spiegazioni

- **Siamo in tre** – There are three of us.

- **Da questa parte** – This way.

- **Si accomodino** – Sit down. This is the formal **Loro** form of the Imperative. (*Grammatica page 115*)

- **Mi piace ...** – I like ... (*Grammatica page 115*)

- **casalinga** – home-made. **Una casalinga** is a housewife.

- **Si mangia / si spende** – One eats / one spends. (*Grammatica page 114*)

- **una collega** – a colleague. **Collega** can be used for both masculine and feminine – **il collega** (pl. **i colleghi**) and **la collega** (pl. **le colleghe**).

- **Non Le dispiace?** – You don't mind?

- **Niente affatto!** – Not at all.

- **Più siamo, meglio è!** – The more the merrier!

- **Scusate** – Excuse me / I'm sorry. **Scusate** is the equivalent of **Scusi** when addressing more than one person.

- **la mia gentilissima collega** – my delightful colleague. When -issimo is added to an adjective (after dropping its final vowel) it corresponds to the English very / most / extremely + adj.

- **Non fa niente** – It doesn't matter.

- **Cosa gradisce?** – What would you like? From **gradire** – to enjoy.

- **Che cosa mi consiglia?** – What do you recommend (for me)? **Che cosa, cosa** and **che** can all be used to translate **what**.

- **Come primo?** – For the first course? You will also hear **Per primo?** and **Di primo?**

- **Per me / per te** – For me / for you. (*Grammatica page 116*)

Vocabolarietto

la cena	evening meal	**consigliare**	recommend
il / la collega	colleague	**gradire (-isc)**	to enjoy
la cucina	cooking / kitchen	**invitare**	invite
il piatto	dish / plate / course	**spendere (speso)**	to spend
il piatto del giorno	dish of the day		
il primo	first course	**meglio**	better
la tavola / il tavolo	table	**quale?**	which? / which one?
il traffico	traffic	**quali?**	which? / which ones?
		bravo!	Bravo / Well said!
buonissimo	excellent		
casalinga	home-made		
gentile	kind, nice		
pronto	ready		

▣ Conversazioni

Francesca raccomanda una specialità siciliana a Peter

Cameriere:	Cosa prendono come secondo?
Francesca:	Io prendo il pesce spada.* È una specialità siciliana, Peter. È delizioso.
Cameriere:	Signore?
Peter:	Non so. Non conosco la cucina siciliana... Pesce spada anche per me, se lo raccomanda Lei, Francesca.
Giancarlo:	Io vorrei la bistecca alla fiorentina,* ben cotta.
Cameriere:	Come contorno? Un'insalata mista?* Bene ... Due ...? Dunque, due insalate miste, e per Lei, signore ..? Spinaci al burro?* Basta ...? Da bere?
Francesca:	Ci porti un buon Frascati* secco, e una bottiglia di acqua minerale.
Cameriere:	Naturale o gassata?
Giancarlo:	Naturale. E un mezzo litro di rosso.
Giancarlo:	Intanto prendiamo l'aperitivo. Ci porti una bottiglia di Orvieto classico abboccato,* per favore.
Cameriere:	Subito, signore.
Francesca:	Che buona idea! Qui in Italia si deve aspettare nei ristoranti.
Giancarlo:	Vuoi dire in Sicilia! Questo è un ristorante siciliano, Peter.
Francesca:	(*a Peter*) Ride sempre di me, perché sono siciliana – sono nata a Palermo. Ma abito a Roma da venticinque anni, e secondo me il Mezzogiorno comincia già a Roma! In ogni caso, il servizio qui non è peggiore che negli altri ristoranti di Roma.
Cameriere:	Minestra* per la signora ... spaghetti alle vongole per Lei, signore, e il risotto. Ecco. Buon appetito!
Francesca:	Buon appetito, Peter, Giancarlo.
Peter:	Grazie, altrettanto.

* *See In Italia ..., page 117.*

Spiegazioni

- **Non so / non conosco** – I don't know. (*Grammatica page 116*)

- **ben cotta** – well cooked

- **Da bere?** – To drink?

- **Basta?** – Will that be all? **Basta,** in the affirmative, means 'that's enough'. **Basta** is often used with an infinitive to mean 'All you need do is ...' (e.g. 'Basta telefonare...').

- **Ci porti** – Bring us.

- **Si deve** + Infinitive – One has to / one must. (*Grammatica page 114*)

- **Vuoi dire** – You mean. (lit. 'you want to say'). Note the Italian for 'What does ... mean?' – **Che cosa vuol dire ...?**

- **Ride sempre di me** – He always laughs at me / makes fun of me.

- **sono nata a Palermo** – I was born in Palermo. **Nascere** (to be born) takes **essere** in the Perfect Tense.

- **secondo me** – in my opinion.

- **Il Mezzogiorno comincia già a Roma** – Southern Italy starts here in Rome. It is a standing joke amongst Italians that the Mezzogiorno, with its connotations of sloth and backwardness, always begins at the next town south of one's own.

- **il servizio qui non è peggiore che negli altri ristoranti di Roma** – the service here is no worse than in the other restaurants in Rome.

- **Buon appetito!** – Enjoy your meal. You will rarely sit down to a meal in Italy without hearing **Buon appetito.**

- **altrettanto** – the same to you.

Vocabolarietto

l'acqua minerale	mineral water	**bere (bevuto)**	to drink
l'aperitivo	aperitif	**nascere (nato)**	to be born
la bottiglia	bottle	**portare**	to bring, carry
il contorno	vegetables	**ridere (riso)**	to laugh
il secondo	second course	**volere dire**	to mean
il servizio	service		
la specialità	speciality	**peggiore**	worse
cotto	cooked	**intanto**	meanwhile
delizioso	delicious	**in ogni caso**	in any case
gassato	sparkling / fizzy		
naturale	natural		
siciliano	Sicilian		

111

⊟ Conversazioni

Mentre mangiano, Francesca rivela che conosce già i prodotti della MK

Francesca:	... e dove si trova la sua ditta – a Londra?
Peter:	Si trova piuttosto in periferia, a dieci chilometri dalla capitale.
Francesca:	Conosco già i vostri prodotti. Li ho visti alla Fiera di Genova l'anno scorso. Non avete agenti in Italia?
Peter:	In questa zona, no. A Milano, a Genova, a Torino, nel Nord, sì, ma attualmente non abbiamo nessuno nel Mezzogiorno.
Giancarlo:	Peter, Roma non è il Mezzogiorno. Il Mezzogiorno comincia a Napoli. Roma è ...
Cameriere:	Tutto bene? Le piace il pesce spada, signore?
Peter:	Mmmm. Squisito... buonissimo!
Francesca	Il Gatto Blu è famoso nella zona per i suoi piatti di pesce...
Cameriere:	... E adesso il dolce. Vogliono sapere che cosa c'è per dolce?
Francesca:	Io vorrei delle fragole. Mi piacciono tanto.
Giancarlo:	Niente dolce per me. Un po' di formaggio, forse. ... Peter?
Peter:	Sì. Vorrei assaggiare un formaggio della regione.
Cameriere:	Allora, fragole, formaggi ...
Giancarlo:	... e un altro mezzo di rosso.
Francesca:	Senta, Peter, Giancarlo mi dice che Lei non è mai stato a Roma. Se non ha niente da fare domani pomeriggio, possiamo fare il giro della città – il Colosseo, il Foro, il Vaticano. Giancarlo, che ne dici?
Giancarlo:	Eh, non so, vediamo ... cioè, c'è la visita dello stabilimento alle dieci, l'incontro con l'ingegnere alle undici e mezzo, pranzo con Antonio alle tredici, dopo di che Peter è libero, mi sembra. Però, io ho un impegno alle tre.
Francesca:	Che peccato! Peter, che ne dice? Andiamo a vedere Roma domani?
Peter:	Volentieri! Non vedo l'ora!

Spiegazioni

- **Li ho visti** – I saw them.
  (*Grammatica page 116*)

- **Non abbiamo nessuno** – We have nobody.
  (*Grammatica page 114*)

- **Vogliono** – Do you want / Would you like.
  The **Loro** form of **volere** (to want).

- **delle fragole** – some strawberries.
  To translate 'some' you use **di** combined
  with the relevant definite article.

- **Mi piacciono tanto** – I like them so much.
  (*Grammatica page 115*)

- **Niente dolce per m**e – No sweet for me.

- **se non ha niente da fare** – if you don't have
  anything to do. (*Grammatica page 114*)

- **Che ne dici? / che ne dice?** –
  What do you say to that?

- **cioè** – that is / I mean. A common and much
  over-used word by many Italians, but useful
  when you are not quite sure what to say!

- **Dopo di che ...** – After which ...

- **Non vedo l'ora** – I'm looking forward to it.

IL GATTO BLU

MENU GASTRONOMICO
L 60.000

tortelloni
spaghetti alle vongole
risotto ai funghi
minestrone

☆★☆★★☆

pesce spada
osso buco
bistecca alla fiorentina
pesce al forno con carciofi

☆★☆★★☆

insalata verde
spinaci alla romana
patatine fritte

☆★☆☆★☆

granita di fragole
zuppa inglese
gelato alla pesca

☆★☆★★☆

formaggi

Vocabolarietto

la capitale	capital	**assaggiare**	to taste
il dolce	sweet	**fare il giro**	to tour
la fragola	strawberry	**rivelare**	to reveal
il gatto	cat	**sembrare**	to seem
l'impegno	engagement, commitment		
la periferia	outskirts	**già**	already
		piuttosto	rather
blu	blue	**tanto**	so much
famoso	famous		
libero	free	**Che peccato!**	What a pity!
squisito	delicious, exquisite		

Grammatica

A Negatives

We have already seen how to say 'not' in Italian

> <u>Non</u> sono italiano – I am not Italian
> <u>Non</u> è arrivata – She has not arrived
> Il signor Russo <u>non</u> parla inglese – Mr Russo does not speak English

We also use **non** with **nessuno, niente** (or **nulla**), and **mai** to say **'nobody'**, **'nothing'**, and **'never'**

> <u>Non</u> abbiamo <u>nessuno</u> – We have nobody
> <u>Non</u> ha <u>niente</u> da fare – He has nothing to do
> <u>Non</u> sono <u>mai</u> stato a Roma – I have never been to Rome

If the negative word begins the sentence, **non** is not used

> Nessuno capisce – No-one understands
> Nulla è impossibile – Nothing is impossible

Watch out for **niente**, used with nouns, meaning **'no'**

> Niente dolce per me – No dessert for me

Niente is used in several idiomatic expressions

> Non fa niente – It doesn't matter
> Niente affatto – Not in the least
> Non serve a niente – It's no use

B Si

Si followed by the **lui / lei** form of the verb corresponds to the indefinite **one, people, you** or **they.**

> Si mangia bene qui – One eats well here
> Come si dice .... in italiano? – How do you say .... in Italian?
> Non si sa mai – One never knows

C Sapere e Conoscere

There are two verbs in Italian for the English 'to know'.

1. <u>SAPERE</u> – to know *a fact*

so	sappiamo
sai	sapete
sa	sanno

2. <u>CONOSCERE</u> – to know *a person or a place*

conosco	conosciamo
conosci	conoscete
conosce	conoscono

So che Francesca abita a Roma – I know that Francesca lives in Rome
Sa dove si trova la banca? – Do you know where the bank is?

Conosco bene il Suo direttore generale – I know your general manager well
Il signor Lawrence non **conosce** Roma – Mr Lawrence doesn't know Rome

D Imperatives

Loro

This is used when addressing more than one person in very formal situations.
It is formed by adding **-no** to the **Lei** form of the Imperative (*page 79*).

Si accomodino, signori – Sit down and make yourselves at home, gentlemen

Voi

The **voi** form is used when addressing more than one friend, acquaintance or business colleague. It is the same form of the verb as the **voi** Present tense form (*page 40*).

Ascoltate! – Listen!   Scusate! – Excuse me!

E Mi piace

The verb 'to like' does not exist in Italian. The way to say 'I like wine' in Italian is '**Mi piace il vino**', which literally means 'The wine is pleasing to me'.
When the object of '**I like**' is plural, as in the sentence 'I like strawberries', you need the equivalent of 'are pleasing' – **mi piacciono**.

Mi piacciono le fragole – (lit. 'The strawberries are pleasing to me')

You can express degrees of liking things by adding **molto** (a lot), **moltissimo** (very much indeed) or **abbastanza** (quite) to **mi piace**.

Mi piace molto questa regione
Mi piace moltissimo la birra tedesca
Mi piacciono abbastanza gli spinaci

You can also use **mi piace** + Infinitive to say you enjoy doing something.

Mi piace viaggiare
Mi piace andare al cinema

To ask someone if they like something, you say **Le piace ...?** or **Le piacciono ...?**

> Le piace il vino rosso?
> Le piacciono le fragole?

To say you do not like something, use **non** in front of **mi piace / mi piacciono.**

> Non mi piace il formaggio.
> Non mi piacciono gli spaghetti.

(As you already know, **mi dispiace** means I am sorry.)

F Me, you, him, her, us, them (object pronouns)

As objects of a verb, normally placed in front of the verb

mi	me	ci	us
ti	you	vi	you
lo	him / it	li	them (m.)
la	her / it	le	them (f.)
La	you		

> <u>Mi</u> capisce? – Do you understand <u>me</u>?
> <u>Lo</u> mando per fax – I'm faxing <u>it</u>.
> <u>Li</u> ho visti* – I saw <u>them</u>.

* When **lo, la, li** and **le** are used with a verb in the Perfect tense, the Past Participle has to agree.

> L'ho vist<u>o</u> – I saw him / it   L'ho vist<u>a</u> – I saw her / it
> Li ho vist<u>i</u> – I saw them (m.)   Le ho vist<u>e</u> – I saw them (f.)

Mi, ti, ci and **vi** can also mean 'to me', 'to you', 'to us' and 'to you'.

> <u>Mi</u> può scrivere? – Can you write <u>to me</u>?
> <u>Ci</u> porti un buon Frascati – Bring (<u>to</u>) <u>us</u> a good bottle of Frascati

Special forms are used where in English we say '<u>to him</u>', '<u>to her</u>', '<u>to you</u> (Lei)', '<u>to them</u>'. These will be explained in Unit 9.

After prepositions

me	noi
te	voi
lui	loro (m. & f.)
lei	
Lei	

Per <u>me</u> la bistecca – The steak for me
E per <u>Lei</u>, signora? – And for you?
Secondo <u>noi</u>. ... – According to us ....
Lavoro con <u>loro</u> – I work with them

All the pronouns are in the Grammar Review on page 205

In Italia ...

Italy possesses one of the world's finest cuisines, with an unsurpassed variety of dishes and wines to accompany them.

The information below should enable you to make an educated choice from a typical Italian menu, but you will need your Italian to ask **Cos'è questo?** for a **piatto locale** or a **specialità della casa**. Waiters are generally far more knowledgeable than in the UK about the preparation of the food they are serving and will often stand proudly at the end of the table and give an account of every item on the menu before you make your choice.

Come antipasto? (Starter, hors-d'oeuvres)

Antipasto misto	Mixed hors-d'oeuvres
Olive / Carciofini	Olives / Artichoke hearts
Prosciutto con melone / fichi	Ham with melon / figs
Frutti di mare	Seafood
Crostini	Bread fried in oil with anchovy / cheese

Come primo? (First course, entrée)

Pasta is the most popular **primo piatto** throughout Italy. It comes in a variety of shapes and sizes – spaghetti, tagliatelle, penne, rigatoni, lasagne, ravioli, tortellini, tortelloni – to name but a few.

These are a few of the sauces you may be offered with your pasta:

al pomodoro – tomato
al ragù – bolognese
ai funghi – mushrooms
alle vongole – clams
in bianco – with butter & parmesan
all'arrabbiata – tomato & chillies
alla carbonara – eggs and bacon

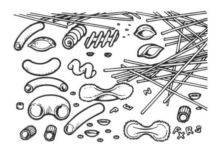

Note that the names for the various pasta shapes are all in the plural. When referring to them you will need the plural forms of verbs and adjectives, e.g. Gli spaghetti <u>sono</u> <u>buoni</u>, mi <u>piacciono</u> molto.

Other **primi piatti** might be:

Risotto	Rice dish
Gnocchi	Potato and flour dumplings
Minestra / zuppa	Soup
Minestrone	Mixed vegetable soup

Come secondo? (Second, main course)

Carne – meat

Manzo (beef), **agnello** (lamb), **pollo** (chicken), **vitello** (veal), **maiale** (pork) may appear on the menu cooked in any of the following ways:

> arrosto – roast
> alla griglia / alla brace – grilled
> al forno – baked
> fritto – fried
> in umido – stewed
> ben cotto – well cooked
> poco cotto – lightly cooked
> giusto – medium

It will also be useful to know:
bistecca (steak), **cotoletta** (cutlet), **braciola** (chop), **fegato** (liver) and **scaloppina** (escalope).

Pesce – fish

Apart from **trota** (trout), **pesce spada** (swordfish), **salmone** (salmon), fish is very likely to appear on the menu as 'pesce del giorno'.

Come contorno? (Vegetables and salads)

There is always such a wide range of fresh vegetables and salads available that it would be impractical to list more than a few of the most common:

Insalata verde / mista	Green / mixed salad
Asparagi	Asparagus
Melanzane	Aubergine
Patatine fritte	Chips
Fagioli / Fagiolini	Broad / French beans
Spinaci	Spinach

Come dolce? (Sweet, dessert)

Frutta di stagione	Fresh fruit (in season)
Macedonia	Fruit salad
Zuppa inglese	Trifle
Torta	Gateau, often **della casa** or **della nonna** (Grandma's cake)
Gelato	Ice-cream

and classic Italian desserts like **tiramisù** or **zabaglione**.

Formaggio (Cheese)

The meal would be incomplete without a selection of **formaggi**. You can choose a mild (**delicato**) cheese such as **Mozzarella, Bel Paese, Dolcelatte, Asiago, Fontina**, or a stronger one (**piccante**) such as **Gorgonzola, Provolone** or the world famous **Parmigiano Reggiano** (Parmesan).

Finally, before asking for the bill (**Mi porti il conto, per favore**), there will be **un caffè** and / or **un digestivo** – a brandy or liqueur to aid the digestion.

Da bere? (To drink)

It would be impossible to do justice to the great tradition of wine-making in Italy in the space available. All we have done here is remind you of some of the great names in Italian wine and provide a few words and phrases which you should know.

Some of Italy's finest wines	
red...	*... and white*
Barolo	Frascati
Chianti Classico Riserva	Orvieto
Vino Nobile di Montepulciano	Soave
Brunello di Montalcino	Pinot Grigio
Barbaresco	Est! Est! Est! di Montefiascone
Valtellina	Colli Albani
	Verdicchio

rosso	red
bianco	white
rosato	rosé
frizzante / spumante	sparkling
secco	dry
amabile / abboccato	sweet
D.O.C. (Denominazione di Origine Controllata)	wines from a precisely-defined area which comply with established standards of production
D.O.C.G. (Denominazione di Origine Controllata e Garantita)	an exclusive category of Italy's most prestigious wines
classico	from the centre of a particular wine-growing area

Wine has a fundamental importance in each of Italy's regions and, even disregarding the great wines, you can usually be assured of a pleasant wine if you ask for **il vino della casa** (the house wine) or **un vino della regione** (a local wine).

> ## *Alla salute! – Cheers!*

119

Pratica

1 *Listen to all the conversations again and answer these questions in Italian.*

(i)   Perché il Gatto Blu piace a Giancarlo Lucarini?

(ii)   Chi arriva in ritardo?

(iii)   Che cosa prende Francesca come primo piatto?

(iv)   Perché Peter prende il pesce spada?

(v)   Che cosa mangia Giancarlo per secondo?

(vi)   Quale aperitivo bevono*?

(vii)   Prendono un dolce?

(viii) Perché Giancarlo ride di Francesca?

(ix)   Dove comincia il Mezzogiorno, secondo Giancarlo e secondo Francesca?

(x)   Dove vanno Peter e Giancarlo alle ore tredici domani?

*From **bere** – to drink, page 207

2 (A) *Listen to someone ordering a meal and decide whether she chooses (a), (b) or (c) for each course.*

(i)   Entrée
- (a) ☐ Ham with melon
- (b) ☐ Mixed hors-d'oeuvres
- (c) ☐ Salmon

(ii) First course – Tagliatelle with
- (a) ☐ Mushroom sauce
- (b) ☐ Bolognese sauce
- (c) ☐ Tomato sauce

(iii) Main course
- (a) ☐ Lamb
- (b) ☐ Chicken
- (c) ☐ Pork

(iv) Vegetables / salads
- (a) ☐ Green beans
- (b) ☐ Green salad
- (c) ☐ Spinach

(v)   To drink
- (a) ☐ Half a litre of white wine
- (b) ☐ A litre of white wine
- (c) ☐ Half a litre of red wine

(B) *The waiter now tells her what is on the menu for dessert. Write down four of the dishes on offer.*

(i) _____   (ii) _____

(iii) _____   (iv) _____

3 *Listen to this radio advertisement.*

(i) What is the advert for?

(ii) What is the nearest city?

(iii) What special attraction is mentioned?

(iv) What is the telephone number?

4 *Match the questions with a suitable answer (e.g. (ii) d).*

(i)	E la bistecca?	(a)	Patatine fritte per me, e per la signorina un'insalata mista.
(ii)	Naturale?	(b)	È deliziosa, grazie.
(iii)	Le piace, signora?	(c)	Sì, ho telefonato ieri sera.
(iv)	Come dolce? Gelato?	(d)	No, gassata, se ce l'ha.*
(v)	Ha una prenotazione?	(e)	No, preferisco la torta.
(vi)	Da bere?	(f)	Ben cotta.
(vii)	E come contorno?	(g)	Un mezzo litro di rosso, e una bottiglia di acqua minerale.

*se ce l'ha – if you have any

5 *Complete these sentences using an appropriate form of SAPERE or CONOSCERE. (Grammatica C)*

(i) Giancarlo è romano, _____ bene la città.

(ii) Scusi, signore, _____dov'è l'ufficio postale?

(iii) Io non _____questa signora. Come si chiama?

(iv) Scusate! Voi _____dove si trova l'Hotel Centrale?

Non lo _____ Non siamo di qui.

(v) È buono questo piatto?

Io non _____ se è buono. Non _____ la cucina siciliana.

(vi) Gli Inglesi non _____ bene i vini italiani.

(vii) Marco! _____ a che ora comincia la riunione?

6 Use SI (meaning 'one', 'people', 'you', etc.) *with the appropriate form of the verb in brackets to complete these sentences. (Grammatica B)*

Esempio In Inghilterra <u>si</u> <u>guida</u> a sinistra. (guidare – to drive)

(i) In Italia _____ molto bene. (mangiare)

(ii) Qui _____francese. (parlare)

(iii) Non _____parcheggiare in centro. (potere)

(iv) _____alla cassa, signore. (pagare)

(v) _____uscire subito? (dovere)

(vi) Senta, _____qui? (firmare – to sign)

7 Fill the blanks with MAI, NESSUNO, NIENTE. *(Grammatica A)*

(i) Non mangio _____la carne.

(ii) _____sa il suo nome.

(iii) Non conosco _____in questa città.

(iv) Non ho _____da fare oggi pomeriggio.

(v) Non sono _____stato in Sicilia.

(vi) _____zucchero per me, grazie.

(vii) Le dispiace aspettare un attimo? _____affatto.

(viii) Oggi non c'è _____nell'ufficio commerciale.

8 How would you say in Italian ... *(Grammatica E)*

– that you really like	Italian cooking red wine baked lasagne
– that you like	fish dishes strong cheese tasting local wines
– that you don't like	sparkling mineral water spinach sweet wine
– that you prefer	dry wine

9 *Answer the questions, as prompted. (Grammatica E)*

(i) Ha visto la signora Rossi questa settimana?
(*Say you see her every day.*)

(ii) Conosce Anna e Sergio?
(*Say that you know them well.*)

(iii) Può parlare più lentamente?
(*Say yes, of course, and ask if they understand you now.*)

(iv) Avete finito, signori?
(*Say yes, and ask him to bring you two coffees.*)

(v) Andiamo allo stabilimento domani.
(*Ask if you can go with them.*)

(vi) Ha ricevuto il contratto?
(*Say yes, and in your opinion it is too long.*)

(vii) Questa lettera è per il signor Merisio?
(*Say yes, it is for him.*)

(viii) E questa?
(*Say no, that one is for him, i.e. the speaker.*)

10 *Take part in this restaurant conversation.*
You have invited two clients to lunch ...

Cameriere:	Buongiorno, signori. Quante persone?
You:	(*Say for three persons and you have a reservation. Give your name and apologise as you are a little late.*)
Cameriere:	Niente, signore. Ecco il vostro tavolo ... e il menù.
You:	(*Order the first course for everyone – spaghetti with mushroom sauce, tagliatelle with bolognese sauce and vegetable soup.*)
Cameriere:	Benissimo. Da bere?
You:	(*Say you would like a red wine from the region. Ask him what he recommends.*)
Cameriere:	Dunque ... non è proprio della regione, ma Le consiglio il Montepulciano d'Abruzzo, signore.
You:	(*Order a bottle and also a half litre of mineral water.*)
Cameriere:	E come secondo?
You:	(*One chicken, one steak (well done) and the roast veal. Ask the waiter what vegetables there are.*)
Cameriere:	Abbiamo patatine fritte, insalata verde o mista, carote e spinaci.
You:	(*You will have chips, and a green salad for both your guests... ... The first course has arrived. Say which is for you and ask the waiter to bring you some bread. Wish your companions a pleasant meal.*)

11 Write these 20 menu items in the correct category. You may need to refer to *In Italia ...* pages 117–19

Risotto al pomodoro	ANTIPASTI
Vitello arrosto	
Gelato	
Insalata verde	PRIMI PIATTI
Frascati secco	
Parmigiano Reggiano	
Gnocchi	SECONDI PIATTI
Melanzane	
Zuppa inglese	
Tortellini al ragù	CONTORNI
Zabaglione	
Prosciutto con melone	
Braciola di maiale	FORMAGGI
Minestrone	
Zucchini all'olio	
Barolo	DOLCI
Penne all'arrabbiata	
Gorgonzola	
Bistecca alla fiorentina	VINI
Scaloppina di vitello	

12 Your colleague who is about to go to Italy has received a leaflet (see opposite) with some information about restaurants and has asked for your help. He wants to know if any of the restaurants in the leaflet...

- advertise accommodation as well as food
- mention conference facilities
- advise advance reservations
- specify that one can pay by credit card
- are closed while he is there (Mon, Tue & Wed)
- specify authentic, traditional Italian cuisine
- advertise regional specialities
- mention local wines
- specialise in fish dishes
- advertise home cooking.

124

le Quattro Stagioni

- ✪ colazioni di lavoro
- ✪ sale per congressi e conferenze
- ✪ aria condizionata
- ✪ ampio parcheggio
- ✪ si accettano carte di credito

Si consiglia di prenotare   Tel (06) 679 32 90

Est Est Est

Cucina casalinga
tutte le specialità romane

Viale Oriolo 21   Tel 761 24 59
giovedì riposo

RISTORANTE
PRIMAVERA

specialità
romane * umbre * abbruzzesi

(06) 349 82 57   lunedì chiuso

Ristorante il Pescatore

* Specialità marinare *
* Frutti di mare *
* Tutti i giorni pesce fresco *

Si consiglia la prenotazione
Tel 578 43 29   Fax 578 44 98

VENERDÌ CHIUSO

Al vigneto RISTORANTE

carne & pesce
alla griglia
servizio all'aperto

Via Colombo, 8
Tel. 635899

Le Rondini
ALBERGO RISTORANTE

Locale rustico ed elegante
Camere con bagno

Si accettano carte di credito
Tel. 557 68 78

Pizzeria
forno a legna
da Franco
aperto fino alle 02.00

La Capricciosa

Ristorante - Tavola calda

domenica sera - chiuso

Di Bartolomeo

Piatti tipici della regione
Vini del Lazio

chiuso mercoledì
Tel (06) 891 46 82

TRATTORIA
Il buongustaio

cucina casalinga italiana

Piazza Ottavia   Tel. 9123759

Unit 7 Buon appetito!

Riassunto

You can now ...

- **order a meal**

  Come primo, secondo, contorno, dolce
  Per me / prendo / vorrei ...
  Da bere, mi porti ...

- **ask advice**

  Che cosa mi consiglia?

- **make the most of regional cuisine**

  Vorrei assaggiare ...
  un formaggio locale / un vino della regione

- **express preferences**

  (Non) mi piace
  Mi piacciono molto

- **use appropriate social courtesies**

  Buon appetito!
  Altrettanto!
  Non Le dispiace?
  Niente affatto
  Non fa niente
  Non vedo l'ora

- **say you know a fact, person, place**

  Non so
  Conosce bene Roma?
  Non conosco la cucina siciliana

- **say 'never', 'nothing', 'nobody'**

  Non sono mai stato a Roma
  Non ho niente da fare
  Non abbiamo nessuno

► ► *Before going on to Unit 8, turn to Assignment 4 on page 188 and practise booking a restaurant in Italy.*

Unit 8

IN TRENO

You will learn to:
- ascertain arrival and departure times
- make enquiries about your journey
- buy tickets
- express hunger, thirst, pain, etc.
- describe people
- give a character reference
- talk about daily routine

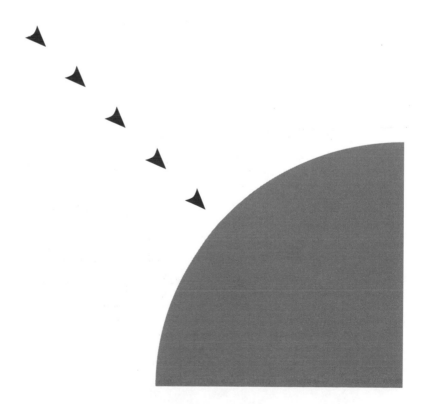

▭ Conversazioni

Alla stazione ferroviaria Peter Lawrence fa il biglietto per Pomezia

Bigliettaio:	Prego?
Peter Lawrence:	Un'andata e ritorno per Pomezia, per piacere.
Bigliettaio:	Quattromilaottocento lire. Grazie ... diecimila ... cinque e due di resto.
Peter Lawrence:	A che ora parte il prossimo treno?
Bigliettaio:	Alle otto e dodici, poi ce n'è uno ogni trenta minuti. Binario sedici.
Peter Lawence:	Quanto tempo ci vuole?
Bigliettaio:	Pomezia? Vediamo ... venti minuti circa.
Peter Lawrence:	Non devo cambiare?
Bigliettaio:	No, è diretto.
Peter Lawrence:	E per il ritorno, a che ora parte l'ultimo treno?
Bigliettaio:	Da Pomezia ... alle ventuno e venticinque.
Peter Lawrence:	Tante grazie.
Bigliettaio:	Prego. Buongiorno.

Sul binario 16

	Attenzione prego! Il rapido per Frosinone, Cassino, Napoli, in arrivo sul binario diciannove, viaggia con dieci minuti di ritardo ... Attenzione! Il locale per Pomezia è in partenza dal binario sedici.
Peter Lawrence:	Scusi signore, ho sentito male. Ha detto 'Pomezia'?
Signore:	Come? Pomezia? Non sono sicuro. È meglio domandare al capotreno.
Peter Lawrence:	Mi scusi. Ferma a Pomezia questo treno?
Capotreno:	Sì, sì. Salga pure.
Peter Lawrence:	Faccio in tempo a comprare un giornale?
Capotreno:	Sì, ma partiamo fra cinque minuti ...!

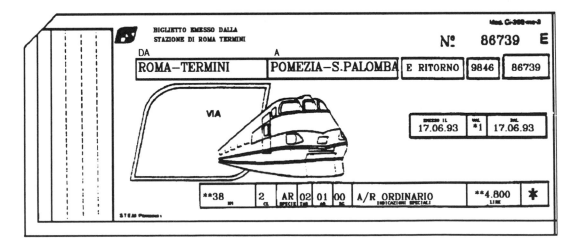

Spiegazioni

- **Prego?** – Can I help you? This is another common use of **prego**.

- **Un'andata e ritorno** – A return ticket. Short for **un biglietto di andata e ritorno**.

- **cinque e due** – a shortened form of **cinquemiladuecento**.

- **Quanto tempo ci vuole?** – How long does it take?

- **Il rapido per ... viaggia ...** – The train for ... is 10 minutes late (there is a list of Italian trains, including the **rapido** (through train) and the **locale** (slow train) in *In Italia ... page 137*).

- **Ho sentito male** – I didn't hear properly (lit. 'I heard badly'). **Male** is the opposite of **bene**.

- **Salga pure** – **Salga** is the **Lei** Imperative form of **salire** (irregular) – to get on (a train, etc.). **Pure** is sometimes added to an Imperative to mean 'by all means', 'go ahead'. You will often hear **Faccia pure** – 'Please do', when you are asking if you may do something.

- **Faccio in tempo a comprare. ..?** – Have I got time to buy ...?

Vocabolarietto

il biglietto	ticket	**cambiare**	to change
il binario	platform	**comprare**	to buy
il capotreno	guard	**domandare**	to ask
il giornale	newspaper	**fermare**	to stop
il resto	change (money)		
il ritorno	return	**circa**	approximately
la stazione ferroviaria	railway station	**male**	badly
il treno	train		
		Attenzione!	Attention!
diretto	direct	**in arrivo**	arriving
prossimo	next	**in partenza**	departing
sicuro	sure		
ultimo	last		

Unit 8 In treno

🔊 Conversazioni

All'edicola

Impiegato:	Dica?
Peter Lawrence:	Che giornali ha?
Impiegato:	*Il Corriere della Sera, La Repubblica, Il Messaggero* ...
Peter Lawrence:	Prendo *Il Corriere*. Quant'è?
Impiegato:	Mille e cinque.
Peter Lawrence:	C'è *Il Mondo Economico*?
Impiegato:	No. È esaurito.
Peter Lawrence:	*L'Espresso?*
Impiegato:	Non ancora. Esce domani.

Peter torna al treno e cerca un posto

Peter Lawrence:	È occupato questo posto?
Signora:	No. È libero. Prego.
Peter Lawrence:	Scusi, signora. Questo treno ferma a Pomezia, vero?
Signora:	Spero di sì. Ci vado anch'io.
Peter Lawrence:	Davvero! A che ora arriva?
Signora:	Verso le otto e mezzo.

Spiegazioni

- **All'edicola** – At the newspaper kiosk. The **edicola** is a common sight on street corners in Italy.

- *Il Corriere della Sera*, etc. – Italian national newspapers. (*In Italia ... page 138*)

- **Esaurito** – sold out.

- **Esce domani** – It comes out tomorrow. **Esce** comes from **uscire** (to come / go out) which is irregular. (*Grammatica page 135.*)

- **Libero / Occupato** – Free / Occupied. **Occupato** can also mean 'busy'.

- **Prego** - Please do sit down.

- **Spero di sì** – I hope so. The same construction is used in the expressions:
  Penso di sì / no – I think so / I don't think so.
  Temo di sì / no – I'm afraid so / not.

- **Ci vado anch'io** – I'm going there too. **Ci** in front of the verb can mean 'there'.

📼 Conversazioni

La signora inizia la conversazione

Signora:	Lei è inglese? Americano?
Peter Lawrence:	Inglese.
Signora:	Ho riconosciuto il suo accento. Ma parla molto bene l'italiano. È qui in vacanza?
Peter Lawrence:	No, per lavoro. Lei non sa per caso dove si trova la ditta Lentini a Pomezia?
Signora:	Ma! Io lavoro proprio per la Lentini. Che coincidenza!
Peter Lawrence:	Straordinario ... Mi permetta di presentarmi – Peter Lawrence.
Signora:	Molto lieta. Laura d'Angelo. Ho sentito dire ieri che deve arrivare questa settimana. Ma non c'è nessuno ad accompagnarLa? Come mai?
Peter Lawrence:	Infatti, l'ingegner Lucarini ha proposto di venire a prendermi all' albergo ma ho preferito venire da solo. Mi piace viaggiare con i mezzi pubblici quando sono all'estero.
Laura d'Angelo:	Sì, capisco. Ha ragione. Così è più facile conoscere il paese e la gente. E a Roma il treno è più rapido della macchina. Dunque, Lei conosce già Lucarini?
Peter Lawrence:	Sì. È molto simpatico. L'ho conosciuto a Londra qualche mese fa e abbiamo cenato insieme ieri sera. Con una vostra collega ... Francesca ... eh, ho dimenticato il cognome. È una donna giovane, molto vivace. Ha i capelli lunghi, castani, gli occhi verdi ...
Laura d'Angelo:	Francesca Bastiani. È molto brava. Eccoci a Pomezia. Lo stabilimento si trova a due passi. Possiamo andarci a piedi.

Spiegazioni

- **Mi permetta di presentarmi** – Let me introduce myself.

- **Ho sentito dire** – I heard (lit. 'I heard say').

- **Venire a prendermi** – To come and fetch me. **Prendere** can mean 'to fetch' as well as 'to take'.

- **Ha ragione** – You are right. (*Grammatica page 134*)

- **la gente** – people. It is a singular noun, and therefore requires a singular verb, e.g. **C'è molta gente** – there are a lot of people.

- **Il treno è più rapido della macchina** – (Going by) train is faster than (going by) car.

- **L'ho conosciuto** – I met him. The Perfect Tense of **conoscere** is used to mean 'to meet ... / to make the acquaintance of ...'.

- **una vostra collega** – a colleague of yours.

- **Ha i capelli lunghi** – She has long hair. Note that 'hair' is in the plural in Italian.

- **Possiamo andarci a piedi** – We can go there on foot.

Vocabolarietto

l'accento	accent	verde	green
i capelli	hair	vivace	lively
la donna	woman / lady		
la gente	people	accompagnare	to accompany
i mezzi pubblici	public transport	iniziare	to start
l'occhio	eye	presentarsi	to introduce oneself
il paese	country	proporre	
il posto	place / seat	(proposto)	to propose
		riconoscere	to recognize
bravo	clever		
castano	chestnut	all'estero	abroad
giovane	young	infatti	as a matter of fact
simpatico	nice	per caso	by any chance
rapido	rapid, fast	proprio	precisely
da solo	alone / on one's own	verso	towards / about
straordinario	extraordinary		

133

Grammatica

A Reflexive verbs

The Infinitive endings of reflexive verbs are **-arsi, -ersi, irsi.**

Present Tense

Reflexive verbs follow the pattern for regular **-are, -ere,** and **-ire** verbs, but require the addition of a reflexive pronoun (underlined in the examples below). For more information on the pronouns, see Grammar Review on page 206.

chiamarsi	mi chiamo ...	my name is ...
ricordarsi	ti ricordi?	do you remember?
alzarsi	si alza alle ...	you/he/she get(s) up at ...
occuparsi	ci occupiamo di	we deal with
sentirsi	vi sentite meglio?	do you feel better?
trovarsi	si trovano	they are (situated)

Perfect Tense

Reflexive verbs take **essere** in the Perfect Tense.

mi sono sbagliato	I made a mistake
Si è alzato	you got up
si è informato	he found out
si è ricordata*	she remembered

*Note that the Past Participle has to agree with a feminine subject.

B Avere

You saw in the dialogue that 'you are right' is '**ha ragione**'.
In fact, there are many common expressions where the English 'to be' is translated by the Italian **avere**. You already know some of them:

Quanti anni hanno? Mio figlio Carlo ha quindici anni. (See Unit 2)

Here are some more **avere** expressions for you to learn:

avere ragione	to be right
avere torto	to be wrong
avere paura	to be afraid
avere bisogno	to need
avere la fortuna	to be lucky enough
avere intenzione	to intend

The above can all be followed by **di** + Infinitive:

Ho intenzione di passare due giorni a Firenze – I intend to spend two days in Florence

avere freddo / caldo	to be cold / hot
avere fame / sete	to be hungry / thirsty
avere male	to have a pain
avere il mal di testa / gola	to have a headache / sore throat

C Fare

The basic meaning of **fare**, introduced in Unit 2, is 'to make / to do'. It occurs in such expressions as:

fare uno sforzo	to make an effort
fare male a ...	to do harm to / to hurt ...

It is also used in many expressions which do not use the words 'make' or 'do' in English:

fare colazione	to have breakfast
fare il biglietto	to buy a ticket
fare una passeggiata	to go for a walk
fare un complimento	to pay a compliment
fare complimenti	to stand on ceremony
fare attenzione	to pay attention
fare una domanda	to ask a question
fare bella / brutta figura	to create a good / poor impression

Perhaps the most common use of **fare** is in weather expressions:

fa caldo / freddo	it is hot / cold

D Uscire

The verb **uscire** is irregular:

esco	usciamo
esci	uscite
esce	escono

E Describing people

You heard Francesca described as 'una donna giovane, molto vivace ...'

Here are some more adjectives you will find useful when describing people.

Anna Chiari –	Mi piace moltissimo. Anna è ...	*Enzo Morelli* –	Non mi piace molto. Enzo è ...
simpatica	nice / likeable	**antipatico**	unpleasant
gentile	kind / nice	**maleducato**	ill-mannered / rude
onesta	honest / straightforward	**difficile**	hard to please
capace	capable / competent	**falso**	two-faced
brava	good / clever	**incapace**	inept / incompetent
seria	serious / reliable		

Many other adjectives are often easily recognisable from the English:

diligente, elegante, efficiente, competente, prudente, intelligente, arrogante, dinamico, sincero, calmo, modesto, stupido, metodico, aggressivo.

Sometimes it is possible to make up an opposite by adding a prefix:

modesto – modest	immodesto – immodest
competente – competent	incompetente – incompetent
contento – satisfied	scontento – dissatisfied

Otherwise use **poco**, meaning 'little', 'not very':

poco intelligente – not very intelligent
poco simpatico – not very likeable

Remember the dictionary gives the masculine singular form only. For the feminine and plural forms refer to page 202 .

In Italia ...

FS – Ferrovie dello Stato – State railway system

Italian trains are generally clean, comfortable, cheap and efficient.
Trains are referred to on timetables according to the following classifications.

Locale	stopping at every station
Diretto	stopping at most stations
Espresso	stopping at main stations only
Rapido	stopping at main towns and cities only. 30% supplement payable, plus extra charge for seat reservations
Intercity (IC)	luxury first-class travel connecting main Italian cities
Super Rapido	supplement and seat reservation obligatory
EC and TEE	Eurocity and Trans-Europe Express as for Intercity trains, linking main cities of Europe

Fares are calculated on a sliding scale according to the distance travelled.
Concessionary tickets include the **biglietto chilometrico** which allows up to five people to travel up to 3000 km at a reduced rate, and the **biglietto turistico libera circolazione** for those who wish to travel extensively over a minimum period of eight days.

At many Italian railway stations you will find an information screen which provides free printouts (see below) for almost any journey on the Italian rail network and even to major cities elsewhere in Europe.

```
15.34     ENTE  FERROVIE  DELLO STATO          14/01/1993
          Sistema di informazioni DIGIPLAN       ROMA TERMINI

          Orario valido : 27 settembre 1992 - 22 maggio 1993
             ROMA TERMINI -----> POMEZIA - SANTA PALOMBA

p. 07.40  Partenza : ROMA TERMINI              1a  £###.###
          Reg 12200    2a                      2a  £  2.400
a. 07.59  Arrivo :   POMEZIA - SANTA PALOMBA   Tempo = 00.19


p. 07.52  Partenza : ROMA TERMINI              1a  £###.###
          Reg 12209    2a                      2a  £  2.400
a. 08.09  Arrivo :   POMEZIA - SANTA PALOMBA   Tempo = 00.17

1a-Carrozza Prima Classe; 2a-Carrozza Seconda Classe; Reg-Treno regionale;
Exp-Treno espresso; Tempo-Durata del viaggio espressa in ORE:MINUTI;
```

La stampa – the press

The Italian press is not dominated in Italy as it is in Britain by national daily newspapers, though three dailies are read all over the country. These are *Il Corriere della Sera*, *La Repubblica* and *L'Unità*.

Many Italians prefer to buy their own provincial daily paper, which also gives coverage to national and overseas news, such as *Il Giornale* (Milan), *Il Messaggero* (Rome), *La Stampa* (Turin), *Il Mattino* (Naples) and *Il Resto del Carlino* (Bologna). *Il Sole 24 Ore* is the equivalent of the *Financial Times*.

Italy also has weekly publications such as *L'Espresso* and *Panorama*, and many specialised trade publications, most of which are published in Milan.

Il Messaggero

Il Sole 24 ORE
Quotidiano Politico Economico Finanziario

la Repubblica

LA SICILIA
del lunedì

il Giornale

LA NAZIONE

Pratica

1 *Listen to all the conversations again and answer these questions in Italian.*

    (i)   Da quale binario parte il treno per Pomezia?

    (ii)   È un rapido?

    (iii) Quanto costa un biglietto di andata e ritorno?

    (iv) A che ora parte l'ultimo treno da Pomezia?

    (v)   Perchè Peter Lawrence non compra *Il Mondo Economico* e *L'Espresso*?

    (vi) Perchè Laura d'Angelo va a Pomezia?

    (vii) Chi ha proposto di venire a prendere Peter in macchina?

    (viii) Perchè Peter preferisce viaggiare in treno?

    (ix) Com'è Francesca Bastiani, secondo lui?

    (x)   Laura e Peter vanno allo stabilimento in tassì?

 2 *Listen to these station announcements from Stazione Termini in Rome and note down the missing information.*

    (A) INTERCITY 505

               Coming from _____

               Due at _____

               Expected at _____

    (B) BORDEAUX EXPRESS

               Leaving at _____

               Platform no. _____

               Last stop before Genoa _____

               Sleeping facilities _____

               Eating facilities _____

 3 *Listen to two people buying their train tickets and note the following details.*

	single / return	cost	destination	type of train
Signora 1				
Signora 2				

4 *Talk about your daily routine using the appropriate form of the following verbs. The first one is done for you. (Grammatica A)*

> alzarsi   andare   arrivare   avere   fare colazione   mangiare
> occuparsi   partire   prendere   svegliarsi   tornare   trovarsi

<u>Mi</u> <u>sveglio</u> ogni giorno alle sette. _____ subito (eccetto la domenica!), e

_____ con la mia famiglia. Di solito _____ un panino e un caffè.

_____ per il lavoro verso le otto meno un quarto. Il Metrò _____ a

cinque minuti da casa mia, dunque ci vado sempre a piedi. _____ all'ufficio

verso le otto e mezzo. _____ di ordinazioni, di contratti, eccetera, fino

all'una. A due passi c'è una piccola trattoria dove _____ spesso a mangiare. Qui si

_____ bene per dodicimila lire. Però, per fare bella figura se _____ clienti

importanti, andiamo in un ristorante più costoso in città. _____ a casa

normalmente verso le sei.

5 *Using AVERE or FARE expressions how would you say in Italian that you .... (Grammatica B & C)*

- intend to go to Milan next week
- would like to ask a question
- are wrong
- are lucky enough to know signora Marotti
- need to telephone a colleague

... and how would you ask someone...

- if they have a pain
- if they intend to go to the meeting
- if they have bought their ticket
- if they are hungry
- what time they have breakfast

6 *Take part in these two conversations at the Stazione Termini.*

(A)

Bigliettaio: Dica, signore.
You: (*Ask for a return ticket to Perugia.*)
Bigliettaio: Prima o seconda classe?
You: (*Say you want second class and ask what time the next train leaves.*)
Bigliettaio: C'è un espresso che parte alle 9.32.
You: (*Find out if there is a train at about 10.30.*)
Bigliettaio: C'è un diretto alle 10.17, poi il rapido delle 11.07.

You:	(*Ask what time the last train leaves Perugia for Rome in the evening.*)
Bigliettaio:	Alle 22.05, signore.
You:	(*Thank him, say you'd like a ticket for the 9.32 and ask how much it costs.*)
Bigliettaio:	Ventiduemila lire ... Grazie. Buon viaggio!

(B)

Bigliettaio:	Dica.
You:	(*Say you'd like to book a seat on the Intercity to Milan tomorrow morning.*)
Bigliettaio:	Ce ne sono tre – alle 6.40, alle 9 e alle 11.10.
You:	(*You choose the 9 o'clock train. Ask what time it arrives.*)
Bigliettaio:	Arriva alle 15.12. Vuole fumatori o non-fumatori?
You:	(*Non-smoking. And say you want first class.*)
Bigliettaio:	Allora, con supplemento Intercity e prenotazione, 168.000 lire.
You:	(*Find out what platform the train leaves from.*)
Bigliettaio:	Binario 2.
You:	(*Thank him and say goodbye.*)
Bigliettaio:	Prego. Buon viaggio!

7 *With a partner, exchange descriptions of yourself, each other, members of your family, friends and colleagues. Use the adjectives from page 136 and remember to make them agree – masculine or feminine. Look in the Vocabulary for tall, short, fat, slim, old, young.*

Esempio   Com'è Luigi? È molto / abbastanza / poco / un po' stupido / difficile / competente

If you are talking about mutual acquaintances, give your description first, then ask **'Chi è?'**

8 *Read these two character references and put a tick in the box overleaf which accurately reflects the reports.*

Stefano Magrelli lavora presso la nostra società da quattro anni. Personalmente lo conosco da tre anni.
Attualmente lavora nell'ufficio assistenza vendite dove si occupa delle vendite estere.
Parla correntemente il francese e l'inglese. È efficiente, dinamico, e il suo lavoro è sempre di alta qualità. Lo raccomando senza alcuna riserva.

Giovanna Colletta fa parte del mio reparto dal febbraio del 1992.
È onesta, aperta e una buona comunicatrice, ma il suo lavoro è poco accurato.
Non è molto puntuale ed è spesso assente dal lavoro. Per questi motivi ho delle riserve nel raccomandarla.

		VERO	FALSO
Stefano is	inefficient	☐	☐
	retiring	☐	☐
	monolingual	☐	☐
Giovanna is	a good communicator	☐	☐
	dishonest	☐	☐
	accurate	☐	☐
	punctual	☐	☐

Now compose a reference for Federico Forlani along similar lines.

He has been working in the Turin branch of your company (Davis Electronics) since 1990 and deals with the marketing. He is very competent, efficient, reliable and honest, and speaks fluent English.

9 *With the aid of a dictionary you should now be able to dip into the Italian press and read some of the news for yourself. Try this article about the latest entrepreneurial activity on the streets of Naples, and answer as many of the following questions as you can. Some of the vocabulary and phrases are translated at the end.*

Un nuovo mestiere

Da qualche giorno c'è un nuovo personaggio ai semafori delle strade di Napoli, accanto ai ragazzi che vendono fazzoletti di carta, cerotti e sigarette di contrabbando.

Si chiama Massimo Colatosti e ha inventato un 'mestiere' decisamente nuovo. Con un telefono cellulare, si avvicina agli automobilisti bloccati dal traffico caotico, e offre telefonate a pagamento.

Colatosti è molto gentile e per tutti i guidatori usa una frase sempre uguale: «Scusi signore» dice «non faccia stare in ansia la sua famiglia o i colleghi di lavoro.

Usi il mio telefono per avvertire che è in ritardo. Mi dà tremila lire e io compongo il numero.»

Effettivamente l'idea è brillante, perché pochi hanno il telefono in macchina e parcheggiare l'auto per raggiungere un telefono pubblico – spesso guasto – è un'impresa disperata. Ma quanto guadagna Colatosti? «Guadagno abbastanza» dichiara «specialmente durante quelle ore della giornata in cui il traffico di Napoli diventa infernale. Il prezzo delle telefonate non è fisso; chi vuole chiamare la famiglia o il posto di lavoro spende infatti tremila lire, ma per parlare con l'amante occorrono quindicimila lire.»

Vocabolarietto

l'amante	lover	avvertire	to warn
il cerotto	elastoplast	avvicinarsi	to approach
il fazzoletto di carta	paper handkerchief	dichiarare	to declare
la frase	phrase / sentence	guadagnare	to earn
il guidatore	driver		
l'impresa	task		
il mestiere	trade /occupation		
il pagamento	payment	accanto a	next to
il ragazzo	boy	bloccato da	blocked by / stuck in
la telefonata	telephone call	caotico	chaotic
il telefono cellulare	cell phone	disperato	desperate
		fisso	fixed
in cui	in which	guasto	out of order
non faccia	don't keep ...	uguale	equal / the same
stare in ansia...	worrying		
chi vuole ...	anyone who wants to ...	decisamente	decidely
occorrono	are required	effettivamente	indeed
compongo	I'll dial the		
il numero	number		

How much did you understand? Answer True or False.

	TRUE	FALSE
(i) Massimo Colatosti invented the cell phone.	☐	☐
(ii) He sells his phones to motorists stuck in traffic jams.	☐	☐
(iii) Motorists pay 3,000 lire to use his phone.	☐	☐
(iv) Cell phones are often out of order.	☐	☐
(v) Motorists have to pay 15,000 lire to talk to their wives.	☐	☐

10 *Rather than depend on the service described above, some motorists might consider installing a car phone. Read this advertisement and decide what it has to offer.*

– What two types of cell phone are on offer?
– How will the company follow up any enquiry?
– What is attractive about their advice service?
– What further inducement is offered to clients who are considering acquiring a new cell phone?
– What three qualities do RO.AL. snc pride themselves on in their dealings with customers?
– Apart from telephones, what other services does the company specialise in?

> **CERCHI UN TELEFONO CELLULARE NUOVO O USATO? RIVOLGITI A NOI!!!**
>
> **PROFESSIONALITÀ - CORTESIA - SERIETÀ**
>
> *Saral visitato, nel tuo ufficio, da professionisti del settore che ti offriranno una consulenza gratuita sui vari modelli. Ti diamo la possibilità di permutare il tuo apparecchio usato.*
>
> Telefonaci al numero **8124942 - 8126626**
>
> **RO.AL.** è: Telefonia – Facsimile – Copiatrici Computers – Arredamenti – Climatizzazione

Riassunto

You can now ...

- **buy a train ticket**

    Un'andata / andata e ritorno per ...
    prima / seconda classe
    con supplemento rapido

- **make enquiries about a journey**

    A che ora parte / arriva...
    il primo / prossimo / treno per ...?
    Per il ritorno a che ora parte l'ultimo treno da ...
    Devo cambiare? / Devo prenotare il posto?
    Da che binario parte il treno?

- **cope on the journey**

    È libero questo posto?
    Faccio in tempo a ...?

- **describe people's appearance ...**

    È alta e snella
    Ha i capelli lunghi e gli occhi verdi

- **... and their character**

    È onesta e efficiente
    È intelligente ma poco simpatico

- **express hunger, thirst, cold, pain, etc.**

    Ho fame / sete / freddo / caldo / male
    Ho il mal di testa / di gola

- **say what you intend to do**

    Ho intenzione di ...

- **talk about your daily routine**

    Mi sveglio alle .... e mi alzo alle ...
    Mi occupo di / del ....

►► *Now, with a partner, try Role Play 4 on page 197.*

ALLO STABILIMENTO

You will learn to:
- describe your company
- show visitors round your company
- make comparisons
- say what you hope to do
- use statistics
- understand some topical issues

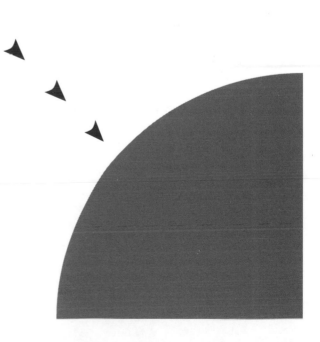

📼 Conversazioni

Arrivato allo stabilimento Lentini a Pomezia, il signor Lawrence, accompagnato dal dottor Bianchi, fa il giro della fabbrica. Innanzitutto fa la conoscenza di Marco Cardella, direttore dei sistemi.

Antonio Bianchi:	Che piacere rivederLa, Peter. Come sta?
Peter Lawrence:	Benissimo, grazie.
Antonio Bianchi:	Benvenuto a Roma! Sa, ho tanti bei ricordi di quel breve soggiorno a Londra. Speriamo di poter fare altrettanto per Lei durante la Sua visita a Roma. Vorrei presentarLe il nostro direttore dei sistemi, l'ingegner Marco Cardella. Cardella, Le presento Peter Lawrence.
Peter Lawrence:	Piacere!
Marco Cardella:	Molto lieto.
Antonio Bianchi:	Allora, se vuole seguirmi, cominciamo dal laboratorio principale di ricerca. Da questa parte ...

Nel corso della visita, Peter si informa della ditta Lentini

Peter Lawrence:	Dunque, la Lentini è una ditta molto grande?
Antonio Bianchi:	Abbastanza. Quest'anno il nostro giro d'affari è di 60 miliardi di lire italiane, cioè 30 milioni circa di lire sterline.
Peter Lawrence:	Avete parecchie fabbriche, vero?
Antonio Bianchi:	Quattro. Questa qui è la più moderna e la più efficiente. Abbiamo fatto investimenti notevoli qui negli ultimi anni.
Peter Lawrence:	Ma la fabbrica di Napoli è più grande di questa, vero?
Antonio Bianchi:	Infatti. È più grande, ci sono ... più di 400 dipendenti, però è meno importante per quanto riguarda il reddito. La qualità dei nostri prodotti è migliore qui a Roma.

Spiegazioni

- **Arrivato ... accompagnato** – Having arrived (lit. 'arrived') ... accompanied ...

- **fa la conoscenza di Marco Cardella** – he meets (lit. 'makes the acquaintance of') Marco Cardella.

- **Tanti bei ricordi** – so many beautiful memories. **Bei** is the plural of **bello** (*Grammatica page 154*)

- **quel breve soggiorno** – that short stay. **Quel** is from **quello**. (*Grammatica page 154*)

- **Speriamo di poter fare altrettanto** – we hope to be able to do the same.
  Sperare + di + Infinitive – To hope to ...
  Poter is a shortened form of **potere**. You will notice that the final -e of an Infinitive is quite often omitted.

- **Vorrei presentarLe ...** – I should like to introduce ... to you.
  Se vuole seguirmi – If you would like to follow me. Pronouns (e.g. **mi** and **Le**) follow the verb when it is in the Infinitive . (*Grammatica page 154*)

- **il nostro direttore dei sistemi** – our systems manager. Nostro means 'our' (*Grammatica page 155*)

- **Da questa parte** – This way.

- **30 milioni circa di lire sterline** – about 30 million pounds sterling. Note that you need **di** after **milione** and **miliardo**.

- **negli ultimi anni** – in the last few years.

- **più grande** – bigger; **meno importante** – less important. (*Grammatica page 152*)

- **per quanto riguarda ...** – as far as ... is concerned.

Vocabolarietto

il giro d'affari	turnover	**notevole**	considerable
gli investimenti	investment	**parecchi(e) pl.**	several
il laboratorio	laboratory	**principale**	principal / main
il reddito	income / yield		
la ricerca	research	**informarsi di**	to enquire about
il ricordo	memory	**seguire**	to follow
il soggiorno	stay		
		durante	during
breve	short	**innanzitutto**	first of all
migliore	better		

📼 Conversazioni

Peter vuole sapere dove si trovano le altre fabbriche e dove vendono i loro prodotti

Peter Lawrence:	Dove sono le altre due fabbriche?
Antonio Bianchi:	Ce n'è una a Verona, e c'è anche quella di Torino, appena acquistata. Ormai siamo uno dei maggiori produttori in questo settore.
Peter Lawrence:	Dove vendete i vostri prodotti?
Antonio Bianchi:	La maggior parte in Italia – i mercati esteri sono sempre più difficili da penetrare. Però recentemente abbiamo esportato negli Stati Uniti ed in Australia. Nei prossimi anni bisogna consolidare la nostra posizione sul mercato estero e svilupparla.

Peter rivela al dottor Bianchi i problemi della MK

Peter Lawrence:	Noi siamo in concorrenza soprattutto con i Giapponesi.
Antonio Bianchi:	Avete problemi di competitività, senza dubbio.
Peter Lawrence:	Eccome! È stato necessario ridurre al minimo le nostre spese. Il maggior problema è tenere bassi i nostri prezzi mentre il prezzo delle materie prime continua ad aumentare.
Antonio Bianchi:	I nostri costi di gestione qui a Pomezia sono altissimi.
Peter Lawrence:	Il nuovo sistema vi permetterà di ridurli significativamente e anche di aumentare la produzione.
Antonio Bianchi:	Speriamo di sì. L'anno prossimo prevediamo una riduzione del 15 per cento, grazie al vostro sistema.

Spiegazioni

- **appena acquistata** – only just acquired.

- **uno dei maggiori produttori** – one of the leading manufacturers.
  la maggior parte – most. **Maggiore** literally means 'greater'. (*Grammatica page 153*)

- **i vostri prodotti** – your products. When 'your' refers to a company rather than to an individual, you use **vostro / vostra** rather than **Suo / Sua**. (*Grammatica page 155*)

- **sempre più difficili da penetrare** – more and more difficult to penetrate. We have seen this use of **da** indicating purpose in '**Se non ha niente da fare**', and '**Da bere?**'.

- **negli Stati Uniti** – to the United States. The Italian names for the majority of countries are feminine, and you use **in** to translate 'in' and 'to', e.g. <u>in</u> Italia, <u>in</u> Australia. The exceptions to this are countries with masculine names, e.g. il Canada, il Giappone, gli Stati Uniti, etc. These require **in** + the definite article , e.g. <u>nel</u> Canada, <u>negli</u> Stati Uniti.

- **nei prossimi anni** – in the next few years.

- **bisogna consolidare la nostra posizione ... e sviluppar<u>la</u>** – we have to consolidate our position and develop <u>it</u>. (*Grammatica page 154*)
  Bisogna + Infinitive is a very useful way of saying that something is necessary, has to be done.

- **Eccome!** – Yes, indeed! And how!

- **ridurre al minimo le nostre spese** – cut our costs drastically.

- **tenere bassi i nostri prezzi** – keep our prices low.

- **i costi di gestione sono altissimi** – the operating costs are extremely high. (*Grammatica page 154*)

- **il nuovo sistema vi permetterà di ridur<u>li</u>** – the new system will allow you to reduce <u>them.</u>

Vocabolarietto

la competitività	competitiveness	**acquistare**	to acquire / purchase
la concorrenza	competition	**aumentare**	to increase
il costo	cost	**consolidare**	to consolidate
le materie prime	raw materials	**esportarre**	to export
la posizione	position	**penetrate**	to penetrate
il prezzo	price	**ridurre (ridotto)**	to reduce
il produttore (m)	producer / manufacturer	**sviluppare**	to develop
la riduzione	reduction	**tenere**	to keep / hold
le spese	costs / expenses		
		appena	just
necessario	necessary	**recentemente**	recently
nuovo	new		

▣ Conversazioni

Prima di tornare all'ufficio, i due uomini parlano dell'ambiente

Antonio Bianchi:	Prima di tornare in'ufficio, vorrei mostrarLe il nostro reparto controllo ambientalc. Da questa parte, prego.
Peter Lawrence:	Incredibile!
Antonio Bianchi:	Come vede, qui alla Lentini prestiamo molta attenzione all'ambiente. In Italia oggi, ridurre i livelli di inquinamento è una priorità.
Peter Lawrence:	Anche in Inghilterra le leggi per la protezione dell'ambiente diventano sempre più rigorose.
Antonio Bianchi:	Ecco, Peter, la nostra visita è finita. Torniamo all'ufficio dell'ingegner Cardella. Avete molto da discutere. Poi, abbiamo previsto un piccolo aperitivo prima di pranzare ...

Incontrano Laura d'Angelo

Laura d'Angelo:	Com'è andata la visita?
Peter Lawrence:	L'ho trovata molto interessante. Tecnologicamente siete già molto avanzati qui alla Lentini.
Antonio Bianchi:	Siamo fierissimi di questo stabilimento. Per sopravvivere in questo mondo bisogna sempre modernizzare, cambiare, migliorare ... È indipensabile tenersi al corrente.
Peter Lawrence:	Esatto. A questo proposito, penso di visitare la Mostra delle Nuove Tecnologie a Napoli prima di tornare in Inghilterra.
Antonio Bianchi:	Ottima idea ... ottima.

Spiegazioni

- **Prima di tornare** – Before going back.
  Prima di + Infinitive – before ...ing.

- **prestiamo molta attenzione a ...** – we pay great attention to.

- **sempre più rigorose** – more and more stringent.

- **Incontrano Laura d'Angelo** – they meet (i.e. by chance) Laura d'Angelo. Compare **incontrare** here with **fare la conoscenza** on page 146.

- **Com'è andata la visita?** – How did the visit go?

- **Siamo fierissimi di ...** – We are extremely proud of ... (*Grammatica page 154*)

- **È indispensabile tenersi al corrente** – It's essential to keep up to date.

- **A questo proposito** – While on this subject.

- **penso di visitare** – I'm thinking of visiting.
  Pensare di + Infinitive – to think of ...ing.

Vocabolarietto

l'ambiente (m)	environment	**incredibile**	incredible
l'inquinamento	pollution	**indispensabile**	indispensable / essential
la legge	law	**interessante**	interesting
il livello	level	**rigoroso**	stringent, strict
il mondo	world		
la priorità	priority	**diventare**	to become
la protezione	protection	**migliorare**	to improve
la tecnologia	technology	**modernizzare**	to modernise
l'uomo (pl. uomini)	man	**pranzare**	to have lunch
		sopravvivere	to survive
ambientale	environmental	**visitare**	to visit
avanzato	advanced		
fiero	proud	**tecnologicamente**	technologically

LEGA PER L'AMBIENTE

Grammatica

A Making comparisons

Adjectives

To say **more / less** .... you use **più / meno** in front of the adjective.

> I mercati esteri sono **più difficili** da penetrare – Overseas markets are more difficult to penetrate
> Lo stabilimento di Napoli è **meno importante** – The plant at Naples is less important

To express **more / less than** you use:

(i) **che** before verbs.

> Prendere il treno è **più** comodo **che** andare in macchina – Taking the train is more convenient than going by car

(ii) **di** before nouns, pronouns and numbers.

> Il treno è **più** rapido **della** macchina – The train is quicker than the car
> Giovanni è **più** competente **di** me – Giovanni is more competent than me
> Abbiamo **più di** 400 dipendenti – We have more than 400 employees

There are a few forms which do not need **più**. You will remember from Unit 7:

> Secondo me, il servizio non è **peggiore** che negli altri ristoranti a Roma – In my opinion the service is no **worse** than in other restaurants in Rome

And in this unit:

La qualità dei nostri prodotti è **migliore** – The quality of our products is **better**

Others you will meet regularly are **maggiore** ('greater') and **minore** ('smaller / lesser'). The final **-e** of **maggiore / minore** is omitted before a noun.

La maggior parte – The greater part / most

more and more + adjective – **sempre più** + adjective

sempre più difficile – more and more difficult

less and less + adjective – **sempre meno** + adjective

sempre meno probabile – less and less probable

Adverbs

The Italian ending **-mente** corresponds to the English **-ly**:

recentemente   recently
continuamente   continually

Just as with adjectives, you use **più / meno** in front of adverbs to compare the way something is done.

Marco parla **più lentamente di** Carla – Marco speaks more slowly than Carla

Note the two special forms: **meglio** (better) and **peggio** (worse). These are often used in sayings such as:

Meglio tardi che mai – Better late than never
Più siamo, meglio è – The more the better
Tanto peggio! – So much the worse!

...and also in reply to '**Come sta?**':

Sto meglio oggi, grazie – I'm (feeling) better today, thank you
Sta peggio – He's (feeling) worse

The most ...

(i)   To say **the most / the least ...** you use:

definite article + **più / meno** + adjective

Il più grande centro – the biggest centre
La più bella città – the most beautiful town / city
I prodotti meno importanti – the least important products
Le migliori segretarie – the best secretaries

(ii) You can also express 'most' in the sense of 'very / extremely' by replacing the final vowel of an adjective with **-issimo** (**-issima, -issimi, -issime**).

buono	buonissimo
alto	altissimo
gentile	gentilissimo

B Bello / quello

Bello ('beautiful', 'fine') and **quello** ('that') have special forms *when they are followed by a noun*. These forms mirror the definite article for that noun.

bel tempo (fine weather)	il	quel giorno	
bello spettacolo	lo	quello stabilimento	
bella notizia (good news)	la	quella settimana	
bell' idea	l'	quell'anno	
bei ricordi	i	quei prodotti	
begli occhi	gli	quegli impiegati	
belle arti (fine arts)	le	quelle donne	

On their own the forms are **bello, bella, belli, belle** and **quello, quella, quelli, quelle.**

C To you, to him / her, to them (Indirect object pronouns)

All the following pronouns are placed in front of the verb:

gli	to him / to them
le	to her
Le	to you (Lei)

Gli telefono spesso – I often phone (to) him / them
E le ho parlato ieri – And I spoke (to) her yesterday

Note that in Italian you telephone to someone, you answer to someone, you give to someone.

Another way of saying 'to them' is to use **loro** *after* the verb.

Mando loro una lettera – I'm sending (to) them a letter

D Object pronouns with the Infinitive

As you know, the object pronoun usually goes in front of the verb:

Le presento Francesca Bastiani

But when the verb is in the Infinitive, the object pronoun is joined on to the end to form one word. (Note: the final -e of the Infinitive is dropped.)

Vorrei presentarLe la signora Bastiani – I would like to introduce Mrs Bastiani to <u>you</u>

Che piacere rivederLa – What a pleasure to see <u>you</u> again

Se vuole seguirmi – If you would like to follow me

Devo telefonargli subito – I must phone <u>(to)</u> <u>him</u> / <u>them</u> immediately

E Possessive adjectives – our, your, their

Nostro (our), **vostro** (your, pl.) and **loro** (their) are preceded by the definite article.

Nostro and **vostro** behave like any other adjectives and change the last vowel to agree with the following noun.

il nostro direttore	our manager
la vostra fabbrica	your factory
i vostri prodotti	your products
le nostre città	our towns

Like **mio, Suo,** etc. they do not need the definite article when referring to a single member of the family (e.g. nostro fratello – our brother).

When 'your' refers to a company or an organisation, **Vostro** is the form to use rather than **Suo**.

All forms of **Vostro** are usually abbreviated to **Vs.** in correspondence.

Abbiamo ricevuto la **Vs.** lettera del 3 aprile – We have received your letter of 3 April

The ending of **loro** does not change.

il loro indirizzo – their address
la loro produzione – their production
i loro prodotti – their products
le loro macchine – their cars

In Italia ...

Names of companies

Throughout this course, you have come accross several Italian words for company, firm or business. **Ditta**, **Azienda** and **Società** are all widely used terms for a company, all virtually interchangeable. You will come across each of them in names such as:

Ditta nazionale, Ditta estera, Ditta offshore
Azienda statale (State company)
Società per Azioni – SpA (*see below*).

You will also hear:

Casa (lit. 'house') as in **casa di spedizioni** (forwarding and shipping agents) and **casa d'esportazione** (export firm). **Casa editrice** is a publishing house.

Compagnia as in **compagnia aerea** (airline company), **compagnia di assicurazione** (insurance company).

Impresa. A small, family firm is **una piccola impresa** or **un'impresa familiare**. **Un'impresa pubblica** is a State / public concern.

The word '**madre**' is the equivalent of the English 'parent' in such phrases as **Ditta madre** and **Azienda madre**. A branch is **una filiale** or **una succursale**.

Aziendale is the equivalent of the English adjective 'company', as in:

la politica aziendale – company policy,
il fondo pensioni aziendale – company pension fund

Various types of business enterprises in Italy

Società per Azioni (SpA) – Public Limited Company, with a minimum capital requirement of 200 million lire.

Società a responsabilità limitata (Srl) - Private Limited Company, with minimum capital requirement of 20 million lire.

Società in nome collettivo (snc) – Unlimited Partnership

Società in accomandita semplice (sas) – Limited Partnership

Società in accomandita per azioni (saa) – Partnership Limited by Shares

Pratica

1 *Listen to all the conversations again and answer these questions in Italian.*

(i)   Dove comincia il giro dello stabilimento?

(ii)   In lire italiane, di quant'è il giro d'affari della ditta Lentini quest'anno?

(iii)   Quale degli stabilimenti Lentini è il più efficiente?

(iv)   Dove si trovano tutte le loro fabbriche?

(v)   Dove vendono la maggior parte dei loro prodotti?

(vi)   La MK è in concorrenza con quale altro paese?

(vii)   Qual è il maggior problema della MK?

(viii) Che riduzione nei costi di gestione prevedono alla Lentini per l'anno prossimo?

(ix)   Prima di tornare all'ufficio, dove vanno Peter Lawrence e Antonio Bianchi?

(x)   Dove ha intenzione di andare Peter Lawrence prima di tornare in Inghilterra?

 2 *Listen to the description of Durantic and decide whether (a)(b) or (c) is correct.*

(i)   Tecnoto is
  (a) a branch of Durantic
  (b) Durantic's parent company
  (c) their international agents

(ii) Durantic has
  (a) three
  (b) fourteen } factories
  (c) two

(iii) Their factories are
  (a) all in Italy
  (b) all in Northern Italy
  (c) all near Bologna

(iv) They export to
  (a) Eastern Europe
  (b) Britain
  (c) USA

(v)   Their export sales are
  (a) as important as
  (b) more important than } domestic sales
  (c) less important than

And now for the statistics.

(vi)   Durantic has

       (a)   300

       (b)   230 employees

       (c)   320

(vii)   This year's turnover is

       (a)   5 million lire

       (b)   5 billion lire

       (c)   5 million pounds

(viii)   This figure represents

       (a)   a 15% increase

       (b)   a 5% reduction

       (c)   a 5% increase

(ix)   They are anticipating a drop in overheads of

       (a)   7%

       (b)   7.5%

       (c)   7.15%

3   *Listen to the radio advertisement.*

(i)   What service is the company offering?

(ii)   What are their telephone numbers?

4   *Antonio Bianchi, Giancarlo Lucarini and Angela Bianchi are discussing the relative merits of Rome, Milan and Naples. (Grammatica A)*
Complete their conversation with:

più	meno	migliore	meglio	di	dei	che

Antonio Bianchi: Evidentemente Roma è ——— grande ——— Milano. Abbiamo ——— ——— quattro milioni di abitanti. Per quanto riguarda l'industria, Milano è ——— forte, ma Roma è la capitale d'Italia; Roma è sempre stata ——— importante nel senso politico.

Giancarlo Lucarini: Sono d'accordo. Ma io preferisco vivere a Milano. Certo, il clima non è ——— ma la gente è ——— simpatica.

Antonio Bianchi: Come? I Milanesi ——— simpatici ———romani? I Milanesi lavorano bene, forse lavorano ——— ——— noi, ma sono ——— simpatici e ——— felici.

Angela Bianchi: Signori! Forse Roma è _____ importante; forse i Milanesi

lavorano _____, ma a Napoli si mangia _____ _____ a

Roma e la nostra città è molto _____ bella _____ Milano!

5 *Answer these questions, using object pronouns as in the example. (Grammatica D)*

Esempio   Ha comprato il giornale? (*Say you hope to buy it this morning.*)
Spero di comprar<u>lo</u> stamattina.

(i)	Ha prenotato la camera?	(*Say you intend to book it today.*)
(ii)	Lei conosce il centro storico?	(*Say you'd like to visit it tomorrow.*)
(iii)	Ha ricevuto i documenti?	(*Say you are hoping to receive them this week.*)
(iv)	Ha finito il progetto?	(*Say you can finish it next week.*)
(v)	Ha noleggiato la macchina?	(*Say you must hire it now.*)
(vi)	Non ha mai visto il Foro?	(*Say you hope to see it today.*)
(vii)	Ha controllato i Suoi impegni?	(*Say you intend to check them now.*)
(viii)	Ha telefonato al signor Lucarini?	(*Say you must phone (to) him tomorrow.*)
(ix)	Ha organizzato l'esposizione?	(*Say you are thinking of organising it soon* (**fra poco**).)
(x)	Benvenuto in Italia!	(*Thank him / her and say what a pleasure it is to see him / her again.*)

6 *Answer the questions using the* **-issimo** *form of the adjective. (Grammatica A)*

Esempio   La signora Bertini è occupata stamattina? Sì, è occupatissima.

(i)   È adatto il contratto? _____

(ii)   Il lavoro della dattilografa è accurato? _____

(iii) I vostri fornitori sono affidabili? _____

(iv) È stata utile la riunione? _____

(v)   I loro prezzi sono alti? _____

(vi) E i vostri prezzi, sono bassi? _____

(vii) Com'è la regione, è bella? _____

(viii) Sono buoni gli spaghetti? _____

(ix) La vita qui in Italia è cara? _____

(x)   Benvenuta, signora! È stanca (tired) dopo il viaggio? _____

7 *Refer to this report from an Italian newspaper giving the inflation and unemployment rates in the industrialised countries over a period of three years.*

PIL (Prodotto Interno Lordo) = GDP

	PIL			INFLAZIONE			DISOCCUPAZIONE		
	1991	1992	1993	1991	1992	1993	1991	1992	1993
USA	−0,7	1,6	3,5	4,2	3,1	3,1	6,8	6,7	6,2
GIAPPONE	4,6	2,8	3,8	3,3	2,6	2,7	2,1	2,2	2,3
GERMANIA	1,2	2,2	3,2	3,5	3,8	3,7	6,5	7,6	7,4
FRANCIA	1,2	1,8	2,6	3,1	2,7	2,5	9,6	10	10
ITALIA	1,0	1,6	2,4	6,4	5	5,2	10,9	10,8	10,7
GRAN BRETAGNA	−2,3	1,4	2,9	5,8	3,8	2,9	8,2	9,6	9,5
CANADA	−1,0	2,7	4,4	5,8	2,7	2,3	10,3	10	9,1

(A) Quale paese?

(i) Nel 1992 la disoccupazione è uguale nel Canada e in _____

(ii) La più alta inflazione del 1991 è in _____

(iii) La più bassa inflazione del 1992 è nel _____

(iv) Nel 1992, la disoccupazione in _____ è del 9.6%.

(v) Nel 1993 il PIL della _____ è del 3.2%.

(B) Vero o falso?

	VERO	FALSO
(i) Dal 1991 al 1992 l'inflazione in Italia è aumentata.	☐	☐
(ii) Negli Stati Uniti fra il 1991 e il 1993 la disoccupazione è scesa.	☐	☐
(iii) C'è stata una riduzione dell'inflazione nel Canada nel 1992.	☐	☐
(iv) Nel 1992 la disoccupazione in Gran Bretagna è più alta che in Germania.	☐	☐
(v) Nel 1992 i paesi con la più bassa inflazione sono la Francia e il Canada.	☐	☐

8 *How would you say in Italian ...*

– It's a pleasure to see you again.
– If you would like to follow me, we'll start here.
– Our plant in Scotland is bigger than this one.
– Our turnover is about £10 million.
– The quality of our products is better this year.
– The operating costs are very high.
– We hope to increase production and reduce costs next year.
– It's essential to keep up to date.

9 *Take part in the following conversation.*

Signor Renzi:	Buongiorno, signora. Come sta?
You:	(*Say you are well and say what a pleasure it is to see him again.*)
Signor Renzi:	Sono contento di poter fare il giro del vostro reparto.
You:	(*Ask him to follow you to the offices.*)
Signor Renzi:	Quante persone lavorano qui?
You:	(*Say you have more than 50 employees.*)
Signor Renzi:	Il reparto commerciale è più grande, vero?
You:	(*Tell him it is smaller. It has less than 40 people.*)
Signor Renzi:	Sembra molto efficiente.
You:	(*Say it's more efficient than the other departments.*)
Signor Renzi:	Ha letto l'ultimo rapporto sull'ambiente?
You:	(*You haven't. Say you hope to read it soon, perhaps next week.*)
Signor Renzi:	È interessante – un po' lungo ma interessante.
You:	(*Say that the visit is over and suggest that you return to your office.*)
Signor Renzi:	Certo.

10 *You are considering applying for a job you have seen advertised in Padua. In answer to your request for more information about the firm you receive the letter overleaf. You need to understand the following from the letter. Do not expect to understand every word, but do refer to the glossary and the Guide to Business Correspondence on page 209 for help.*

(i) In which sector do Santini Fratelli specialise?

(ii) Where is their head office?

(iii) How many sites do they have?

(iv) How many employees work at Padua?

(v) What is their turnover this year?

(vi) How does this compare with 1992?

(vii) What does the letter say about the salary and the conditions of work?

(viii) What qualifications must the successful applicant have?

Unit 9 Allo stabilimento

Società Fratelli Santini
Viale Vittoria, 35
00157 - Torino

31 maggio 1993
Alla cortese attenzione di John Smith
Oggetto: Invio Informazioni

Con riferimento alla Sua lettera, alleghiamo delle informazioni sulla nostra società.

La Società Santini Fratelli è una società pubblica a responsabilità limitata (Srl), fondata nel 1972. Leader nel settore sanitario, la società è specializzata nell'ingegneria ortopedica.

La nostra sede principale si trova a Torino. Abbiamo tre fabbriche a Piacenza, Padova e Treviso. Lo stabilimento di Padova (centocinquanta impiegati) è tecnologicamente avanzato, tutto computerizzato e molto efficiente. Il giro d'affari quest'anno è di circa 6 miliardi di lire italiane, un aumento del trenta per cento rispetto al 1992.

Per la posizione di direttore alle vendite, siamo disposti ad offrire uno stipendio competitivo, commisurato all'età ed all'esperienza. Le condizioni di lavoro sono ottime – la settimana lavorativa di trentacinque ore, trenta giorni di ferie all'anno, fondo pensioni aziendale.

È indispensabile l'esperienza nel settore e la conoscenza della lingua inglese.

La preghiamo di inviare il curriculum dettagliato all'indirizzo di cui sopra entro il 30 giugno.

Distinti saluti,

Dott. ROSSETTI Massimo, Direttore del personale.

11(A)   *You are an employee of Bailey & Sons.*
Using the dialogues, and the above letter to help you, write a brief presentation of the company. It should include the following information.

- a family concern
- founded in 1965
- manufacturers of laser printers ('**stampanti laser**')
- factory in Bristol
- 24 employees
- turnover of £1 million
- considerable investment this year
- quality of products high

(B)   *If you work for a company, describe it in general terms along the same lines.*

12 *Look at these headlines from the Italian press. Which ones are about:*

(a) The environment   No _____
(b) Labour costs   No _____
(c) Imports   No _____
(d) Exports   No _____
(e) Inflation   No _____
(f) Job losses   Nos _____ and _____

1. •IN **ITALIA**

   Il consumatore sceglie più prodotti esteri

2. •IN **ITALIA**

   L'inflazione nel '92

3. *Nei prossimi tre anni* **Bankamerica taglia 12.000 posti di lavoro**

4. **Un'ora di lavoro costa il 9% in più**

5. **emergenza inquinamento**

6. **I greci boicottano le merci italiane**

   «Non comperate più gli spaghetti italiani». Le organizzazioni dei consumatori, i mass media e i commercianti greci hanno lanciato un boicottaggio nei confronti delle merci italiane e di quelle olandesi.

7. **Boeing taglia 8mila posti di lavoro**

   ■ Il colosso aerospaziale Boeing ha annunciato l'eliminazione di 8mila posti di lavoro negli Stati Uniti entro la fine del 1992, nell'ambito del piano già annunciato, per far fronte soprattutto al forte calo delle spese del Pentagono

13 *Look at this newspaper advertisement.*

(i) What service is the company offering?
(ii) Give any three claims the company makes about its service.

VOLETE ACQUISTARE UN'AZIENDA? VOLETE VENDERE UN'AZIENDA?

"Allora Vi interessa mettervi in contatto con noi"

Tra i clienti SIAE Vi sono nomi importanti del mondo imprenditoriale e finanziario interessati ad operazioni di qualunque dimensione ed ovunque.

La SIAE Vi mette a disposizione una organizzazione efficiente; tecnici qualificati soddisferanno tutte le Vostre esigenze, in tempi eccezionalmente brevi.

SIAE SOCIETÀ INTERMEDIAZIONE AZIENDALE EUROPEA

☎ 02/29516130 r.a. Fax 02/29527504 **MILANO**

163

Riassunto

You can now ...

- **describe your company**

  La nostra società è abbastanza grande.
  Siamo produttori di ...
  Siamo uno dei maggiori produttori di ...
  Siamo in concorrenza con ...
  Esportiamo in ...
  Prestiamo molta attenzione a...
  Siamo fieri di questo stabilimento.
  I nostri costi di gestione sono altissimi.

- **talk about statistics**

  Il giro d'affari è di un milione di lire sterline.
  Prevediamo una riduzione delle spese del 5 per cento.

- **show visitors round your company**

  Da questa parte, signori.
  Se vuole seguirmi, andiamo a ...
  Vorrei mostrarLe / mostrarVi il reparto ... / il laboratorio ...

- **make comparisons**

  La fabbrica di Napoli è più grande di questa.
  È meno importante.
  La qualità dei prodotti qui è migliore.

- **say what you hope to do / are thinking of doing**

  Spero di / penso di andare a ... prima di tornare a ...
  Ho intenzione di visitare la Mostra.

- **understand some topical issues**

  Il prezzo delle materie prime continua ad aumentare.
  Bisogna ridurre i livelli di inquinamento.
  Le leggi per la protezione dell'ambiente sono rigorose.
  Nel 1992 l'inflazione è scesa nel Canada.
  La disoccupazione è aumentata negli Stati Uniti.

►► *Now turn to Assignment 5 on page 190.*

164

Unit 10

IN RIUNIONE

You will learn to:
- follow a formal business meeting
- express agreement & disagreement
- invite an opinion
- express an opinion
- talk about the future

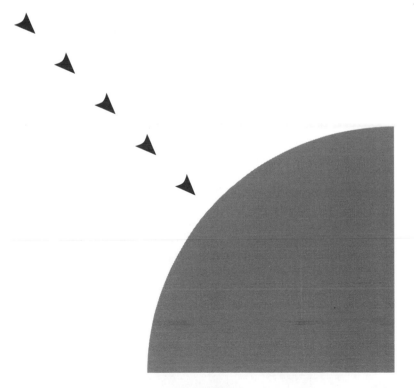

📼 Conversazioni

Il Direttore Generale ha convocato una riunione riguardo al nuovo sistema. La prima questione all'ordine del giorno è la specificazione del sistema

Antonio Bianchi:	Signori, buongiorno. Ho il piacere di dare il benvenuto a Peter Lawrence della società MK. Lo conoscete già tutti, credo. Incomincerò subito – c'è molto da discutere oggi. Avete tutti una copia dell'ordine del giorno…? Allora, prendiamo la prima questione – la specificazione del nuovo sistema. Russo, vuole dare un giudizio sui dati tecnici?
Salvatore Russo:	In complesso, questa specificazione è accettabile. C'è qualche dettaglio da modificare, e ieri allo stabilimento il signor Lawrence e l'ingegner Cardella hanno compilato un elenco di tutte le modifiche necessarie. Secondo me, possiamo approvare questi dati.
Antonio Bianchi:	Grazie, Russo. Siamo tutti d'accordo? Qualcuno desidera aggiungere qualcosa? … Nessuno? Bene.

La seconda questione è il tempo di consegna

Antonio Bianchi:	Passiamo adesso alla questione della consegna. Peter, quando potrete effettuare la consegna?
Peter Lawrence:	La nostra consegna è di 150 giorni – cinque mesi circa.
Antonio Bianchi:	Qual è la prima data possibile? La nuova sala di computer sarà pronta alla fine di settembre.
Peter Lawrence:	La prima data possibile sarà il 30 novembre.
Antonio Bianchi:	Possiamo accettare questa data, mi sembra, ma dovrete rispettarla. Dovremo ricevere la merce non oltre il 1 dicembre. Un ritardo ci causerà problemi gravissimi.
Peter Lawrence:	Sì, sì, capisco. Se riusciremo a raggiungere un accordo questa settimana potrò garantire la consegna entro il 30 novembre.

Spiegazioni

- **Incomincerò subito** – I will begin straightaway. **Incomincerò** is the Future form of **incominciare** (to start). (*Grammatica page 172*)

- **l'ordine del giorno** – the agenda. As you know from Unit 4, **l'agenda** means 'a diary'. You will occasionally come across Italian words which look and sound similar to English words but which have a different meaning. In this dialogue you also have **la questione** which, in this context, means 'item'. The Italian for 'a question' is **una domanda**.

- **Vuole dare un giudizio sui dati tecnici?** – Would you like to comment on the technical data?

- **In complesso** – On the whole / all in all.

- **Secondo me** – In my opinion. (*Grammatica page 173*)

- **Siamo tutti d'accordo?** – Are we all agreed?

- **Quando potrete effettuare la consegna?** – When will you be able to deliver? **Potrete** is the Future of potere. Note that the **Voi** form is being used throughout the meeting, not Lei. Similarly, they all say **noi**, not **io**.

- **La nostra consegna è di 150 giorni** – Our delivery time is 150 days.

- **La nuova sala computer sarà pronta** – The new computer room will be ready. **Sarà** is the Future of **essere**. (*Grammatica page 172*)

- **mi sembra** – it seems to me / I think.

- **non oltre il 1 dicembre** – no later than 1 December.

- **Un ritardo ci causerà problemi gravissimi** – A delay will cause us very serious problems.

- **Se riusciremo a ...** – If we manage to ...

- **entro il 30 novembre** – by 30 November.

Vocabolarietto

la consegna	delivery	**causare**	to cause
la copia	copy	**compilare**	to compile
i dati	data	**convocare**	to convene/call
il dettaglio	detail	**effettuare**	to effect
l'elenco	list	**garantire (-isc)**	to guarantee
il giudizio	judgement	**incominciare**	to begin / start
la merce	the goods	**modificare**	to modify / alter
la modifica	modification	**passare**	to pass / call
il ritardo	delay	**raggiungere**	
la specificazione	specification	**(raggiunto)**	to reach
		rispettare	to respect
accettabile	acceptable	**già**	already
grave	serious	**oltre**	later than / beyond
		qualcosa	something
aggiungere		**qualcuno**	someone
(aggiunto)	to add	**riguardo a**	relating to
approvare	to approve		

📼 Conversazioni ▨▨▨▨▨▨▨▨▨▨▨▨▨▨

La questione del pagamento diventa piuttosto problematica

Antonio Bianchi:	Parliamo dei termini di pagamento.
Peter Lawrence:	È nostra prassi richiedere il pagamento a trenta giorni.
Antonio Bianchi:	Signora d'Angelo, vuole per cortesia confermare i nostri termini.
Laura d'Angelo:	Normalmente le nostre condizioni di pagamento sono di trenta giorni dopo la consegna. Ma in questo caso vogliamo ritenere il trenta per cento fino a centoventi giorni.
Peter Lawrence:	No, non posso essere d'accordo. Non potremo assolutamente accettare una dilazione di tre mesi. Però, posso suggerire un compromesso.

Il compromesso del signor Lawrence riguarda il servizio assistenza dopo vendita

Peter Lawrence:	Vorrei a questo punto dettagliare il nostro servizio assistenza dopo vendita. È eccezionale – per un periodo di sei mesi dopo la consegna garantiamo di occuparci di qualsiasi problema entro ventiquattro ore.
Laura d'Angelo:	Ma non avete un agente locale, vero?
Peter Lawrence:	Attualmente non abbiamo un agente nella zona, ma siamo in trattative con una ditta proprio qui a Pomezia. Entro settembre ci sarà un agente sul campo. Allora, potremo prolungare l'assistenza fino a nove mesi.
Antonio Bianchi:	Dunque, per riassumere...

Riunione 09.30 il 17 giugno 1993
Ordine del giorno

1. Dati tecnici

2. Data di consegna

3. Termini di pagamento

4. Trasporto / costi di trasporto

Spiegazioni

- **È nostra prassi richiedere il pagamento a trenta giorni** – Our policy is to request payment at 30 days.

- **non posso essere d'accordo** – I can't agree.

- **il nostro servizio assistenza dopo vendita** – our after sales service.

- **garantiamo di occuparci di qualsiasi problema entro ventiquattro ore** – we guarantee to deal with any problem within 24 hours.
  Entro can mean 'by' as in **entro il 30 novembre** (*page 166*) or 'within' / 'in' a period of time.

- **siamo in trattative con ...** – we are negotiating with ...

- **una ditta proprio qui a Pomezia** – a company right here in Pomezia.

- **ci sarà** – there will be. **Ci sarà** is the Future of **c'è**.

- **sul campo** – on the spot.

Vocabolarietto

il caso	case
il compromesso	compromise
la dilazione	delay / extension
il periodo	period
la prassi	policy / procedure
i termini	terms
eccezionale	exceptional
problematico	problematic
dettagliare	to detail
prolungare	to extend
riassumere (riassunto)	to sum up
richiedere (richiesto)	to request
riguardare	to concern
ritenere	to retain
suggerire (-isc)	to suggest
assolutamente	absolutely
normalmente	usually
qualsiasi	any

⏸ Conversazioni

Finalmente, dopo una discussione lunga e complicatissima, raggiungono un accordo

Antonio Bianchi:	Signori, abbiamo raggiunto un accordo. Adesso possiamo concludere la discussione. Vi ringrazio tutti per la vostra collaborazione. Vorrei anche ringraziare Peter Lawrence d'esser venuto.
Peter Lawrence:	È stato un piacere. Ci metteremo in contatto con voi al più presto. Grazie. Arrivederci!

Uscendo, Peter incontra Francesca Bastiani

Francesca Bastiani:	Allora, Peter, la tua visita è finita. Non verrai domani a Pomezia?
Peter Lawrence:	Purtroppo, no, Francesca. Non avrò tempo. Dovrò partire presto per Napoli.
Francesca Bastiani:	Ci vai in treno o in aereo?
Peter Lawrence:	Ho intenzione di noleggiare una macchina.
Francesca Bastiani:	E quando ritornerai a Roma?
Peter Lawrence:	Chissà? ... Forse l'anno prossimo. Arrivederci, Francesca. Alla prossima volta!
Francesca Bastiani:	Arrivederci, Peter. E buon viaggio.

DOVE VA L'ECONOMIA ITALIANA
(Variazioni percentuali su anno precedente)

	BILANCIO ALLA DERIVA					FRENA LA SPESA PUBBLICA					FRENATA PIÙ FISCALIZZAZIONE				
	1992	1993	1994	1995	1996	1992	1993	1994	1995	1996	1992	1993	1994	1995	1996
Pil	1,6	2,0	2,0	1,9	1,9	1,3	1,8	2,5	2,7	3,1	1,3	2,0	2,8	3,0	3,3
Bilancia corrente	-2,4	-2,8	-3,1	-3,5	-3,7	-2,3	-2,1	-1,7	-1,5	-1,1	-2,3	-2,1	-1,7	-1,5	-1,2
Inflazione al consumo	5,6	4,5	4,4	4,6	4,6	5,7	3,1	2,3	2,0	1,5	5,7	3,0	2,2	1,9	1,5
Retribuzioni	6,1	4,8	4,4	4,4	4,5	5,3	3,5	2,3	2,1	1,9	5,3	3,5	2,3	2,0	1,9
Fabbisogno pubblico (*)	11,4	12,5	12,9	13,2	13,4	10,5	8,5	6,5	4,9	3,7	10,5	8,5	6,6	5,0	3,8
Occupazione	-0,5	0,1	0,6	0,9	1,0	-0,7	-0,3	0,2	0,9	1,2	-0,7	-0,2	-0,3	1,0	1,4

(*) In percentuale del Pil

Fonte: Centro studi Confindustria

Spiegazioni

- **abbiamo raggiunto un accordo** – we have reached an agreement. **Raggiunto** is the irregular Past Participle of **raggiungere** (to reach).

- **Vi ringrazio per ...** – I thank you for ...
  Vorrei ringraziare Peter Lawrence d'esser venuto – I would like to thank Peter Lawrence for coming (lit. 'for having come').
  Ringraziare and **Grazie** can be followed by **per** or **di**.

- **È stato un piacere** – It has been a pleasure.

- **Ci metteremo in contatto... al più presto** – We will be in touch ... as soon as possible.

- **Uscendo...** – On his way out (lit. 'Going out').

- **verrai, avrò, dovrò, ritornerai** – these are all examples of the Future tense. (*Grammatica page 172*)

- <u>Ci</u> **vai in treno ...?** – Are you going <u>there</u> by train ...?

Vocabolarietto

la bilancia	balance
il bilancio	budget
la collaborazione	contribution
il consumo	consumption
l'economia	economy
il fabbisogno	requirement
la fiscalizzazione	(tax) exemption
l'inflazione	inflation
l'occupazione	employment
la percentuale	percentage
Pil (prodotto interno lordo)	gross domestic product
la retribuzione	salary
la spesa	expenditure
la variazione	variation
corrente	current
precedente	preceding
concludere (concluso)	to conclude
frenare	to brake, control
noleggiare	to hire
ringraziare	to thank
alla deriva	adrift
chissà	who knows?

Grammatica

A Future tense

The Future tense in Italian is easy to recognise because of its distinctive / r / sound in the suffix.

parl_are_	scriv_ere_	part_ire_
parl_erò_	scriv_erò_	part_irò_
parl_erai_	scriv_erai_	part_irai_
parl_erà_	scriv_erà_	part_irà_
parl_eremo_	scriv_eremo_	part_iremo_
parl_erete_	scriv_erete_	part_irete_
parl_eranno_	scriv_eranno_	part_iranno_

1. The endings of -**are** and -**ere** verbs are the same.

2. There is a written accent on the **io** and the **Lei / lui / lei** forms.

3. The Future tense in Italian expresses the English 'shall / will', and 'am / is / are going to'.

   Un ritardo ci <u>causerà</u> problemi gravissimi – A delay will / is going to cause us very serious problems

   <u>Partirò</u> alle due – I shall leave / I am going to leave at two o'clock

   Quando <u>ritornerai</u> in Italia? – When will you / are you going to return?

4. When talking about future events, Italians use the Future tense even when the English use the Present, e.g. after 'when' and 'if'.

   Chiederò l'informazione quando lo vedrò domani – I'll ask for the information when I see him tomorrow

Irregular future forms

In the dialogues you have met some irregular future forms:

   Ci sarà (from **essere**)
   Dovrò (from **dovere**)

Note that only the stem of the verb is irregular; the endings always follow the regular pattern shown above.
For a complete list of the commonest irregular Future forms, see Grammar Review, page 208.

B quale qualche qualcuno qualcosa qualsiasi

By now you have met a number of words beginning with 'qual-' which can cause confusion. It is worth making an effort to learn them.

1. **Quale** (sometimes shortened to **qual**) means 'which'
    Qual è la Sua macchina? – Which is your car?

    The plural form is **quali.**
    Quali giornali legge? – Which newspapers do you read?

2. **Qualche** means 'some / a few'. It is always followed by a singular noun.
    C'è *qualche* dettaglio da modificare – There are a few details to modify
    Qualche volta – Sometimes

3. **Qualcosa** means 'something'. It is an abbreviated form of **qualche cosa**.
    Desidera *qualcosa* da bere? – Would you like something to drink?

4. **Qualcuno** means 'someone / somebody'.
    Aspettiamo *qualcuno* – We're waiting for somebody

5. **Qualsiasi** means 'any / whatever'.
    Possiamo occuparci di *qualsiasi* problema – We can deal with any problem

C Expressing / asking an opinion

You can express an opinion by using:

-   **secondo me** – in my opinion

    Secondo me, possiamo approvare questi dati – In my opinion, we can approve these specifications

-   **penso/credo** – I think / I believe

    Lo conoscete già tutti, credo – I think you all know him

Note that '**credo**' appears at the end of the sentence. Do not start your sentence with '**penso che**' or '**credo che**' (I think / believe that ...) as these normally require the Present Subjunctive.
A full treatment of the Subjunctive is outside the scope of this book. It poses few problems in understanding spoken or written Italian, since for most verbs the Subjunctive forms do not differ markedly from the Present tense endings you have already learnt.
However, you should listen out for two very distinctive, commonly used Subjunctive forms: **sia** (from **essere**), and **abbia** (from **avere**).

> Penso che <u>sia</u> troppo tardi – I think it is too late
> Non credo che mi <u>abbia</u> capito bene – I don't think you have understood me properly

-   the Future tense. Italian uses the Future tense to express supposition. English has a similar colloquial usage:

Dov'è Francesca? <u>Sarà</u> in ufficio – Where is Francesca? She'll be in the office
('I suppose' / 'probably' implied.)

To ask someone else's opinion, use **secondo Lei** or **secondo te**

Secondo te, Anna, qual è il migliore? – Which is the best in your opinion, Anna?
Quando potremo tornare, secondo Lei? – When will we be able to return, do you think?

D Expressions of time

It will now be useful to remind yourself of the commonest expressions of time – and learn
some new ones – so that you can use them appropriately with each of the three tenses you
have met: Present, Past and Future.

Present

ora / adesso	now
in questo momento	at this moment
attualmente	at present / at the present time
oggi	today
questa mattina / sera / notte	this morning / evening / tonight
stamattina / stasera / stanotte	
da tre anni	for three years
da settembre	since September
ogni tanto	now and then

Past

allora	then
nel passato	in the past
ieri (mattina / sera)	yesterday (morning / evening)
ieri l'altro	the day before yesterday
la settimana scorsa	last week
l'anno scorso / l'anno passato	last year
due anni fa	two years ago
poco fa	a short while ago

Future

domani (pomeriggio)	tomorrow (afternoon)
dopodomani	the day after tomorrow
l'anno prossimo	next year
fra poco	soon
fra un mese	in a month's time
entro il 22 maggio	by 22 May
non oltre il 22 maggio	no later than 22 May
subito	straightaway

In Italia ...

Agents – Agenti

Many British companies prefer to conduct their business in Italy through an agent. Local knowledge and connections still play a significant part in business success. Before appointing an Italian agent a company would be well advised to seek specialist advice. The Economic Department of the Italian Embassy in London gives some general information on agency agreements in its booklet *Developing Business in the Italian Market*, and a memo on the subject of agency legislation and practice in Italy is available from the Overseas Trade Division, DTI, (address on page 194).

Quite apart from the distances involved, there are good reasons for not attempting to appoint one agent for the whole of Italy. The differences in outlook, business practice and standards of living between the North and the South render it unlikely for an agent in Milan to be able to deal successfully in southern Italian cities and vice versa. If you wish to do business throughout Italy, it could therefore be more profitable to appoint one agent in the North, and another in the South. You should be aware, however, that an agency agreement in Italy is generally presumed to be on an exclusive basis unless the contract specifically states otherwise. Because of the complexity of Italian legislation on agency agreements you should always seek legal advice before entering into any such agreement.

Business negotiations and payment terms

Business meetings in the workplace in Italy tend to be more formal than is now usual in Britain. Full academic titles are used, first names are avoided and the informality now prevalent elsewhere is not expected.

A large proportion of Italian companies are small- or medium-sized and family controlled. Negotiations over contracts, delivery dates, payment terms, etc. are helped by knowing the right people and it is here that local knowledge is invaluable.

Payment terms tend to be longer in Italy than in most other countries, and it is not unusual for a company to press for 180 days. The best procedure for securing payment on a due date is via the banks either on a documentary collection basis or by opening an external collection account with a British bank in Italy. A paper on this subject, prepared by the British Consulate-General in Milan, is available from the DIT's Italian Desk Branch (address on page 194).

Pratica

1 *Listen to all the conversations again and answer these questions.*

(i)   Perché vuole incominciare subito Antonio Bianchi?

(ii)   Qual è la prima questione all'ordine del giorno?

(iii)   Qual è la seconda?

(iv)   Di quanto tempo è la consegna?

(v)   Qual è la prima data possibile?

(vi)   Perché, secondo Antonio Bianchi, è importante rispettare questa data?

(vii)   Quali sono i termini di pagamento della MK?

(viii) Fino a quando la Lentini vorrà ritenere il 30 per cento?

(ix)   Dove avrà un agente fra poco la MK?

(x)   Perché Peter Lawrence non potrà vedere Francesca domani?

 2 *Listen to the discussion and decide whether (a), (b) or (c) is correct for each of the statements below.*

(i)   Normal delivery time is

    (a) 50 days

    (b) 60 days

    (c) 70 days

(ii) They agree to the delivery of 50% by

    (a) 4 June

    (b) 5 June

    (c) 14 June

(iii) And the other 50%

    (a) on 30 July

    (b) no later than 30 July

    (c) after 30 July

(iv) Seller's normal payment terms are

    (a) 15 days after delivery

    (b) 30 days after delivery

    (c) 50 days after delivery

(v)   Buyer suggests retaining

    (a) 30% until after whole delivery

    (b) 50% until after whole delivery

    (c) 100% until after whole delivery

3 *Answer the questions as in the example. (Grammatica A and D)*

Esempio   Ha scritto la lettera? (*Say you will write it tomorrow.*)
   La scriverò domani.

(i)	Ha già telefonato?	(*Not yet – you'll phone this evening.*)
(ii)	Siete andati a Pomezia ieri?	(*You'll go tomorrow morning.*)
(iii)	Ha confermato la prenotazione?	(*No, but your secretary will confirm it right away.*)
(iv)	Il signor Menucci è uscito?	(*Yes, but he'll return in a short while.*)
(v)	Lei è mai stata in Sicilia?	(*No, but you'll be in Palermo next year for a trade fair.*)
(vi)	Hanno incominciato?	(*Say they're going to start in five minutes.*)
(vii)	È arrivata la signora Botticelli?	(*She'll arrive this morning.*)
(viii)	Verrà a Londra l'anno prossimo?	(*Say next year it won't be possible.*)
(ix)	Hai fatto il lavoro?	(*Say you'll do it as soon as possible.*)
(x)	Può visitare la nuova fabbrica oggi?	(*No, you won't have time until next week.*)

4 *A managing director is outlining his company's plans for the coming year to Italian visitors, with a view to setting up a collaborative venture ... Complete this extract from his report, using the appropriate Future form of the verb in brackets. The first is done for you. (Grammatica A)*

L'anno prossimo <u>avremo</u> (avere) un agente locale a Milano. Questo ci _____

(aiutare) a trovare clienti nel Nord Italia. Il nostro agente _____

(mettersi) in contatto con le ditte più importanti e _____

(organizzare) la nostra campagna pubblicitaria per tutta la zona.

Il nostro direttore commerciale, il signor Craven, _____ (visitare) l'agenzia a

Milano in aprile. In questo modo noi_____ (potere) capire direttamente il

mercato italiano e _____ (essere) in grado di fare concorrenza ai

Tedeschi, agli Americani e ai Giapponesi.

Per quanto riguarda il prodotto stesso, la nostra gamma di computer _____

(essere) pronta per la Fiera di Torino. Sono sicuro che noi _____ (fare) tutti

del nostro meglio per assicurare il successo.

5 *Match the questions and answers.*

(i)   Avete mangiato qualcosa?

(ii) Aspetta da molto tempo?

(iii) Conosce qualcuno a Napoli?

(iv) Lei va spesso a Venezia?

(v)   Quale birra è la Sua?

(vi) Qualcosa da bere?

(a) No, nessuno.

(b) Questa qui.

(c) Una birra, grazie.

(d) No, niente.

(e) No, solo da qualche minuto.

(f) Ci vado qualche volta per lavoro.

6 *Fill in the blanks in the dialogue with one of the following: (Grammatica B)*

qualche qualcuno qualcosa qualsiasi quale

Alida: Allora, Enzo, parti domani? Conosci _____ a Roma?

Enzo: Sì, un amico di famiglia, Sergio, che abita proprio vicino all'aeroporto.

Alida: _____ aeroporto? Fiumicino?

Enzo: No, Ciampino. _____ volta Sergio viene a Londra per affari e l'ultima volta mi ha invitato a Roma per _____ giorno.

Alida: Posso aiutarti in _____ modo? Farò _____ cosa. Hai fatto la valigia? Se hai dimenticato _____ !

Enzo: Non ti preoccupare. Tutto è a posto. Vuoi _____ da bere?

7 *How would you ask / say in Italian*

– Have you all got a copy of the agenda?
– Let's take the first item on the agenda.
– Would anyone like to add anything?
– To sum up ...
– Are we all agreed?
– I can't agree.
– We have reached an agreement.
– Thank you for your participation.
– I would like to thank ...
– It's been a pleasure.

8 *Working with a partner, compare views on the subjects in the first column below. Use **secondo me / credo / mi sembra**, and select appropriate words from the second and third columns. (Grammatica C)*

Esempio   Roma / Parigi

Roma è molto bella!
Certo, ma secondo me Parigi è più romantica.

(i)	L'aereo / il treno	molto	comodo
			difficile
(ii)	La cucina cinese /	abbastanza	bello
	la cucina italiana		rapido
		poco	famoso
(iii)	Il giapponese / il francese		leggero
		troppo	interessante
(iv)	Il vino italiano /		caro
	il vino inglese	più	romantico
			importante
(v)	Milano / Napoli	meno	

9 *When you and a colleague return to your hotel the receptionist hands you these three phone messages. Tell your colleague what the messages are.*

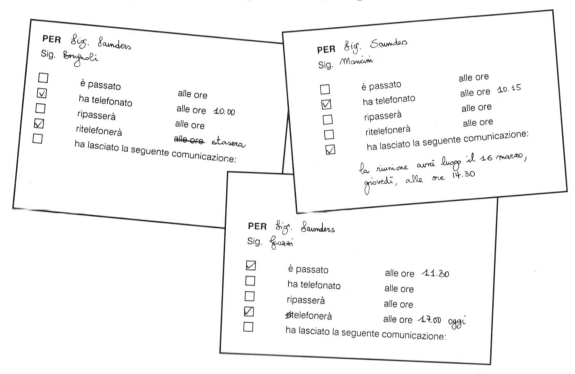

PER *Sig. Saunders*
Sig. *Brugnoli*

- [ ] è passato — alle ore
- [x] ha telefonato — alle ore 10.00
- [ ] ripasserà — alle ore
- [x] ritelefonerà — ~~alle ore~~ stasera
- [ ] ha lasciato la seguente comunicazione:

PER *Sig. Saunders*
Sig. *Mancini*

- [ ] è passato — alle ore
- [x] ha telefonato — alle ore 10.15
- [ ] ripasserà — alle ore
- [ ] ritelefonerà — alle ore
- [x] ha lasciato la seguente comunicazione:

la riunione avrà luogo il 16 marzo, giovedì, alle ore 14.30

PER *Sig. Saunders*
Sig. *Grozzi*

- [x] è passato — alle ore 11.30
- [ ] ha telefonato — alle ore
- [ ] ripasserà — alle ore
- [x] ~~ri~~telefonerà — alle ore 17.00 oggi
- [ ] ha lasciato la seguente comunicazione:

10 *Take part in the following conversations.*

(A) *During a business meeting.*

Signor Mancini:	Signore, Lei vuole aggiungere qualcosa a questo punto?
You:	(*Say no, nothing, thank you.*)
Signor Mancini:	Ha tutti i dati tecnici?
You:	(*Say that you will have all the information by Friday.*)
Signor Mancini:	E queste macchine sono adatte, secondo Lei?

179

You:	(*Say that in your opinion they are extremely suitable.*)
Signor Mancini:	Avete, senza dubbio, un servizio assistenza dopo vendita?
You:	(*Tell them that your service is excellent.*)
Signor Mancini:	Quando potrete effettuare la consegna?
You:	(*Say you can deliver by 25 January, and ask if that is all right.*)
Signor Mancini:	Sì, sì, va benissimo.
You:	(*Ask when you will be able to meet the engineer.*)
Signor Mancini:	Domani mattina, se Lei non ha impegni.
You:	(*Ask if it will be possible the day after tomorrow.*)
Signor Mancini:	Non so – gli telefonerò più tardi. E adesso prendiamo la prossima questione all'ordine del giorno ...

(B) *Hiring a car*

Impiegato:	Buongiorno. Mi dica.
You:	(*Say you would like to hire a car.*)
Impiegato:	Piccola? Media? Grande?
You:	(*Say you want a small one.*)
Impiegato:	Per quando la desidera?
You:	(*Say you want it from Thursday morning until Saturday afternoon.*)
Impiegato:	Va bene. Allora, innanzitutto Lei deve avere almeno 21 anni e deve essere in possesso di una patente di guida valida.
You:	(*Say there is no problem and hand over your driving licence.*)
Impiegato:	E dove vuole riconsegnare la macchina – qui in città?
You:	(*Say you would like to return it at the airport in Naples.*)
Impiegato:	Va bene. Signore, se vuole per cortesia riempire questo modulo.
You:	(*Say yes, of course, and thank him.*)

11 *Peter Lawrence is considering hiring a car in Rome for his trip to Naples.*
He needs the following information from the brochure opposite. Can you tell him:

(i) What would be the price for a Fiat Tipo, collected on Friday morning in Rome and returned on Saturday evening in Naples airport?

(ii) Do prices include – insurance?
                     – VAT?
                     – petrol?

(iii) Is there a limit on mileage?

With compliments of Budget

GRUPPO E TIPO DI VETTURA		PRESA E CONSEGNATA NELLA STESSA CITTÀ		RICONSEGNA IN CITTÀ DIVERSA	
		1/3 giorni al giorno	4 + giorni al giorno	1/3 giorni al giorno	4 + giorni al giorno
A	Fiat Panda/Seat Marbella	87.000	70.000	103.000	95.000
B	Opel Corsa/Peugeot 205/Peugeot 106	105.000	84.000	124.000	99.000
C	Fiat Uno/Ford Fiesta/Renault Clio	119.000	95.000	138.000	111.000
D	Ford Escort 1.4/Volkswagen Golf 1.4	142.000	114.000	161.000	129.000
E	Fiat Tipo 1.4 DGT/Opel Vectra 1.4	162.000	130.000	175.000	140.000
F	Peugeot 405 GR/Fiat Tempra 1.6	170.000	133.000	189.000	155.000
G	Fiat Talento Minibus/Ford Transit M	195.000	156.000	209.000	192.000
H	Lancia Dedra 1.8 I/BMW 316 I	195.000	156.000	209.000	192.000
I	Audi 80 2.0 E/Lancia Thema 2.0 16V	209.000	187.000	221.000	199.000
K	Mercedes 200 E/Mercedes 190 E	209.000	187.000	221.000	199.000
J	Mercedes 300 SE	380.000	304.000	420.000	401.000

La tariffa comprende:
* *Chilometraggio illimitato.*
* *Protezione Kasko (CDW).*
* *Garanzia infortuni conducente e passeggeri (PAI).*
* *Copertura franchigia incendio e furto (ALW).*
* *Tasse (IVA 19%).*
A carico del cliente rimane esclusivamente il carburante.
Le tariffe sono valide negli aeroporti e in città.
Le tariffe non sono ulteriormente scontabili
e rimangono in vigore fino al 31/3/93.
Le condizioni generali di noleggio sono quelle riportate sul depliant ufficiale.
Per i noleggi che iniziano in Campania ed in Puglia sarà addebitata al cliente
la somma di L. 7.500+IVA per tutti i gruppi. Nel caso, comunque, in cui
avvenga un furto sarà addebitata una franchigia di L. 300.000+IVA.

12 *More headlines from the Italian press.*

Which ones are about ...

(a) Eastern Europe   Nos ____ and ____

(b) The EC   No ____

(c) Labour disputes   Nos ____ and ____

(d) Industrial agreement   No ____

(e) Rising prices   No ____

(f) Recession   Nos ____ and ____

181

Riassunto

You can now ...

- **follow a formal business meeting**

  Avete tutti una copia dell'ordine del giorno?
  Prendiamo la prima / la seconda / la prossima questione.
  Qualcuno desidera aggiungere qualcosa?
  Quando potrete effettuare la consegna?
  Parliamo dei termini di pagamento.
  Per riassumere ...
  Possiamo concludere la discussione.
  Vi ringrazio per la vostra collaborazione.

- **express agreement / disagreement**

  (Non) Sono d'accordo.
  Non posso essere d'accordo.
  Abbiamo raggiunto un accordo.
  Credo di sì / no.

- **invite an opinion**

  Secondo Lei ...?
  Signore, vuole dare un giudizio su ...
  Siamo d'accordo?

- **express your opinion**

  Secondo me ...
  Possiamo accettare questa data, mi sembra.
  Lo conoscete già, credo.
  Francesca sarà in ufficio.
  È nostra prassi ...
  Vorrei suggerire un compromesso.

- **talk about the future**

  Entro settembre ci sarà un agente nella zona.
  Un ritardo ci causerà problemi gravissimi.
  Potrò garantire la consegna entro il ...
  Dovremo ricevere la merce non oltre il ...
  Ci metteremo in contatto con voi al più presto.

- **relay messages**

  La signora Rossi ha telefonato alle ore 10.00, ritelefonerà stasera.
  Il signor Gozzi è passato, ripasserà dopodomani.

►► *Now turn to Assignment 6 on page 191*

182

Assignments

Assignment 1
Welcoming an Italian visitor

Situation

You are PA to Peter Lawrence, the Sales Manager at MK Systems.
An Italian visitor from Rome, signor Bianchi, has arrived early for an 11 a.m. appointment with Mr Lawrence. Mr Lawrence has been informed of signor Bianchi's arrival, but has been detained and will not be free until 11.15.
Knowing that you have been learning Italian and that your visitor has little English, Mr Lawrence has asked you to welcome signor Bianchi and keep him talking until he arrives.

Task 1

Greet your visitor and introduce yourself.
Offer him a seat.
Offer him some coffee.

Task 2

Tell him you do not speak Italian very well and explain how long you have been learning the language.
Find out if he speaks English, and enquire where he is from in Italy.
He has seen the company photograph on the wall. Tell him the names and the positions of some of the management team and invent some details about each one.

Task 3

Mr Lawrence arrives. Introduce the two men and say goodbye.

Assignment 2
Letters, faxes and telephone calls

Situation

You are working in the general office of Broadway plc, a large electronics company in Cheshire. You receive this request from the Sales Department.

MEMO

I have received the attached letter from signor Bergami. I presume it confirms his forthcoming visit, but I would be grateful if you would let me have a translation. Also would you please fax him a reply confirming the visit and indicating the arrangements for his stay.

He is due to arrive at Manchester airport at 7.30 p.m. on Monday 4 Oct.

We have booked him a single room with *en suite* bathroom at The Excelsior until Thursday 7 Oct.

On Tuesday signor Bergami will be in Warrington. He has an appointment with Linda Patel, the Commercial Manager, at 9.30 and a meeting in the Design & Development Department an hour later. Lunch (1.30 p.m.) is at the Old Hall Restaurant with Export Manager John Perrett who will take him round the works at 2.30.

He will spend all day Wednesday at Head Office in Chester with Peter Burgess, the Managing Director.

On Thursday there is a visit arranged to the Riverside works at 9 a.m. and another meeting with Linda Patel at 11.30. His flight back to Italy is at 4.15 p.m. so he will need to leave for the airport at about 2.30.

* Tomorrow will do for the translation and fax, but please ring his office this afternoon to say you are sending the info.

Letter from signor Bergami

Spett. Ditta Broadway plc

Alla cortese attenzione del signor G. Milton,

A seguito della ns. telefonata, vorrei confermare la mia visita alla ditta Broadway dal 4 al 7 ottobre.

Arrivo all'aeroporto di Manchester lunedì sera, alle 19.30.

Vi prego di comunicarmi via fax le disposizioni per la visita.

Vi porgo distinti saluti,

E Bergami

Edoardo Bergami.

Task 1

Translate signor Bergami's letter into English. You may need to refer to the *Guide to Business Correspondence* on *page 209*

Task 2

Phone signor Bergami's office to say the information is on its way.
(Listen to the cassette after Unit 4 for guidance on what to say.)

Task 3

Reply in Italian and include full details of the arrangements which have been made for his visit. Use the fax in Unit 4, page 66, as your model.

Assignment 3 – Part 1
Making travel arrangements

Situation

You are an employee of MK Systems.
You are required to make travel arrangements for the Commercial Manager who is attending a trade fair in Venice.
You have received a memo from his secretary, Ms Donnington:

From: C. Donnington   **To:**

Richard Craven has decided to combine the Venice Trade Fair in July with a week's vacation with his family on the Venetian Riviera.

Mr Craven will be accompanied by his wife, son aged 8 and daughter aged 11.

He wants to leave the first Wednesday in July, returning one week later.

Could you read through attached Wasteels brochure and let me have the following information, please.

– Departure and arrival times both ways.
– What will the price of the flight be, and what are the terms of payment?
– Could Mr Craven be reimbursed if he should be forced to cancel his flight?
– Is it possible to change the booking later, to another day if necessary?
– Mr Craven and his family may be away from London the week before his departure. What are the arrangements for getting the tickets to him? Are they sent? If so, when?

Attached: Wasteels brochure

Task

Gather information as requested from the brochure shown below and reply in full to Ms Donnington's memo.

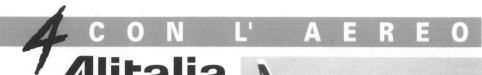

Alitalia, la compagnia aerea Italiana...anche quest' anno Wasteels vi offre voli su tutte le principali citta' Italiane servite direttamente dall' aeroporto di Londra Heathrow, con possibilita' di coincidenze a Roma Fiumicino per le isole e tutte le altre destinazioni.

Un' opportunita' da non perdere quindi, per volare in stile ad un prezzo eccezionale!!!

PREZZI

LONDON	£ 1 APRILE – 9 APRILE / 19 APRILE – 30 GIUGNO / 1 OTTOBRE – 31 OTTOBRE	£ 10 APRILE – 18 APRILE / 1 LUGLIO – 30 SETTEMBRE
Milano	163	188
Roma	183	226
Pisa	183	219
Bologna	155	177
Napoli	190	231
Torino	162	193
Venezia	200	237
Alghero*	242	286

PREZZI

LONDON	£ 1 APRILE – 9 APRILE / 19 APRILE – 30 GIUGNO / 1 OTTOBRE – 31 OTTOBRE	£ 10 APRILE – 18 APRILE / 1 LUGLIO – 30 SETTEMBRE
Cagliari*	242	286
Bari*	253	308
Brindisi*	253	308
Catania*	253	308
Reggio Calabria*	253	308
Lamezia*	253	308
Palermo*	253	308

*Via Roma

LONDON HEATHROW – TERMINALE 2

PARTENZE				ARRIVI			
PARTENZA	ARRIVO	VOLO	FREQUENZA	PARTENZA	ARRIVO	VOLO	FREQUENZA
08.05	MILANO 11.00	AZ 285	Giornaliero	MILANO 09.05	10.00	AZ 458	Giornaliero
10.55	MILANO 13.50	AZ 459	Giornaliero	MILANO 14.35	15.30	AZ 266	Giornaliero
16.30	MILANO 19.25	AZ 267	Giornaliero	MILANO 17.00	17.55	AZ 304	Giornaliero
18.45	MILANO 21.40	AZ 305	Giornaliero	MILANO 20.30	21.25	AZ 284	Giornaliero
07.25	ROMA 10.55	AZ 287	Giornaliero	ROMA 09.50	11.25	AZ 282	Giornaliero
12.25	ROMA 15.55	AZ 281	Giornaliero	ROMA 16.55	18.30	AZ 280	Giornaliero
19.30	ROMA 23.00	AZ 279	Giornaliero	ROMA 18.40	20.15	AZ 286	Giornaliero
09.40	PISA 12.45	AZ 1263	Giornaliero	PISA 07.40	08.45	AZ 262	Giornaliero
20.00	PISA 23.05	AZ 263	Giornaliero	PISA 18.10	19.15	AZ 1260	Giornaliero
17.00	BOLOGNA 20.00	AZ 1263	Giornaliero	BOLOGNA 15.50	16.10	AZ 1262	Giornaliero
06.55	NAPOLI 10.30	BM 1294	Giornaliero	NAPOLI 18.35	20.20	BM 1294	Giornaliero
18.50	TORINO 21.35	AZ 1293	Giornaliero	TORINO 17.05	18.00	AZ 1292	Giornaliero
12.00	VENEZIA 15.10	AZ 295	Giornaliero	VENEZIA 09.55	11.05	AZ 294	Giornaliero
17.00	VENEZIA 20.10	AZ 261	Sabato	VENEZIA 14.40	15.50	AZ 260	Sabato

Per le coincidenze a Roma Fiumicino, a destinazione Alghero/Cagliari/Bari/Brindisi/Catania/Lamezia/Palermo e Reggio Calabria potete telefonare al nostro ufficio (071.834 7066) e saremo lieti di darvi tutte le informazioni necessarie.

Si prega notare che tutte le partenze da/per la Gran Bretagna saranno un' ora piu' tardi dal 27 Settembre al 24 Ottobre.

CONDIZIONI E INFORMAZIONI GENERALI

DURATA Tutti i viaggi devono contenere almeno un sabato notte a destinazione, a possono avere la durata massima di 14 giorni.

PAGAMENTO Il pieno pagamento e' richiesto al momento della prenotazione.

BIGLIETTI Il vostro documento di viaggio vi verra' consegnato entro la settimana di partenza. In casi eccezionali e/o urgenti e' possibile ritirare il biglietto presso lo sportello Alitalia, al terminale 2 dell'aeroporto di Londra Heathrow.

CANCELLAZIONE/CAMBIO DATE DI VIAGGIO Il cambio della prenotazione fatta e' consentito solo se fatto prima della data di partenza, e previo pagamento di una penale del 50% del costo totale del biglietto.

Dopo la partenza nessuna modifica alla prenotazione fatta e' consentita.

RIMBORSI In nessun caso é permesso il rimborso del biglietto dopo la prenotazione.

BAMBINI I bambini fino all' eta' di 2 anni pagano il 10% della tariffa pubblicata. I bambini di eta' compresa tra i 2 e i 12 anni pagano il 67% della tariffa pubblicata.

Assignment 3 – Part 2
Arranging accommodation

You receive a second memo from Ms Donnington relating to Mr Craven's accommodation in Italy. You have been asked to make use of your reading and speaking skills to reserve hotel accommodation for the family.

MEMO

From: C. Donnington   **To:**

A contact from Lentini has recommended that Mr Craven & family might like to stay at the Hotel Napoli, and has sent him the brochure. Mr Craven likes the sound of the hotel (see attached leaflet) but is anxious to clarify a number of points.
Could you check:

– that the hotel is within easy walking distance of the beach; has amenities (shops, restaurants, etc.) close by; serves Italian, not English food in the hotel restaurant.
– that this room has shower and TV and has a sea view.

Please check the price for half board for the four of them (children 8 and 11).
If the brochure is not clear on any of these points, would you telephone the hotel, and if there are no problems, reserve a room for the week.

Task 1

Gather information as requested from the hotel brochure opposite. List points requiring clarification.

Task 2

Telephone Hotel Napoli (listen to the cassette after Unit 6). If answers to your questions are satisfactory, make the reservation.

Task 3

Confirm the booking in writing. (Refer to the *Guide to Business Correspondence, page 209*.)

Task 4

Reply to Ms Donnigton's memo, giving details of final accommodation arrangements.

Hotel Napoli

Situato direttamente sul mare in posizione tranquilla a due passi dal centro. Negozi, bar, ristoranti a 500 m.

Cucina casalinga con tipiche specialità locali.

Ascensore, piscina, giardino, stanza dei giochi. Spiaggia a 100 m.

Tutte le camere hanno TV e telefono diretto. La maggior parte con balcone e vista sul mare.

		7 notti 31/3–2/6	7 notti 3/6–30/8
Singola	Pensione completa	428.000	500.000
	Mezza pensione	380.000	430.000
Doppia	Pensione completa	360.000	410.000
	Mezza pensione	310.000	380.000

Bambini 0–4 anni: lettino gratuito, pasti a pagarsi direttamente.
Bambini 5–8 anni in camera con i genitori: 50%

Assignment 4
Booking a restaurant

Situation

You are in Rome with a colleague negotiating a contract. To help retain the goodwill of your clients you have invited the Purchasing Manager, signor Perini, and his wife to dinner at a restaurant which has been recommended to you, the Quattro Fontane.

Task 1

Ring the Quattro Fontane to make a phone booking for yourself and colleague and your two Italian guests for 8 p.m. (listen to the cassette after Unit 7).
Bear in mind the following points:

- you have budgeted for a maximum L.300,000 for the evening.
- you have been recommended their 'menu gastronomico' at L.55,000 per person, but you need to check if this is all inclusive ('tutto compreso'). Remember to allow for drinks as well as service and VAT, if not included.

Task 2

You need to check that the menu is suitable for your colleague who does not eat fish, and for signor Perini who you know likes shellfish.
Make a note in English of the items on the menu.

Task 3

Your colleague will be out of town during the day, and as he may not return to your hotel until late, he will make his own way by taxi or tube and meet you at the restaurant. In case he takes the tube, find out from the Quattro Fontane how to get there from your hotel near the Via Cavour underground station and *leave him a note of the directions* (in English).

(Listen to the cassette after Unit 7 for instructions and follow the directions on the street plan and tube map as illustrated opposite)

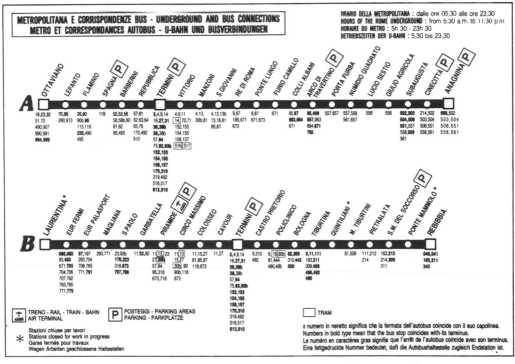

Assignment 5
Routine letters

Situation

Ian Renshaw, the Sales Manager of the company for which you work, has sent you the letter shown below. He needs a translation for the files and also wants you to deal with the request.
(Refer to the *Guide to Business Correspondence* on page 209 for help in completing these tasks.)

Task 1

Translate the letter for Mr Renshaw.

Task 2

Compile a letter which will be sent out with your company's latest brochure and price list in response to the request. Make sure that it includes the name of the Sales Manager as the person to whom to write for further information.

Make a copy for the Sales Manager's files. Mark this 'For information only'.

Task 3

Write the address label for the envelope.

ISDI
Via Dante, 164
50136 Prato

Ns/Rif EG/CarEl

Spett. Ditta Mallam & Sons,
Bankside Business Park,
Norford NF5 8AD
Inghilterra

Alla cortese attenzione del Direttore alle Vendite

Oggetto: Informazioni

Vogliate inviare appena possibile all'indirizzo di cui sopra informazioni e prezzi dei Vs. prodotti.

Vi porgo distinti saluti,

E. Giannotti

Ing E. GIANNOTTI Direttore produzione

Assignment 6
Curriculum Vitae

Situation

With the arrival of the Single Market Joanna Rossi is considering the possibility of spending a few years working in Italy. She has seen the Professional Data-bank application form (*see* below) in the 'Affari e Finanza' section of *La Repubblica* and decided to fill it in and send it off. She is looking ideally for a position as purchasing manager for a company in Northern Italy.

PROFESSIONAL DATA-BANK®
Sistema computerizzato per la ricerca di lavoro qualificato

Se desiderate migliorare il Vostro ruolo nel mondo del lavoro o «semplicemente» pianificare la Vostra carriera, compilate **SENZA ALCUN IMPEGNO ECONOMICO** il nuovo questionario **PROFESSIONAL DATA-BANK**, il curriculum che mette in evidenza le Vostre qualità professionali. **PROFESSIONAL DATA-BANK**, il sistema computerizzato per la ricerca di personale qualificato, è operativo **QUALUNQUE SIA LA POSIZIONE PRESA IN ESAME.** Il Vostro nome sarà inviato solo

alle aziende che si sono impegnate a mantenere la massima riservatezza e sarete **AUTOMATICAMENTE ESCLUSI DALLE RICHIESTE DELLA VOSTRA AZIENDA**, naturalmente se indicata sul questionario. Leggete attentamente l'intero questionario, compilatelo in ogni sua parte e, nel Vostro interesse, firmatelo. **SPEDIRE A: SOMEDIA - PROFESSIONAL DATA-BANK - CASELLA POSTALE 1141 - 20121 MILANO.** Per informazioni telefonare allo 02/57300237 dalle 16 alle 18.

A - DATI ANAGRAFICI

1 COGNOME

2 NOME

3 INDIRIZZO E NUMERO CIVICO

4 COMUNE

5 CAP   6 PROVINCIA (sigla automob.)

7 TELEFONO

8 SESSO:
01 ☐ maschile
02 ☐ femminile

9 NAZIONALITÀ:
01 ☐ italiana
02 ☐ straniera

10 ANNO DI NASCITA
1 9

11 LUOGO DI NASCITA (sigla automobilistica della prov. o dello stato, se estero)
provincia   stato estero

12 STATO CIVILE
01 ☐ coniugato
02 ☐ non coniugato

13 SERVIZIO MILITARE
01 ☐ assolto/esente
02 ☐ da assolvere

14 PATENTE AUTO ☐ sì   Auto propria ☐ sì

B - FORMAZIONE SCOLASTICA

15 TITOLO DI STUDIO CONSEGUITO
01 ☐ licenza di scuola media   02 ☐ Diploma   03 ☐ Laurea

16 TIPO E INDIRIZZO DEL DIPLOMA CONSEGUITO (es. perito meccanico, maturità classica ecc.)

17 VOTO DI DIPLOMA   18 ANNO DI CONSEGUIMENTO
su 60   1 9

19 LAUREA CONSEGUITA E INDIRIZZO SCELTO

20 EVENTUALE SECONDA LAUREA E INDIRIZZO SCELTO

21 DOVE HA CONSEGUITO LA LAUREA?
università

città

22 VOTO DI LAUREA   23 ANNO DI CONSEGUIMENTO
su   Lode ☐ sì   1 9

24 CORSI ED ESPERIENZE DI SPECIALIZZAZIONE O TITOLO TESI
(dopo il diploma o post universitaria)

25 LINGUE STRANIERE

LIVELLO DI CONOSCENZA

		Scolastico	Professionale	Madrelingua
Francese	=	11 ☐	12 ☐	13 ☐
Inglese	=	21 ☐	22 ☐	23 ☐
Spagnolo	=	31 ☐	32 ☐	33 ☐
Portoghese	=	41 ☐	42 ☐	43 ☐
Tedesco	=	51 ☐	52 ☐	53 ☐
Altra (specificare sotto)				

26 CONOSCENZE INFORMATICHE

01 ☐ da specialista   02 ☐ da utilizzatore   03 ☐ nessuna

Settore o area di specializzazione per specialisti EDP
(es.: Assicurazioni, bancaria, Amm.ne, Gestione del personale, ecc.)

Sistemi operativi:

01 ☐ DOS	04 ☐ CICS	07 ☐ UNIX
02 ☐ VM	05 ☐ CPF	08 ☐ VMS/VAX
03 ☐ MVS	06 ☐ OS/2	09 ☐ Altro (Spec. sotto)

Hardware:

Linguaggi di programmazione:

01 ☐ ASSEMBLER	04 ☐ COBOL	07 ☐ SQL
02 ☐ BASIC	05 ☐ DBXX	08 ☐ PL
03 ☐ C	06 ☐ FORTRAN	09 ☐ RPGXX

Altri:

Applicazioni e sviluppi
(Word processors, Fogli elettronici, 4GL, Reti, Case, Data Base, CAD, CAM, CAE ecc.)

C - ATTUALE ESPERIENZA PROFESSIONALE

27 QUALIFICA PROFESSIONALE

Lavoro dipendente
01 ☐ Operaio
02 ☐ Impiegato
03 ☐ Funzionario/Quadro
04 ☐ Dirigente

Lavoro autonomo
05 ☐ Agente/Rappresentante
06 ☐ Libero professionista
07 ☐ Attività in proprio

IL LAVORO

INDICHI L'AREA AZIENDALE ENTRO CUI SVOLGE LA SUA ATTIVITÀ RIPORTANDO UN SOLO CODICE NELLA CASELLA

A - Top Management	L - Logistica
B - Amministrativa	M - Acquisti
C - Finanziaria	N - Commerciale
D - Legale	O - Vendita
E - Personale	P - Marketing
F - Organizzazione	Q - Comunicazione/Pubblicità
G - Ricerca	R - EDP
H - Tecnica	S - Documentazione
I - Produzione (di manufatti)	T - Segretariale
J - Produzione (di servizi)	U - Didattica
K - Manutenzione	

☐ Codice area

TITOLO DELL'ATTUALE POSIZIONE RICOPERTA (es: Agente di vendita, Direttore commerciale, Process Eng., Analista di sistema, ecc.)

INDICHI LA SUA ATTUALE RETRIBUZIONE LORDA:
(solo per i lavoratori dipendenti)

01	fino a 28 mil./anno	☐
02	da 29 a 35 mil./anno	☐
03	da 36 a 45 mil./anno	☐
04	da 46 a 60 mil./anno	☐
05	da 61 a 90 mil./anno	☐
06	oltre 91 mil./anno	☐

L'AZIENDA

(o Ente o datore di lavoro)

(Chi svolge lavoro autonomo, risponda comunque a tutte le domande)

28 AZIENDA
L'informazione serve ad escludere i dipendenti di una Azienda dalle richieste della Azienda stessa.

29 SEDE (di lavoro)

30 TIPO DI AZIENDA

01 ☐ in proprio   03 ☐ a part. statale   05 ☐ multinazionale
02 ☐ privata   04 ☐ pubblica

31 L'AZIENDA OPERA IN:
(identificare LA casella di pertinenza)

01 ☐ Produzione   02 ☐ Commercio   03 ☐ Servizi

32 IDENTIFICHI IL SETTORE MERCEOLOGICO DELL'AZIENDA BARRANDO UNO DEI SETTORI CHE SEGUONO:
(se l'Azienda opera in più settori, indicare quello che ha maggiore rilevanza con l'attività da lei svolta)

01 ☐ AGRICOLTURA	10 ☐ ALIMENTARE E BEVANDE	20 ☐ TRASPORTI, VIAGGI, COMUNICAZIONI
02 ☐ MINERARIO PETROLIFERO	11 ☐ TESSILE E ABBIGLIAMENTO	21 ☐ CREDITO E FINANZA
03 ☐ ENERGIA produzione e distribuzione	12 ☐ LEGNO E ARREDAMENTO	22 ☐ ASSICURAZIONI
		23 ☐ IMMOBILIARE
04 ☐ SIDERURGIA produzione e prima trasform. metalli	13 ☐ CARTOTECNICO E TIPOGRAFICO	24 ☐ PROGETTAZIONE E ENGINEERING
05 ☐ CHIMICO E FARMACEUTICO	14 ☐ GOMMA E PLASTICA	25 ☐ CONSULENZE E SERVIZI ALLE IMPRESE
06 ☐ MECCANICO manufatti, macchine e utensili per l'industria	15 ☐ EDILIZIA E OPERE PUBBLICHE	26 ☐ INFORMATICA, TELEMATICA, ELABORAZIONE DATI - Servizi
07 ☐ ELETTROTECNICO ELETTRONICO	16 ☐ VARI ARTICOLI di largo consumo	27 ☐ ISTRUZIONE
		28 ☐ RICERCA
08 ☐ ATTREZZATURE E MACCHINE per ufficio e elaborazione dati	17 ☐ MATERIALI E COMPONENTI per l'edilizia	29 ☐ EDITORIA E PUBBLICITÀ
	18 ☐ IMPIANTISTICA	30 ☐ SPETTACOLO
		31 ☐ SERVIZI SOCIALI Sanità, assistenza, ecc.
09 ☐ MEZZI TRASPORTO civili e industriali	19 ☐ ALBERGHI E RISTORAZIONE	32 ☐ ALTRI SERVIZI nella Pubblica Amministrazione

33 INDICHI CON PRECISIONE CHE COSA PRODUCE O DI CHE COSA SI OCCUPA L'AZIENDA (O ENTE O ALTRO) PRESSO CUI LAVORA

34 INDICHI QUANTI DIPENDENTI HA ATTUALMENTE L'AZIENDA
01 ☐ meno di 10   03 ☐ 50/99   05 ☐ 500/999
02 ☐ 10/49   04 ☐ 100/499   06 ☐ più di 1000

40 DA QUANTO TEMPO LAVORA NELLA SUA AZIENDA ATTUALE?
mesi
☐

E - ASPIRAZIONI PROFESSIONALI

58 IN QUALE AREA AZIENDALE SI COLLOCA L'ATTIVITA' CUI LEI ASPIRA?
☐ ☐

59 PUÒ INDICARE LA POSIZIONE PROFESSIONALE PER LA QUALE È DISPOSTO A CANDIDARSI? (es: Assistente al controller, Agente di vendita, Progettista hardware, ecc.)

61 DOVE È DISPOSTO A LAVORARE
01 ☐ Nord Italia
02 ☐ Centro Italia
03 ☐ Sud Italia
04 ☐ Ovunque   05 ☐ Estero

Il sottoscritto autorizza la società SOMEDIA ad inserire il presente questionario nel sistema informativo "Professional Data Bank" e a diffonderlo presso le aziende in cerca di personale con le qualifiche equivalenti a quelle da me offerte.

Data ....

Firma ....

192

Task

Fill in the Data-bank form as though you were Joanna Rossi, taking as your facts her curriculum vitae (*see* below), and using as much Italian in answering the questions as seems appropriate. Make full use of the vocabulary at the back of *Pronto!*, the list of abbreviations on page 18 and, where necessary, your dictionary.

The following sections on the form need some some further explanation:

(6) **Provincia (sigla automobile)**
For Italian nationals only. Refers to the number on car licence plates in Italy indicating the province where the vehicle was registered.

(13) **Servizio militare**
Obviously Joanna Rossi would leave this blank or tick the 'esente' (exempt) box.

(16) **Diploma (di maturità)**
Roughly equivalent to English 'A' Levels.

(17) and (22) **Voto di ...**
Best left blank since English examinations are not marked 'out of' as in Italy.

(24) **Titolo tesi**
Refers to post-graduate study. Joanna Rossi would mention her MA from Rugby in this section. English terms such as 'Business Administration' are widely understood without translation in Italian business circles.

CURRICULUM VITAE   *   JOANNA ROSSI

NAME	Joanna Rossi
DATE OF BIRTH	21 March 1964
PLACE OF BIRTH	London, England
ADDRESS	21 York Road, Leighton Buzzard, Hertfordshire, England LB4 8QT
TEL.	0632 87582
NATIONALITY	British
SITUATION	Married, no children
EDUCATION & QUALIFICATIONS	1975–1982 Heathgrove Grammar School, 'A' levels in French, Spanish, English 1982–1986 University of Livingham, BA in French (1st class) 1986–1988 University of Rugby, MA in Business Administration
PROFESSIONAL EXPERIENCE	1988–1990 Marketing Researcher, Ledbury Sportswear, Chester 1990–present i/c Exports, MK Information Systems (UK) Ltd
PRESENT SALARY	£31,000
SUBSIDIARY SKILLS	Driving licence since 1987 Languages: French – fluent. Good working knowledge of German and Japanese. Learning Italian. IT – experience of DOS

Useful addresses

For students of Italian (Examining & Validating Boards)

The Institute of Linguists
24 Highbury Grove
London N5 2EA
071 359 7445

The London Chamber of Commerce
  & Industry (LCCI)
Marlowe House, Station Rd
Sidcup, Kent DA15 7BJ
081 302 0261; 081 309 5169

The City & Guilds Examining Board
74 Portland Place
London W1N 4AA
071 278 2468

The Pitman Institute
Cattleshell Manor
Godalming, Surrey GU7 1UU
0483 415311

The Royal Society of Arts (RSA)
Progress House,
Westwood Way, Coventry CV4 8HS
0203 470033

The Business & Technology Education
  Council (BTEC)
Central House, Upper Woburn Place
London WC1H 0HH
071 388 3288

The Scottish Vocational Education Council
  (SCOTVEC)
Hanover House, 24 Douglas St
Glasgow G2 7NQ
041 248 7900

For travellers to Italy

The Italian Tourist Board
1 Princes St
London W1R 8AY
071 408 1254

For business people

The Italian Embassy Commercial Office
14 Three Kings Yard
London W1
071 629 8200

The Italian Consulate General
38 Eaton Place
London SW1X 8AN
071 235 9371

The Italian Chamber of Commerce
296 Regent St
London W1R 5HB
071 637 3153

The Italian Trade Centre (Istituto Nazionale
  per il Commercio Estero)
37 Sackville St
London W1X 2DQ
071 734 2412

90 St Vincent St
Glasgow XG2 5UB
041 221 0503

The Italian International Bank plc
45 Monmouth St
London WC2
071 836 3010

The Department of Trade and Industry
  (Italian Desk)
1 Victoria Street
London SW1H 0ET
071 215 5000

General interest

The Italian Cultural Institute
39 Belgrave Square
London SW1
071 235 1461

Accademia Italiana Bookshop
7 Cecil Court
London WC2N 4EZ
071 240 1634

Role plays

Role play 1
Informazioni

Role A

While in Milan on a work placement, you are asked to help out as delegates arrive for an international seminar.

Greet them as they arrive and ask them the questions which will allow you to fill in the following forms. ('Il Suo nome?' is used instead of 'Come si chiama?' in a formal situation such as this.)

Cognome _____
Nome _____
Nazionalità _____
Professione/ _____
Posizione

Cognome _____
Nome _____
Nazionalità _____
Professione/ _____
Posizione

Cognome _____
Nome _____
Nazionalità _____
Professione/ _____
Posizione

Cognome _____
Nome _____
Nazionalità _____
Professione/ _____
Posizione

Role play 2
Una telefonata

Role A

You are Mr / Ms Austin in Italy on business for a week, and you need to arrange an appointment with signor/a Innocenti. Your diary for the week (shown below) is already quite full.
Decide on a time convenient for both of you, allowing an hour for the appointment. Any time between 8.30 and 18.00 will do. You will need such questions as:

Ci vediamo martedì alle dieci? *or*
Lei è libero/a (free) martedì alle dieci?

Monday 18 October	Tuesday 19 October
9.00 - 12.30 *Visit to Sansoni factory*	8.30 - *Meeting in Technical Dept-* *Vanoni Flli* *Exhibition-p.m.*
Wednesday 20 October	**Thursday 21 October**
9.00 - 11.30 *Meeting in Piacenza* 2.00 - 4.30 *Appointment-sig.Menucci*	12.30 *Lunch with Enrico Dolce* 3.45 *Vist to factory in Monza*
Friday 22 October	**Saturday 23 October**
3.30 *Appointment with Giorgio Martini*	

Role play 1
Informazioni

Role B

Play the part of each of these four delegates in turn as they arrive at an international seminar. Your partner will ask you for some information about yourself.

1. Sig. Alessandro MAGNANI (Commercial Manager from Italy)

2. Sig.ra Maria MEIER (Accountant from Germany)

3. Sig. Pedro SANTOS (Representative from Portugal)

4. Sig.na Francesca ROSA (Sales Manager from the USA)

Role play 2
Una telefonata

Role B

You are Signora Innocenti, an Italian working in Milan. Your partner is Mr / Ms Austin, an English contact who rings you in order to fix an appointment for one day next week. Here is your diary for the week.

Decide on a time convenient for both of you, allowing an hour for the appointment. Any time between 8.30 and 18.00 will do. You will need such questions as:

Ci vediamo martedì alle dieci? *or*
Lei è libero/a (free) martedì alle dieci?

lunedì 18 ottobre	martedì 19 ottobre
12.00 Pranzo con Elena Ruggieri 14.30-17.30 Mostra MITAS	9.00 Riunione-Ufficio Vendite 13.00 Pranzo-Ristorante Roma
mercoledì 20 ottobre	**giovedì 21 ottobre**
11.45-13.30 Incontro con il capoufficio	9.00 - 12.00 Riunione
venerdì 22 ottobre	**sabato 23 ottobre**
15.45 Appuntamento con sig.ra Alessandra	

Role play 3
In albergo

Role A

With a partner, enact a typical scene at the reception desk of an Italian hotel. Play the part of each of the following in turn:

1. Giuseppe Santoro coming from Milan. Single room required with shower and telephone. Leaving early next morning for Rome, so 6.30 call with breakfast at 7.00.
   Needs to know parking arrangements – car is on the street at the moment.

2. Raymond Bates, English from London, with wife and two children.
   Requires room with bath & shower and with TV if possible, for two nights. Leaving on Friday for Venice. Maximum £80 per night including breakfast.

3. Raffaella Galli from Naples travelling to Trieste. Staying one week.
   Requires room for self and invalid mother, so ground floor essential. Bath not shower. TV in room. Breakfast late – about 9 o'clock.

Role play 4
Alla stazione ferroviaria

Role A

Enact this scene at the **Biglietteria** at the Stazione Termini in Rome.
Play the part of each of three passengers in turn as they buy their tickets to Florence.

1. One single ticket, first class, to arrive in Florence before midday. Find out departure and arrival times.

2. Three return tickets, second class. You need to know the price of the tickets, how long the journey will take and whether you have to change.

3. Two second-class returns, leaving about 1 p.m. Find out which platform the train leaves from, whether there is a supplement to pay for Intercity and if it is necessary to book seats in advance.

Role play 3
In albergo

Role B

> *10% reduction for guests staying one week. Free car park behind hotel.*

Play the part of a receptionist in a hotel in Italy. There are five rooms remaining:

Camera No.	Persone	Piano	Bagno	Doccia	TV	Tel	Prezzo Lit. camera	colaz
4	3	terr.	sì	no	sì	sì	110.000	8.000
11	4	1	sì	sì	no	no	120.000	8.000
17	1	1	no	sì	sì	sì	90.000	8.000
21	4	2	sì	sì	sì	sì	150.000	8.000
22	3	2	no	sì	no	no	100.000	8.000

Ask guests questions to obtain the following information for the hotel register (details of Marie Dural, a previous guest, have been left as a guide):
Ask guests to spell names.

Camera no:	15		
Cognome:	Duval		
Nome:	Marie		
Nazionalità:	Francese		
Documento:*	Passaporto		
Sveglia alle:	07.00		
Prima colazione:	07.45		
Destinazione:	Ravenna		

*An Italian guest would give his **carta d'identità** (identity card) or his **patente di guida** (driving licence).

Role play 4
Alla stazione ferroviaria

Role B

You work at the Biglietteria at the Stazione Termini in Rome. Answer the enquiries using the timetable and the list of fares.

ORARIO

	Roma	Firenze
	6.40 pend.	8.19 Rifredi*
Roma Tib.	6.48 Exp	9.23
	7.15 EC	9.15
	8.00 EC	10.00
	8.10 EC	10.10
	8.55 pend.	10.34 Rifredi
	9.00 IC	11.15
Roma Tib.	10.13 IC	12.19
	11.10 IC	13.10**
	11.50 IC	13.50
	12.00 EC	14.00
	13.10 IC	15.10
	13.50 IC	15.50
	14.10 IC	16.10
Roma Tib.	15.12 IC	17.10
	15.40 IC	17.40
	16.10 IC	18.10
	17.00 IC	19.08
	17.06 Exp	19.32
	18.00 IC	20.09
	19.00 pend.	20.39 Rifredi
	19.10 pend.	20.49 Rifredi
	19.15 Exp	21.33
	19.45 pend.	21.24 Rifredi***
	20.55 Exp	23.45
	21.20 Exp	0.02 Firenze CM

* Soppresso nei giorni festivi
** Soppresso la domenica e nei giorni 25 dicembre e 1 gennaio
*** Soppresso nel giorno lavorativo precedente i festivi e nei giorni 8, 25 dicembre e 31 marzo

RADIO TAXI 5798
400 vetture al vostro servizio per 24 ore

TARIFFA

<u>1a classe</u>

andata   41.200 lire
andata/   82.400 lire
ritorno

<u>2a classe</u>

andata   28.400 lire
andata/   56.800 lire
ritorno

Grammar review

Glossary of grammatical terms used in *Pronto!*

Grammatical Term	Example English	Italian	Explanation
Noun	train, student, company, day	treno, studente, ditta, giorno	Names a person, object or idea
Gender	Masculine and feminine. In Italian, every noun is either masculine or feminine.		
Indefinite article	a, an	un, uno, una	Masculine or feminine to agree with noun
Definite article	the	il, lo, l', la, i, gli, le	
Partitive article	some	del, della, dei, degli, delle	Masculine, feminine, singular or plural to agree with the noun or pronoun
Possessive adjective	my, our	mio/a/e/miei, nostro/a/i/e	
Preposition	in, to, with	in, a, con	
Verb	come, speak	venire, parlare	A 'doing' word denoting an action or an event
Subject pronoun	I, we	Io, noi	The person/thing performing the action
Object pronoun	me, us	mi, ci	The person/thing on the receiving end of the action
Reflexive pronoun	myself, himself	mi, si	Refers back to the subject
Infinitive	to see, to go	vedere, andare	Only expresses the idea, not the subject or tense. (Infinitive of verb is given in dictionary)
Imperative	Wait! Say!	Aspetta! Dica!	Command or instruction
Tense	The form of the verb which shows when the event occurs, i.e. present, past or future		
Adverb	today, easily	oggi, facilmente	Says how/when the action is performed
Adjective	good, easy	buono/a/i/e, facile/i	Describes the noun or pronoun and agrees with it (see below)
Agreement	Using different endings for the adjective to show the gender or number of the noun it is describing, or for the verb to show the subject or the tense		

199

The indefinite article ('a', 'an')

Masc $\begin{cases} \text{un} \\ \text{uno}^* \end{cases}$ Fem $\begin{cases} \text{una} \\ \text{un'+} \end{cases}$

un bar   una cassa
uno sportello   un'agenda

The definite article

	Sing	Pl
Masc	il	i
	lo*	gli
	l'+	gli
Fem	la	le
	l'+	le

il centro   the centre   i centri   the centres
lo stato   the state   gli stati   the states
la carta   the card   le carte   the cards
l'agente   the agent   gli agenti   the agents

* Before s and another consonant (sp, sv, etc.), before z or gn.
+ Before a vowel

Uses of definitive article

(i)   For titles of people

Le presento **la** signora Rossi Let me introduce you to Mrs Rossi

but not when talking to them

'Buongiorno, signora Rossi' 'Good morning, Mrs Rossi'

(ii)   For continents, countries, large islands and regions of Italy

l'Italia, la Sardegna, il Veneto, l'Europa

but *not* after **in** if the noun is feminine

nel Veneto, *but* **in** Italia, **in** Sardegna, **in** Europa

(NB: two masculine regions also omit the article: **in** Piemonte, **in** Trentino)

The definite article is always used with an adjective:

in Inghilterra *but* **nell'**Inghilterra centrale

(iii)   For languages, except with **parlare**:

        L'inglese non è difficile   English is not difficult

but Parlo italiano   I speak Italian

(iv)   For the time of day, the year, and for percentages:

        alle due   at two o'clock
        nel 1994   in 1994
        il 50 per cento   50 per cent

(v)   With the possessive adjective, except for singular members of the family:

        la mia macchina   my car
but **mia** moglie   my wife

and the article is always used with **loro**:

        la loro macchina   their car
        il loro figlio   their son

(vi)   Frequently used in general statements:

        il caffè italiano è delizioso Italian coffee is delicious
        la vita non è un gioco   life is not a game

Prepositions

Some common prepositions combine with the definite article to produce contracted forms:

	IL	LO	LA	L'	I	GLI	LE
A (to, at)	al	allo	alla	all'	ai	agli	alle
DA (from, by)	dal	dallo	dalla	dall'	dai	dagli	dalle
DI (of)	del	dello	della	dell'	dei	degli	delle
IN (in)	nel	nello	nella	nell'	nei	negli	nelle
SU (on)	sul	sullo	sulla	sull'	sui	sugli	sulle

    dalle otto **alle** nove   from eight to nine o'clock
    Ferrovie **dello** Stato   State Railways
    nel 1993   in 1993
    con vista **sul** mare   with a sea view

The definitive article combines with **di** to express 'some', 'any'.

    Vorrei **del** pane e **dell'**acqua   I'd like some bread and some water

Adjectives

Adjectives agree with the noun they describe. The ending changes to show masculine, feminine, singular or plural agreement:

Type one

	Singular	Plural
Masc	buono	buoni
Fem	buona	buone

Type two

	Singular	Plural
Masc/Fem	inglese	inglesi

Generally, the adjective comes *after* the noun it describes:

la moda **italiana**   un'esposizione **importante**   i mercati **esteri**

But the following adjectives usually precede the noun:

grande – big   bello – beautiful   lungo – long
piccolo – small   brutto – ugly   buono – good
giovane – young   vecchio – old   breve – short

una **grande** città   il **brutto** tempo   le **piccole** imprese

The adjectives **bello**, **buono**, and **grande** show other changes when they precede the noun:

- **Bello** changes in the same way as the definitive article:

  i **bei** laghi   i **begli** animali   le **belle** donne

- **Buono** changes in the same way as the indefinite article:

  il **buon** amico   una **buon'**amica

- **Grande** shortens to **grand'** before a singular word beginning with a vowel and to **gran** before a masculine word beginning with a consonant (except for **z** and **s** together with another consonant):

  una **grand'**idea   un **gran** favore   *but*   un **grande** sviluppo

Possessive adjectives

Singular			Plural	
Masc	Fem		Masc	Fem
mio	mia	my	miei	mie
tuo	tua	your (fam)	tuoi	tue
suo	sua	his/her	suoi	sue
Suo	Sua	your (formal)	Suoi	Sue
nostro	nostra	our	nostri	nostre
vostro	vostra	your (plural)	vostri	vostre
loro	loro	their	loro	loro

The above are preceded by the definite article, except when referring to one member of the family.

Demonstrative adjectives ('this', 'that')

(i) **Questo** (this, this one)

	Singular	Plural
Masc	questo	questi
Fem	questa	queste

(ii) **Quello** (that, that one)

	Singular	Plural
Masc	quel quello quell'	quei quegli
Fem	quella quell'	quelle

Note the forms of **quello** are the same as those of the definite article and of the adjective **bello**.

Le piace **questo** ristorante?   Do you like this restaurant?
Si, ma preferisco **quello**   Yes, but I prefer that one.

Comparison of adjectives

To make comparisons use **più** ('more') or **meno** ('less') in front of the adjective:

importante – important
più importante – more important
meno importante – less important
una città più importante – a more important city

As with the English 'better', 'worse', etc. there are a few special comparative forms in Italian which frequently replace the forms with **più**:

migliore – better   peggiore – worse

A few others are used to a more limited degree, often in set phrases:

maggiore – greater   minore – smaller, lesser
superiore – higher, upper   inferiore – lower

Istruzione Superiore   –   Higher Education
la maggior parte   –   mostly

To express a preference ('more/less ... than') use **più/meno** with the adjective followed by **che** or **di:**

È meglio prendere un tassì **che** aspettare l'autobus – It is better to take a taxi rather than wait for the bus

Si mangia meglio qui **che** in quel ristorante – You eat better here than in that restaurant

Use **di** before a noun, a pronoun, or a number:

Firenze è **più bella di** Milano   Florence is more beautiful than Milan
Mario fa **meno errori di** Giorgio   Mario makes fewer mistakes than Giorgio
Ho **più di** centomila lire   I have more than 100,000 lire

To say 'most', 'the most', simply put the definite article in front of più:

la citta **più** interessante   –   the most interesting city

Similarly with **meno:**

la regione **meno** ricca   –   the least wealthy region

Finally, to say 'most' with the meaning 'very', 'extremely', Italian makes frequent use of the ending **-issimo:**

Questa piazza è **bellissima**   This square is very (most) beautiful
un uomo **richissimo**   an extremely rich man

Adverbs

Apart from the many adverbs which answer the questions 'when?' or 'where?' (e.g. **ora** – 'now', **oggi** – 'today', **ieri** – 'yesterday', **lontano** – 'far', **qui** – 'here', etc.) most adjectives can become adverbs to describe how something happens. This is done by adding **-mente**, in the same way as we add '-ly' in English. *The feminine form of the adjective is always used:*

rapida – quick	rapidamente – quickly
certa – certain	certamente – certainly

Adjectives ending in **-le** or **-re** first drop the **-e:**

naturale – natural	naturalmente – naturally
particolare – particular	particolarmente – particularly

Two adverbs need to be noted separately:

bene – well	male – badly

their comparative forms are **meglio** ('better') and **peggio** ('worse'):

Lei parla **meglio** di me	You speak better than me
Tanto **peggio**	Too bad, so much the worse

Personal pronouns

Subject	Object of verb		Object of preposition	Indirect Object
io (I)	mi	me	me	mi
tu (fam. you)	ti	you	te	ti
lui (he)	lo	him / it	lui	gli
lei (she)	la	her / it	lei	le
Lei (form. you)	La	you	Lei	Le
noi (we)	ci	us	noi	ci
voi (you pl.)	vi	you	voi	vi
loro (they)	li / le	them	loro	loro

Lo conosco	I know him
Mi capisce?	Do you understand me?
Non li vedo	I don't see them
Andiamo con **loro**	Let's go with them

Pronoun objects of verbs *always precede the verb*, except **loro**.

Reflexive pronouns

mi – myself		**ci** – ourselves	
ti – yourself (fam.)		**vi** – yourselves	
si – him/her/one/itself/ yourself (form.)		**si** – themselves	

Uses of the reflexive pronoun

(i)   When the reflexive pronoun refers back to the subject:

Mi chiamo Gina Cinotti	My name is Gina Cinotti (lit. I call myself ...)
Si è alzato alle sette	He got up at seven (lit. he raised himself ...)

(Note: reflexive verbs always form the Perfect tense with **essere**)

(ii)   Certain verbs require the reflexive pronoun:

Ti senti male?	Do you feel bad?
Mi sono sbagliato/a	I have made a mistake
Non **mi** ricordo	I don't remember

(iii) To express the passive:

I nostri prodotti **si** vendono anche in Francia	Our products are also sold in France
Questa carta di credito non **si** accetta qui	This credit card is not accepted here

(iv) In certain general expressions **si** is used to mean 'one', 'we', or 'people':

Si mangia bene qui	You eat well here
Come **si** dice ...?	How do you say ...?

Verbs

The Present Tense

(i)   Three *regular* forms: -**are**, -**ere**, and -**ire** verbs:

PARLARE	parlo	parli	parla	parliamo	parlate	parlano
VENDERE	vendo	vendi	vende	vendiamo	vendete	vendono
PARTIRE	parto	parti	parte	partiamo	partite	partono

NB: some -**ire** verbs insert -**isc**- before the ending

CAPIRE	capisco	capisci	capisce	capiamo	capite	capiscono

(ii) *Irregular verbs*

Here is a list of some of the most common irregular verbs:

ANDARE	vado	vai	va	andiamo	andate	vanno
AVERE	ho	hai	ha	abbiamo	avete	hanno
BERE	bevo	bevi	beve	beviamo	bevete	bevono
DARE	do	dai	da	diamo	date	danno
DIRE	dico	dici	dice	diciamo	dite	dicono
DOVERE	devo	devi	deve	dobbiamo	dovete	devono
ESSERE	sono	sei	è	siamo	siete	sono
FARE	faccio	fai	fa	facciamo	fate	fanno
POTERE	posso	puoi	può	possiamo	potete	possono
SALIRE	salgo	sali	sale	saliamo	salite	salgono
SAPERE	so	sai	sa	sappiamo	sapete	sanno
STARE	sto	stai	sta	stiamo	state	stanno
USCIRE	esco	esci	esce	usciamo	uscite	escono
VENIRE	vengo	vieni	viene	veniamo	venite	vengono
VOLERE	voglio	vuoi	vuole	vogliamo	volete	vogliono

The Perfect Tense

Formed with the present tense of **avere** or **essere** followed by the past participle.
Use the perfect tense to talk about any single, completed action in the past.

- The past participle of **-are** verbs ends in **-ato** (e.g. **parlare** -> **parlato**)
- The past participle of **-ere** verbs ends in **-uto** (e.g. **vendere** -> **venduto**)
- The past participle of **-ire** verbs ends in **-ito** (e.g. **partire** -> **partito**)

NB: irregular past participles are shown in the vocabulary at the end of the book.

The following verbs form the perfect tense with **essere**:

ANDARE	to go	sono andato/a
ARRIVARE	to arrive	sono arrivato/a
CADERE	to fall	sono caduto/a
ENTRARE	to enter	sono entrato/a
PARTIRE	to leave	sono partito/a
SALIRE	to go up	sono salito/a
SCENDERE	to go down	sono sceso/a
TORNARE	to return	sono tornato/a
USCIRE	to go out	sono uscito/a
VENIRE	to come	sono venuto/a

Notice that these are all verbs of *movement*.

A few more common verbs form the perfect tense with **essere**:

NASCERE	to be born	sono nato/a
RESTARE	to remain	sono restato/a
RIMANERE	to remain	sono rimasto/a
RIUSCIRE	to succeed	sono riuscito/a
DIVENTARE	to become	sono diventato/a
MORIRE	to die	è morto/a

Ho parlato con Mario	I spoke/have spoken to Mario
La signorina Bastiani ha telefonato	Miss Bastiani phoned/has phoned
Sono arrivato/a	I arrived/have arrived
Siamo rimasti/e	We remained/have remained
I clienti sono partiti	The clients left/have left

With **essere** verbs the past participle must agree with the subject.

The Future Tense

Formed by adding the following endings to the verb:

-ò,   -ai,   à   -emo,   -ete,   -anno

-**are** and -**ere** verbs:	erò,	erai,	erà,	eremo,	erete,	eranno
-**ire** verbs:	irò,	irai,	irà,	iremo,	irete,	iranno

e.g. parlerò   –   I shall speak
prenderà   –   he/she will take
partiremo – we shall leave
finiranno – they will finish

A few common verbs are irregular:

ANDARE	andrò	andrai	andrà	andremo	andrete	andranno
AVERE	avrò	avrai	avrà	avremo	avrete	avranno
DARE	darò	darai	darà	daremo	darete	daranno
DOVERE	dovrò	dovrai	dovrà	dovremo	dovrete	dovranno
ESSERE	sarò	sarai	sarà	saremo	sarete	saranno
FARE	farò	farai	farà	faremo	farete	faranno
POTERE	potrò	potrai	potrà	potremo	potrete	potranno
RIMANERE	rimarrò	rimarrai	rimarrà	rimarremo	rimarrete	rimarranno
SAPERE	saprò	saprai	saprà	sapremo	saprete	sapranno
TENERE	terrò	terrai	terrà	terremo	terrete	terranno
VEDERE	vedrò	vedrai	vedrà	vedremo	vedrete	vedranno
VENIRE	verrò	verrai	verrà	verremo	verrete	verranno

Guide to business correspondence

This section contains the basic guidelines and some of the phrases and expressions useful in routine business correspondence with Italy. It covers requests for brochures, price lists and information, and booking accommodation.

The sample letter illustrates the conventional layout of an Italian formal letter. (*See* below)

MK Information Systems (UK) Ltd
Ledbury House
42 Greenfields
London WC2 6LA

Tel. 071 836 0023   Fax. 071 836 0487

Vs/Rif.   PL/24
Ns/Rif.   GL/4DR

21 marzo 1993

Spett. Ditta Brusotti & F.gli
Corso Umberto
50134 Firenze

Alla cortese attenzione del dott. P. SALVETTI, Direttore Sistemi

OGGETTO: Informazioni

Con riferimento alla Vs. lettera del 4 marzo, Vi inviamo il ns. ultimo opuscolo e il ns. listino prezzi.

Vorremmo invitarVi a visitare il ns. stand alla Mostra Informatica di Bologna il 25 aprile.

Vi porgiamo i nostri più distinti saluti.

Peter Lawrence
Direttore alle Vendite

all/2

- Keep your letters and faxes formal and impersonal. You should address the letter to the company rather than to any individual. Instead of beginning your letter with 'Dear' followed by a person's name, you use **Spettabile Ditta** followed by the name of the company, e.g. Spettabile Ditta Lentini SpA. This is often abbreviated to **Spett. Ditt.**

- This is followed by **Alla cortese attenzione di** followed by the name of the person for whom the letter is intended, e.g. Alla cortese attenzione dell'ing. G. Lucarini. You can substitute this with **Gentile signor(a) XX** or **Egregio(a) signor(a) XX** only if you are personally acquainted with them. **Caro** ('dear') is only used in informal letters.

- When writing to a hotel, bank or similar organisation use **Spettabile Direzione** as the equivalent of the English 'Dear Sir/s' after the name of the institution.

- The emphasis on the company rather than the individual is also apparent in the use of **Voi**, **Vostro** and related forms to translate 'you' and 'your'. Do not forget to write **Voi** and all associated forms such as **Vostro/Vi/Vs.** with a capital letter. Only when writing a letter to one person on a matter of relevance to him/her alone should you use **Lei** and **Suo**.

- When writing on behalf of your company, use **noi** and associated forms. **Nostro** is usually abbreviated to **ns**.

- The envelope should be addressed to **Spettabile Ditta XX**. Remember to include the **CAP** (postcode).

Useful expressions

Spettabile Ditta XX	Dear Sirs
Spettabile Direzione	Dear Sirs
alla cortese attenzione di	f.a.o.
oggetto	re.
Vs./ns. Rif.	Your/our reference
a seguito della ns. telefonata	further to our telephone call
con riferimento alla Vs. lettera del	with reference to your letter of + date
vorrei/vorremmo	I would like/we would like
vogliate	would you please
prenotare	to reserve
confermare	to confirm
annullare/disdire	to cancel
ricevere	to receive
inviare	to send
Vi prego di comunicarmi	please let me know
Vi preghiamo di comunicarci	please let us know
Vi preghiamo di inviare	please send
a giro di posta	by return of post
all'indirizzo di cui sopra	to the above address
alleghiamo	please find enclosed
il Vs./ns. ultimo catalogo/opuscolo	your/our latest catalogue/brochure
il Vs./ns. listino prezzi	your/our price list
i Vs./ns. prezzi	your/our prices
i Vs./ns. tempi di consegna	your/our delivery times
il prezzo tutto compreso	the inclusive price
un modulo	a form
una prenotazione	a booking
una camera singola/doppia	a single/double room
con bagno/doccia	with bath/shower
dal 22 al 29 agosto	from August 22 to 29
per una camera	for a room
con/senza colazione	with/without breakfast
se è necessario versare un acconto	if you require a deposit
per ulteriori informazioni	for further information
telefonate/scrivete a	telephone/write to
in attesa di Vostra conferma/risposta	awaiting your confirmation/reply
Vi porgo/porgiamo distinti saluti	Yours faithfully
Cordiali saluti	Yours sincerely
all./alleg.	enc.

Vocabulary

Nouns – The gender is indicated for all nouns ending in -e (e.g. filiale (f)) and for a few exceptions (e.g. programma (m)). Otherwise, assume all nouns ending in -o are masculine, and those ending in -a are feminine.

Adjectives – These are given in their masculine singular form.

Verbs – These are given in their infinitive form. Refer to Grammar Review, page 207 for tenses of irregular verbs. Verbs ending in **-ire** which form their present tense with -isc- are indicated (e.g. capire (capisco)). Irregular past participles are given (e.g. dire (pp. detto)). Verbs forming the perfect tense with **essere** are marked with an asterisk.

Abbreviations – (m) masculine; (f) feminine; (pl) plural; (adj) adjective; (n) noun; (irreg) irregular verb; (pp) past participle; (invar) invariable, i.e. ending does not change.

Stress – The stress in Italian is normally on the penultimate syllable. Stressed final vowels are accented (e.g. nazionalità, caffè, però). Irregular stress is indicated in this vocabulary with underlining (e.g. telefono).

a to, at, in
abbastanza enough, quite, fairly
abboccato sweet (of wine)
abitare to live
abituarsi*(a) to get used (to)
abbreviato abbreviated
accento accent
accesso access
accettabile acceptable
accettare to accept
accettazione (f) check-in, acceptance
accomodarsi* to settle in, to make oneself comfortable
accompagnare to accompany, to go with
accordo agreement
accurato accurate
acqua water
acquistare to buy, to acquire
acquisto acquisition, purchase
adesso now
aereo plane
aeroporto airport
affari (m pl) business
affatto completely, entirely
affidabile reliable
agenda diary
agente (m / f) agent
aggiornato up to date
aggiungere (pp aggiunto) to add
aggressivo aggressive
agnello lamb
agosto August
aiutare to help
albergo hotel
alcuno some, any
allegare to enclose
allora so, well, then
alto tall, high
altrettanto likewise, the same to you
altro other
alzarsi* to get up
amabile sweet (of wine)
ambasciata embassy
ambientale environmental
ambiente (m) environment
ambulanza ambulance
americano American
amministratore (m) manager
amministratore delegato managing director

amministrazione (f) management
ampio ample
analisi (f) analysis
analista (m / f) analyst
anche also, too, even
ancora again, more, yet
andare (irreg) to go
andata single (ticket)
andata e ritorno return (ticket)
angolo corner
anno year
anticipo advance
antipasto hors-d'oeuvre
antipatico unpleasant
aperitivo aperitif
aperto open
apparecchio appliance
appartamento apartment, flat
appena hardly, scarcely
appetito appetite
approvare to approve
appuntamento appointment
aprile (m) April
architettura architecture
aria condizionata air conditioning
arrabbiato angry
arredato furnished
arrivare to arrive
arrivederci goodbye
arrivo arrival
arrogante arrogant
arrosto roast(ed)
arte (f) art
artista (m / f) artist
ascensore (m) lift
ascoltare to listen
asparagi (m pl) asparagus
aspettare to wait (for)
assaggiare to taste, to try
assente (da) absent (from)
assicurazione (f) insurance
assistenza assistance, care
assolutamente absolutely
Atene Athens
attenzione (f) attention
attimo moment
attività activity
attività in proprio self-run business
attraversare to cross
attualmente at present

aumentare* to increase, rise
aumento increase, rise
autonoleggio car hire
autonomo independent
avanti forward
avanzato advanced
avere (irreg) to have
azienda firm, company
aziendale company (adj)
bagaglio luggage
bagno bath
balcone (m) balcony
bambino child
banca / banco bank
bancomat (m) cash dispenser
bar (inv) bar
barista (m / f) barman/maid
basso low, short (of people)
bastare to be enough, sufficient
bello beautiful
bene well, fine, good
benvenuto/a welcome
bere (irreg) (pp **bevuto**) to drink
Berlino Berlin
bevanda drink
bianco white
bigliettaio ticket seller
biglietteria ticket office
biglietto ticket
binario (railway) platform
birra beer
bisogna ... it is necessary to
bisogno need
bistecca steak
bolognese from Bologna
bottiglia bottle
braciola chop
bravo good, honest, capable
breve brief, short
brutto ugly, bad, unpleasant
Bruxelles (f) Brussels
buongiorno good morning, good afternoon
buono good
cabina telefonica telephone box
caffè coffee, café
caldo hot
calmo calm, quiet
cambiare to change
cambio (valuta) (rate of) exchange

camera room
campanile (m) bell tower
campione (m) sample
capace capable
capelli (m pl) hair
capire (capisco) to understand
capitale (f) capital city
capitale (m) capital (econ.)
capo chief, head
caposquadra (m) foreman
capotreno guard
cappella chapel
carabiniere (m) policeman
carburante (m) fuel
carciofo artichoke
carico burden, responsibility
carne (f) meat
caro dear, expensive
carote (f pl) carrots
carta paper, card, map
carta di credito credit card
casa house, firm, company
casalinga housewife
casalingo home-made, home-cooked
caso case
casella postale PO box
cassa cash-desk, till
castano chestnut, brown
causare to cause
cena dinner, supper
cenare to have dinner, supper
cento hundred
centrale central
centralinista (m/f) (telephone) operator
centro centre
centro storico old city centre
cercare to search, to look for, to try
certo certain, certainly, by all means
che what, that, then
chi who
chiamare to call
chiamarsi to be called
chiamata (telephone) call
chiave (f) key
chiedere (irreg) to ask
chilometro kilometre
chimico/a chemist
chissà? who knows?
chiuso closed
ci here, there
ci us, ourselves, each other
ciao hello, goodbye
cifra figure, number
cinema (m invar) cinema
cinese Chinese
cioè that is (to say), in other words
circa about, around, approximately
città (f invar) town, city
classico classical
cliente (m/f) client, customer
clima (m) climate
coordinatore co-ordinator
coincidenza coincidence, connection
  (rail / air)
colazione (f) breakfast, lunch
collaborazione (f) cooperation
collega (m/f) colleague
colore (m) colour
Colosseo Colosseum
colpire (colpisco) to strike
come how, as, like
cominciare to begin, to start
commerciale commercial, trade

commercio commerce, trade
commisurato commensurate, appropriate
comodo comfortable, convenient, handy
compagnia company
competente competent
competitività competitiveness
competitivo competitive
compilare to compile
complimento compliment
componente (m) component
comprare to buy
compreso included
compromesso compromise
computerizzato computerised
comunicatore communicator
comunicazione (f) communication
con with
concludere (pp concluso) to conclude
concorrenza competition
condizione (f) condition
conferenza talk, conference
confermare to confirm
confidenziale confidential
confusione (f) confusion, embarrassment
conoscenza knowledge, acquaintance
conoscere to know (a person or place)
consegna delivery
consigliare to advise
consiglio (piece of) advice
consolidare to consolidate
consulenza consultation
contabile (m) accountant
contabilità accountancy
contatto contact
contento pleased, content, happy
continuamente continually
continuare to continue, to carry on
conto account, (restaurant) bill
contorno vegetable side dish
contratto contract
controllare to check
controllo check, control
conversazione (f) conversation
copertura cover
copia copy
corrente current
correntemente fluently
corso course
cortese courteous, polite
cortesia courtesy
cosa thing
costo cost
costoso expensive
costruire to build, construct
costruzione (f) construction
cotoletta cutlet
cotto cooked
credere to believe
croce rossa (f) red cross
crostino crouton
cucina kitchen, cooking, cuisine
da from, by, since, for
Danimarca Denmark
dare (irreg) to give
data date
dati (m pl) data
dattilografo / a typist
davvero really, indeed
delicato delicate, mild
delizioso delicious
dente tooth
depliant (m) leaflet, brochure
desiderare to want, to wish

destinatario recipient
destinazione (f) destination
destra right
dettagliare to detail
dettaglio detail
di of, from, than
dire (irreg) (pp detto) to say, to tell
dicembre (m) December
differita postponed
difficile difficult
difficoltà difficulty
diffondere to promote, distribute
dilazione (f) delay, extension
diligente diligent
dimensione (f) dimension
dimenticare to forget
dinamico dynamic
dipendente (m / f) employee
diretto direct, non-stop, through (train)
direttore (m) manager, director
direzione (f) direction; management
dirigente (m / f) executive
discutere (pp discusso) to discuss
disdire (irreg) (pp disdetto) to cancel
disoccupazione (f) unemployment
disporre (irreg) (pp disposto) have,
  arrange
disposto a prepared to, ready to
distrettuale district
distribuzione (f) distribution
ditta firm company
ditta madre parent company
diventare* to become
doccia shower
documento document
dogana customs
dolce sweet
dolce (m) dessert
domanda question
domandare to ask
domani tomorrow
domenica Sunday
donna woman
dopo after, then, later
dopodomani the day after tomorrow
doppio double
dottore (m / f) doctor
dove where
dovere to have to
dritto straight
dunque so, then, therefore, well
durante during
e and
eccetera etcetera
eccetto except
eccezionale exceptional
ecco here is / are / I am; that's just it,
  that's just what I mean
economia economy
edicola (newspaper) kiosk
edilizia building trade
Edimburgo Edinburgh
effettuare to effect
efficiente efficient
egregio eminent, distinguished
elaborazione (f) preparation
elaborazione (dei) dati data processing
elegante elegant, smart
elenco list
elettrico electric
elettronico electronic
emergenza emergency
ente (m) corporation, authority

entrare to enter, to go in
esaurito sold out
esclusivo exclusive
esempio example
esente exempt
esigenza need, demand
esperienza experience
esportare to export
esportazione (f) export, exporting
esposizione (f) exhibition
espresso express
essere* (irreg) (pp stato) to be
estero foreign, overseas
età age
Europa Europe
europeo European
eventuale possible, future
evidentemente obviously
fa ago
fabbrica factory
facile easy
fagiolini (m pl) green beans
fagiolo bean
falso false, wrong, insincere
fame (f) hunger
famiglia family
familiare family, familiar, friendly
famoso famous
fare (irreg) (pp fatto) to do, to make
farmaceutico pharmaceutical
farmacia chemist's
fattura invoice, bill
favore (m) favour
febbraio February
fegato liver
felice happy
femmina daughter, girl, female, woman
feriale working (day)
ferie (f pl) holidays
fermare to stop
ferrovie (f pl) railways
festivo holiday
fettuccine (f pl) fettuccine (pasta)
fico fig
fiera (trade) fair
fiero proud
figlia daughter
figlio son
figura shape, figure, appearance
filiale (f) branch (of company)
finalmente finally, at last
finanziario financial
finire (finisco) to finish
fino a as far as, until
fiorentino Florentine
Firenze (f) Florence
firmare to sign
fisico physicist
fissare to fix, arrange
fondare to found, to establish
fondo end; bottom; fund
formaggio cheese
formazione (f) formation, training
formazione scolastica education
fornire (fornisco) to supply
fornitore (m) supplier
forno oven
foro forum
forse perhaps
forte strong; loud
fortuna fortune, luck
fotografia photograph
fra between

fragola strawberry
francese French
Francia France
francobollo (postage) stamp
Francoforte (f) Frankfurt
fratello brother
freddo cold
fresco fresh
fritto fried
frizzante sparkling
frutta fruit
fungo mushroom
funzionario civil servant
fuori outside
fuori sede out of the office
furto theft
gallese Welsh
garantire (garantisco) to guarantee
garanzia guarantee
gassato carbonated, fizzy
gatto cat
gelato ice-cream
generale general
gennaio January
Genova Genoa
gente (f sing inv) people
gentile kind
Germania Germany
gestione (f) management
gettone (m) telephone token
già already
giapponese Japanese
giornale (m) newspaper
giornaliero daily
giornalista (m/f) journalist
giorno day
giovane young
giovedì (m) Thursday
girare to turn
giro tour
giro d'affari business turnover
gita tour
giudizio judgement
giugno June
giusto right, fair, correct
gola throat
gomma rubber
gradire (gradisco) to enjoy, to like
grafico graphic designer
grande large
granita water ice
grasso fat
gratuito free
grave serious
grazie thank you
greco Greek
grigio grey
griglia grill
guardare to look (at)
guardia guard, watch
guardia medica hospital emergency
   service
idea idea
ieri yesterday
immobiliare property
imparare to learn
impegno engagement, commitment
impiegato / a clerk, employee
importante important
importanza importance
impossibile impossible
imprenditoriale (adj) entrepreneurial
impresa firm, business

in in
incapace incapable
incassare to cash
incendio fire
incominciare to begin
incompetente incompetent
incontro meeting
indirizzo address
indispensabile indispensable
industria industry
infatti in fact
inflazione (f) inflation
informarsi* to find out
informatica information technology
informazioni (f pl) information
ingegnere (m) engineer
ingegneria engineering
inglese English
ingrandirsi* to grow (bigger)
ingresso entrance
iniziare to start up
innanzitutto first of all
innovazione (f) innovation
inoltre furthermore, besides
inquinamento pollution
insalata salad
inserire (inserisco) to insert
insieme together
insomma in other words, in short
installazione (f) installation
intanto meanwhile
intelligente intelligent
intenzione (f) intention
interessante interesting
internazionale international
interno internal, interior, (telephone)
   extension
intero entire, whole
investimento investment
inviare to send
invitare to invite
io I
irlandese Irish
isola island
Italia Italy
italiano Italian
là there
laboratorio laboratory
lagnarsi* to complain
lasciare to leave, to let
latte (m) milk
laurea (university degree
laureato / a graduate
lavorare to work
lavoro work
lega league
leggere (irreg) (pp letto) to read
leggero light
legno wood, timber
lentamente slowly
lettera letter
letto bed
lì there
libero free
libero professionista self-employed
   person
lieto pleased
limitato limited
limone (m) lemon
linea line
lingua language
lira lira (unit of currency)
litro litre

livello level
locale local
località locality
Lombardia Lombardy
Londra London
lontano far
luglio July
lunedì Monday
lungo long
luogo place
ma but
macchina machine, car
macedonia fruit salad
madre (f) mother
madrelingua mother tongue
magari I wish, if only, perhaps
magazzino shop, warehouse
maggio May
mai never, ever
maiale (m) port
mal(e) (m) pain
maleducato impolite, ill-mannered
mandare to send
mantenere to maintain
manutenzione (f) maintenance
manzo beef
mare (f) sea
marito husband
martedì Tuesday
marzo March
maschio boy, son, male
massimo maximum
materia prima raw material
matrimoniale matrimonial; double
mattina morning
meccanico mechanic
meglio better
mela apple
melanzane (f pl) aubergines
melone (m) melon
meno less, minus
mensile monthly
mentre while
menù (m) menu
mercato market
merce (f) goods, merchandise
mercoledì Wednesday
mese (m) month
messaggio message
metodico methodical
metropolitana underground, tube
mettere (pp messo) to put
mezz'ora half hour
mezzanotte (f) midnight
mezzi pubblici public transport
mezzo means
mezzo (adj) half
mezzogiorno midday
Mezzogiorno south (of Italy)
migliorare to improve
migliore better, best
milanese Milanese
Milano (f) Milan
minestra soup
minestrone (m) minestrone (soup)
mio my
misto mixed
modello model
modernizzare to modernize
moderno modern
modesto modest
modifica alteration, modification
modificare to modify

moglie (f) wife
molto much, a lot, very
momento moment
mondo world
moneta coin
morire* (irreg) (pp morto) to die
mostra exhibition
mostrare to show
motivo reason, purpose
motore (m) engine, motor
multinazionale multinational
museo museum
napoletano Neapolitan
Napoli (f) Naples
nascere* (irreg) (pp nato) to be born
nascita birth
naturale natural
naturalmente naturally
nazione (f) nation
necessario necessary
nessuno nobody, not any
niente (m) nothing
no no
noleggiare to hire
nome (m) name
non not
normalmente normally
notare to note
notevole considerable, sizeable
notizia news item, piece of news
notte (f) night
novembre (m) November
nulla (m) nothing
numerazione (f) enumeration
numero number
nuovo new
o or
occhio eye
occuparsi* (di) to be busy with, involved with
occupato busy, occupied
offerta offer
offrire (pp offerto) to offer
oggetto object, reference (in correspondence)
oggi today
ogni each, every
olio oil
oliva olive
oltre over, in excess of
omaggio gift
onesto honest
opera work, opera
operaio / a worker
operativo operative
opuscolo leaflet, brochure
ora (adv) now
ora hour
orario timetable
orario di sportello opening/duty hours
ordinazione (f) order
ordine (m) order
ordine del giorno (m) agenda
organizzare to organise
organizzazione (f) organisation
ortopedico orthopaedic
ospite (m/f) guest, host
osso bone
ottimo best, excellent
ottobre (m) October
ovunque anywhere, everywhere
ovviamente obviously
Padova Padua

padre (m) father
paese (m) country, village
pagare to pay
pagina page
pagine gialle yellow pages
palazzo palace
Palazzo dei Congressi Conference Centre
panino bread roll
parcheggiare to park
parecchi / e (m/f pl) several, quite a few
Parigi Paris
parlare to speak, to talk
parte (f) part
partecipazione (f) partnership
partecipazione statale state shareholding
partenza departure
partire* to leave, depart
passaporto passport
passare to spend (time), to pass (by)
passeggero passenger
passeggiata walk, stroll
passo step
pasta pasta, cake, pastry
patate (f pl) potatoes
patatine fritte chips
paura fear
pazienza patience
peccato sin, pity
peggio worse
peggiore worse, worst
penale (f) penalty, fine
penetrare* to penetrate
pensare to think
pensione (f) guesthouse, board
per for, through
perché why, because
perfetto perfect
periferia suburb, outskirts
periodo period
perito expert
permutare to exchange
però however, but, and yet
persona person
personale personal
personale (m) personnel, staff
pesce fish
piacere* (pp piaciuto) to please
piacere (m) pleasure
Piacere! Pleased to meet you
pianificare to plan
piano floor, storey
piano (adv) slowly
pianterreno ground floor
piatto plate, dish, course
piazza (town) square
piccante spicy
piccolo small
piede (m) foot
Piemonte (m) Piedmont
pieno full
più more, most
piuttosto rather
poco, po' little
poi then
politica politics, policy
politica aziendale company policy
politico political
polizia police
polizia stradale traffic/highway police
pollo chicken
pomeriggio afternoon
pomodoro tomato
ponte (m) bridge

portare to carry, to bring, to wear
portoghese Portuguese
posizione (f) position
possibile possible
posta post, mail, post office
posto place, seat
potere (irreg) to be able
pranzare to have lunch
pranzo lunch
prassi (f) practice
prestigiosa prestigious
preferire (preferisco) to prefer
pregare to ask, to request, to beg
prego please (do), can I help you?
prendere (pp preso) to take
prenotare to book, reserve
prenotazione (f) booking, reservation
preoccuparsi* to worry
presentare to introduce
presentarsi* to introduce oneself
presso near, for, with
presto early, soon
prevedere (pp previsto) to plan, envisage
preventivo estimate
previo (adj) subject to
prezzo price
primo first
principale main
priorità priority
privato private
probabile probable
problema (m) problem
prodotto product
produzione (f) production
professore teacher, professor
progettazione (f) design
progettista (m / f) design engineer
progetto project, plan
programma (m) program(me)
programmatore (m) programmer
prolungare to extend
pronto ready
Pronto! Hello (on telephone)
proporre (irreg) to suggest, to offer
proposito subject
proprietario owner
proprio (adj) own
proprio (adv) just, precisely, really
prosciutto ham
prossimo next
protezione (f) protection
prudente prudent, careful, wise
pubblicare to publish
pubblicità publicity, advertising
pubblico public
punta point
punto point, dot
puntuale punctual
purtroppo unfortunately
quadro executive, manager
qualche some
qualcosa something
qualcuno someone
quale which (one)
qualità quality
qualsiasi any, whatever
qualunque whatever, whichever
quando when
quanto how much
quarto quarter
quasi almost, nearly
quello that (one)
questo this (one)

qui here
raccomandare to recommend
raggiungere (pp raggiunto) to reach
ragione (f) reason, right
ragioniere / a accountant
ragù (m) meat sauce
rapido rapid, fast
rapporto report, relationship
rappresentante (m) representative
rappresentare to represent
recentemente recently
reddito income, yield
regione (f) region
regolazione (f) regulation
Regno Unito United Kingdom
reparto department, section
responsabilità reponsibility
resto change
retribuzione (f) income, payment
retribuzione lorda gross income
riassumere (pp riassunto) to sum up
ricerca research
ricercare to seek
ricercatore researcher
ricevere (pp ricevuto) to receive
ricezione (f) reception
richiamare to call back
richiedere (pp richiesto) to require
richiesta request
riconoscere (pp riconosciuto) to recognise
ricordarsi* to remember
ricordo memory, recollection
ridere (pp riso) to laugh
ridurre (pp ridotto) to reduce
riduzione (f) reduction
rigoroso stringent
rimanere (irreg) (pp rimasto) to remain
rimborso reimbursement
ringraziare to thank
riparazione (f) repair
ripetizione (f) repetition
ripieno stuffed, filled
riposo rest
rischiare to risk
riserva reservation
risolvere (pp risolto) to solve
risoluzione (f) resolution
rispettare to respect
rispetto a with respect to, regarding
ristorante (m) restaurant
ritardo delay
ritenere to retain
ritirare to withdraw, collect
ritiro bagagli baggage reclaim
ritornare* to return
ritorno return
riunione (f) meeting
riuscire* (irreg) to succeed
rivedere (pp rivisto) to see again
rivelare to reveal
Roma Rome
romano Roman
romantico romantic
rosato rosé (wine)
rosso red
ruolo role
rustico rustic
sabato Saturday
sala room, hall
salire* (irreg) to go up, to climb on
salone (m) lounge; exhibition
salotto sitting room
salute (f) health

sanità health
sapere (irreg) to know (a fact)
Sardegna Sardinia
sbagliare to mistake
sbagliarsi* to make a mistake, to be wrong
scalo stop
scaloppina escalope
scappare* to dash
scatola box
scegliere (irreg) (pp scelto) to choose
scelta choice
scendere* (irreg) (pp sceso) to go down, get off, descend
schema (m) design, plan
scienziato scientist
sciopero strike
scontento unhappy, dissatisfied
scontrino receipt
scorso last
Scozia Scotland
scozzese Scottish
scrivere (pp scritto) to write
scuola school
scusare to apologise
se if
seccatura bother, nuisance
secco dry
secondo second; according to
sede (centrale) (f) head-office
segnale acustico (m) (telephone) tone
segretaria secretary
segreteria telefonica telephone answering machine
segreto secret
seguente following
seguire to follow
selezione (f) selection
semaforo (sing) traffic lights
sembrare* to seem
semplice simple
sempre always
senso sense
sentire to hear, to feel
senza without
sera evening
serietà reliability
serio serious
servire to serve
servizio service
sete (f) thirst
settimana week
settimana lavorativa working week
settore (m) sector
sforzo effort
sì yes
Sicilia Sicily
siciliano Sicilian
sicuro sure
sigla initials
sigla automobile car registration number
signora Mrs, Madam, lady
signore (m) Mr, Sir, gentleman
signorina Miss, young lady
simpatico pleasant, likeable
sincero sincere
singolo single
sinistra left
sistema (m) system
snello slim
soccorso help
soccorso stradale vehicle breakdown service

215

società company, society
soddisfare* (pp soddisfatto) to satisfy
soggiorno stay
solamente only
solito usual, same
solo only
sopravvivere (pp sopravvissuto) to survive
soltanto only
sorella sister
sotto under
sottoscritto undersigned
spagnolo Spanish
speciale special
specialità speciality
specializzato specialised
specificazione (f) specification
spedire (spedisco) to send
spendere (pp speso) to spend
sperare to hope
spese (f pl) costs, expenses
spesso often
spettabile ditta Dear Sirs
spettacolo entertainment, show
spiegare to explain
spinaci (m pl) spinach
sportello counter, cashier's window
sposato married
spumante sparkling
squisito exquisite, delicious
stabilimento factory, plant
stagione (f) season
stamattina this morning
stampa press
stampante (f) printer
stanco tired
stanotte tonight
stare to be, to stay
stasera this evening
statale state (adj)
stato state
stazione (f) station
stazione ferroviaria railway station
stella star
sterlina pound sterling
stesso same
stipendio salary
stomaco stomach
storico historic(al), old
strada street
straniero (adj) foreign
straniero / a foreigner
straordinario extraordinary
studiare to study
stupido stupid
su on
subito immediately, right away
succursale (f) subsidiary

suggerire (suggerisco) to suggest
suo his / her / its
Suo your (formal)
supplemento supplement, extra charge
sveglia alarm call
sviluppare to develop
sviluppo development
Svizzera Switzerland
svizzero Swiss
tagliare to cut
tanto so much, a lot
tariffa price list
tassa tax
tassì (m inv) taxi
tasso rate
tavola table
tavolo table
tè (m) tea
tecnico (adj) technical
tecnico (m) technician
tecnologia technology
tedesco German
telecomunicazioni (f)
   telecommunications
telefonare to telephone
telefonia telephony
telefono telephone
teleselezione (f) direct dialling
televisione (f) television
temere to fear
tempo time, weather
tenere (irreg) to keep, hold
termini (m pl) terms
terzo third
tesi (f) thesis
testa head
tipico typical
tipo type, kind, sort
tiramisù (m) tiramisu (dessert)
titolare (m / f) owner
titolo title
tonno tuna
Torino (f) Turin
tornare* to return
torta tart, cake
torto wrong
Toscana Tuscany
traffico traffic
tranquillo quiet
trasferire (trasferisco) to transfer
trasformabile changeable
trasmettere (pp trasmesso) to send,
   transmit
trasmissione (f) transmission
trasporto transport
trattoria small, family restaurant
treno train

troppo too, too much
trovarsi* to be situated
turismo tourism
tutto all, every(thing)
ufficio office
ufficio postale post office
ultimo last
umbro Umbrian
umido damp, humid
un(o), una a(n), one
usare to use
uscire* (irreg) to go out, come out
uscita exit
vacanza holiday
valido valid
valigia suitcase
vantaggioso advantageous
Vaticano vatican
vecchio old
vedere (pp visto / veduto) to see
vendere to sell
vendita sale(s)
venditore (m) salesman
venerdì Friday
Venezia Venice
veneziano Venetian
venire* (irreg) to come
verde green
vero true
verso towards
via street
via by, via, away
viaggiare to travel
viaggio journey
viale (m) avenue
vicino (a) near (to)
vigile (vigilessa) policeman (woman)
vigore (m) strength, force
visita visit
visitare to visit
vitello veal
vivace lively, vivacious
vivere (pp vissuto) to live
volare to fly
volentieri willingly
volere (irreg) to want, to wish
volo flight
volta time, occasion
vongola clam
zona district
zucchero sugar
zucchini (m pl) courgettes
zuppa soup
zuppa inglese trifle
Zurigo (f) Zurich